Parties, Politics, and Public Policy in America

Parties, Politics, and Public Policy in America
Fifth Edition

William J. Keefe
University of Pittsburgh

CQ
PRESS

A Division of Congressional Quarterly Inc.
1414 22nd Street N.W., Washington, D.C. 20037

Library of Congress Cataloging-in-Publication Data

Keefe, William J.
    Parties, politics, and public policy in America.

    Includes index.
    1. Political parties—United States. I. Title.
JK2265.K44   1988   324.273   87-14655
ISBN 0-87187-424-5

For Martha, Kathy, Nancy, Jodi, and John

Table of Contents

c h a p t e r   t h r e e
Political Parties and the Electoral Process   79

c h a p t e r   f o u r
Political Parties and the Electorate   151

c h a p t e r   f i v e
The Congressional Party and the
Formation of Public Policy   191

c h a p t e r   s i x

The American Party System: Problems and Perspectives

Tables and Figures

Tables

Figures

Preface

THE AMERICAN party system is neither comatose nor moribund. But it is not in the best of health. Among social organizations, the parties occupy an unenviable position. Few people take them seriously. The reality is that voters generally ignore the parties, politicians often dismiss them, activists typically bypass them, and the media usually demean them. Almost everyone, it seems, distrusts them—if they think about them at all. The weakness of the parties shows up in both the government and, especially, the electorate. Key outsiders—political action committees (PACs), the media, campaign management firms, political consultants, and direct-mail fund raisers—often play a more important role in campaigns than the parties. The hard truth is that party organizations frequently find themselves in the uneasy role of bystander. As candidates struggle to win office, they use party money and intelligence, if available, and advertise the party label, if appropriate, but count on victory through use of techniques validated in mass merchandising. Even the most ingenuous candidates know that "the image" is more important than "the party." In this highly individualistic, entrepreneurial system of electing public officials, sometimes the most influential fact about candidates is whether they are incumbents, not whether they are Democrats or Republicans.

The weakness of the parties is pronounced in the presidential election process. Reforms, ironically, have contributed to this condition. The reforms introduced in the presidential nominating process have diminished the independent role of the national convention. All recent experience shows that the convention meets largely to ratify the results of the preconvention struggles in primary and caucus-convention states. Convention proceedings are dominated by candidate organizations rather than state party delegations. Party spending in presidential campaigns has been subordinated to public financing, as provided by the Federal Election Campaign Act. In the process of nominating presidential candidates in the new participatory system, the preferences of party leaders count for less and less, the preferences of amateur activists and assorted enthusiasts for more and more. The presidential campaign itself has become a major media event. In shaping presidential elections, the media are the closest thing the nation has to parties. For candidates and public officials alike, more often than not, it is the party label that matters, not the party mission.

In the electorate, where the parties are in serious trouble, independence and split-ticket voting flourish while strong partisanship and straight-ticket voting decline. If party depended mainly on widespread popular support, the days would be numbered for both major parties. But happily for party advocates, including myself, this is not the case. Inertia, the lack of alternatives, traditional infrastructure, and public law support and protect the two-party system about as well as could be done. The major parties are thus not about to fade away.

One has to look hard to find signs of party vitality, but they can be uncovered. Of most importance, they appear in the growing capacity of the national parties to raise campaign funds and, as a result, to increase their services to candidates and state party organizations. The long-run impact of these changes on the party role in recruitment, nominations, campaigns, voter mobilization, and governing remains to be seen. It would be difficult to make a case that the parties today are doing well, playing a dominant role in any of these activities. "Hanging on" is more like it, particularly in the electorate's domain.

The parties have suffered from prolonged neglect by the public and from overattention by the reformers. Scholars, meanwhile, continue to be intrigued by them. Numerous books, monographs, and articles have been published on American parties in recent years. I have drawn extensively on this interesting literature. The scholarship tracks that I followed are amply reflected in the footnotes.

When a book comes up for a fifth edition and, additionally, is moved from one publishing house to another, it deserves a substantial revision. This one got it. Large parts of each chapter have been rethought, reworked, and rewritten. Much new material has been added. Among the topics to receive new and significantly expanded treatment are the nominating process, campaign finance, candidate-centered campaigns, law and the parties, interparty conflict during the Reagan administration, "loyalists" and "irregulars" in Congress, court rulings on the parties, twists and turns of party reform, change and continuity in voting behavior, racial polarization in voting, the disruption of the Democratic coalition, increasing efforts to professionalize party organizations, and the characteristics of strong parties.

Despite the numerous additions made, this book is still on the lean side. One justification for brevity emerges from the observation of E. E. Schattschneider, a scholar whose work touches all who write about American politics: "The compulsion to know everything," he wrote, "is the road to insanity." Based on that firm ground, this book leaves some lesser aspects of party unexplored, some things unsaid.

It may be that the American party system needs to be rescued from its detractors, but that is not the main purpose of this book. Nor is it to sketch a blueprint showing where the best opportunities lie for making further changes. The central purpose is rather one of exegesis: to bring into focus the major features of the parties, to account for party form and functions, and to examine and interpret the parties' present condition.

For helping on one or more of the first four editions, I thank Paul A. Beck, Keith Burris, Holbert N. Carroll, Edward F. Cooke, Stephen Craig, William J. Crotty, Robert L. Donaldson, John Havick, Charles O. Jones, Paul Lopatto, Roger McGill, Michael Margolis, Russell Moses, Morris S. Ogul, Bert A. Rockman, Robert S. Walters, and Sidney Wise.

For the fifth edition, I especially acknowledge the assistance and advice of two colleagues at the University of Pittsburgh: Holbert N. Carroll and Morris S. Ogul. Graduate student Eugene Torisky ran down, looked up, and tabulated one thing after another for me. Another graduate student, Brooke Harlowe, helped to prepare certain graphs. Josie Raleigh and Donna Woodward typed numerous tables for this edition. Herbert E. Alexander provided data and guidance on campaign finance. David M. Olson and Sidney Wise offered valuable suggestions for revising the book. And Robert L. Donaldson, Jon Hurwitz, Jodi Keefe-McCurdy, David C. Kozak, James M. Malloy, Thomas E. Mann, Michael Margolis, Raymond E. Owen, and Guy Peters were helpful in various ways. All the people mentioned in this and the previous paragraph should know how much I appreciate their thoughtfulness and friendship. But they are not perfect, not by a long shot. Despite their assistance and good intentions, errors of fact and interpretation may somehow have crept into a page here and there. If this turns out to be the case, I suggest the responsibility is properly theirs.

I owe special thanks to Joanne D. Daniels, director of CQ Press, for her advice and support. Everyone familiar with her work knows she is one of the best in the business. The suggestions of Colleen McGuiness, a singularly talented editor, greatly improved the book.

Finally, I thank my wife, Martha, for her valuable work on each of the editions. She is indefatigable, a consummate revisionist, a master in manuscript preparation. Every page reflects her contributions.

Parties, Politics, and
Public Policy in America

Political Parties and the Political System

THE AMERICAN political party system is not an insoluble puzzle. But it does have more than its share of mysteries. The main one, arguably, is how it has survived for so long or, perhaps, how it survived at all, in a difficult and complicated environment. The broad explanation, arguably as well, is that the party system survives because parties are an inevitable outgrowth of civil society ("factions . . . sown in the nature of man," thought James Madison[1]); because parties perform functions important to democratic polities ("democracy is unthinkable save in terms of parties," wrote E. E. Schattschneider[2]); and because the American public has never held particularly high expectations of parties or made particularly rigorous demands upon them—thus in truth their survival has not been contingent on performance.

A logical starting point for understanding the political party system, an enduring institution of American society, is to recognize that parties are less what they make of themselves than what their environment makes of them.[3] Put another way, in language social scientists sometimes invoke, parties typically are the dependent variable. That is, to a marked extent the party owes its character and form to the impact of four external elements: the legal-political system, the election system, the political culture, and the heterogeneous quality of American life. Singly and in combination, these elements contribute in significant and indelible ways to the organizational characteristics of the parties, to the manner in which they carry on their activities, to their internal discipline, to the behavior of both their elite and rank-and-file members, and to their capacity to control the political system and to perform as policy-making agencies.

1

The Parties and Their Environment

The Legal-Political System

The Constitution of the United States was written by men who were apprehensive of the power of popular majorities and who had scant sympathy for the existence of party. Their basic intent, evident in the broad thrust of the Constitution and in line after line of its text, was to establish a government that could not easily be brought under the control of any one element, whatever its size, that might be present in the country. The underlying theory of the founders was both simple and pervasive: power was to check power, and the ambitions of some men were to check the ambitions of other men.* The two main features in this design were federalism and the separation of powers—the first to distribute power among different levels of government, the second to distribute power among the legislative, executive, and judicial branches. Division of the legislature into two houses, with their memberships elected for different terms and by differing methods, was thought to reduce further the risk that a single faction (or party) might gain ascendancy. Schattschneider developed the argument in this way:

> The theory of the Constitution, inherited from the time of the Glorious Revolution in England, was legalistic and preparty in its assumptions. Great reliance was placed in a system of separation of powers, a legalistic concept of government incompatible with a satisfactory system of party government. No place was made for the parties in the system, party government was not clearly foreseen or well understood, government by parties was thought to be impossible or impracticable and was feared and regarded as something to be avoided.... The Convention at Philadelphia produced a constitution with a dual attitude: it was proparty in one sense and antiparty in another. The authors of the Constitution refused to suppress the parties by destroying the fundamental liberties in which parties originate. They or their immediate successors accepted amendments that guaranteed civil rights and thus established a system of party tolerance, *i.e.,* the right to agitate and to organize. This is the proparty aspect of the system. On the other hand, the authors of the Constitution set up an elaborate division and balance of powers within an intricate governmental structure designed to make parties ineffective. It was hoped that the parties would lose and exhaust themselves in futile attempts to fight

---

* In addition to using terms such as "candidate," "legislator," "member," and "representative" to apply to men and women in politics, I have referred to them in the masculine gender—"he," "him," "his." This is simply a matter of style. These pronouns are employed generically.

their way through the labyrinthine framework of the government, much as an attacking army is expected to spend itself against the defensive works of a fortress. This is the antiparty part of the constitutional scheme. To quote Madison, the "great object" of the Constitution was "to preserve the public good and private rights against the danger of such a faction [party] and at the same time to preserve the spirit and form of popular government." [4]

Federalism also works at cross purposes with the development of centralized parties. As an organizational form, federalism guarantees that there will be not only fifty state governmental systems but also fifty state party systems. No two states are exactly alike. No two state party systems are exactly alike. The prevailing ideology in one state party may be sharply different from that of another state—contrast the state Democratic party of Mississippi with its counterpart in New York, the state Republican party of Utah with its counterpart in Connecticut. And within each state all manner of local party organizations exist, sometimes functioning in harmony with state and national party elements and sometimes not. There are states (and localities) where the party organizations are well financed and active and those where they are not, those where the organizations are easily penetrated by outsiders and those where they are not, those where factions compete persistently within a party and those where factional organization is nonexistent, those where the parties seem to consist mainly of the personal followings of individual politicians and those where traditional party organizations and their leaders exercise significant influence.[5] Parties differ from state to state and from community to community, and the laws that govern their activities and shape their influence also differ. A great variety of state laws, for example, governs nominating procedures, ballot form, access to the ballot, campaign finance, and elections. On the whole, northeastern states are most likely to have statutes that foster stronger parties, while southern states tend to have statutes that weaken them.[6] Similarly, strong ("monopolistic") local party organizations have been more prominent and durable in the East than anywhere else.[7] The broad point is that the thrust of federalism is dispersive and parochial, permitting numerous different forms of political organizations to thrive and inhibiting the emergence of cohesive and disciplined national parties.

The Election System

The election system is another element in the environment of political parties. So closely linked are parties and elections that it is difficult to understand much about one without understanding a great deal about the other. Parties are in business to win elections. Election systems shape the way the parties compete for power and the success with which they do it. Several examples will help to illustrate this point.

Although a state's election calendar may appear neutral, even innocuous, it has a substantial bearing on party fortunes. Many state constitutions establish election calendars that separate state elections from national elections—for example, gubernatorial from presidential elections. The singular effect of this arrangement is to insulate state politics from national politics. Similarly, the behavior of voters also weakens state and national political linkages. Even in those states in which governors are elected at the same time as the president, the chances are about four out of ten that the party that carries the state in the presidential contest will lose at the gubernatorial level. (The outcomes in presidential-gubernatorial voting from 1964 to 1984 are indicated in Table 1-1.) In addition, the national tides that sweep one party into the presidency may be no more than ripples by the time a state election is held two years later. Although the Democratic party won presidential election after presidential election during the 1930s and 1940s, a great many governorships and state legislatures remained safely Republican. Recent Republican success in presidential elections (1968, 1972, 1980, 1984) was not translated into major gains for the party at the state level. Prior to the 1984 presidential election, for example, the Democratic party held majorities in sixty-six state legislative chambers. Despite President Ronald Reagan's landslide reelection, the Democrats lost control of only four state chambers. And at the same time, Republicans picked up only one additional governorship in thirteen gubernatorial elections. (In 1986 Democrats gained four legislative chambers and lost eight governorships, leaving Democrats in control of twenty-six governorships and Republicans in control of twenty-four.)

The use of staggered terms for executive and legislative offices diminishes the probability that one party will control both branches of government at any given time. When the governor is elected for four years and the lower house is elected for two years—the common pattern—chances are that the governor's party will lose legislative seats, and sometimes its majority, in the off-year election. The same is true for the president and Congress. Whatever the virtues of staggered terms and off-year elections, they increase the likelihood of divided control of government.

The use of single-member districts with plurality elections for the election of legislators carries important ramifications for the parties.

TABLE 1-1   Split Outcomes in Presidential-Gubernatorial Voting: States
Carried by Presidential Candidate of One Major Party and by
Gubernatorial Candidate of Other Major Party, 1964-1984

Year	Gubernatorial elections	Split outcomes	Percentage
1964	25	9	36
1968	21	8	38
1972	18	10	56
1976	14	5	36
1980	13	4	31
1984	13	5	38

When an election is held within a single-member district, only one party can win; the winning candidate need receive only one more vote than the second-place candidate, and all votes for candidates other than the victor are lost. Although the single-member district system discriminates against the second party in each district, its principal impact is virtually to rule out the possibility that a minor party can win legislative representation. Indeed, only a handful of minor party candidates have ever held seats either in Congress or in the state legislatures. The device of single-member districts with plurality elections has long been a major bulwark of the two-party system.[8]

Single-member districts distort the relationship between the overall vote for legislative candidates within a state and the number of seats won by each party. The discrepancy may be sizable. The majority party nearly always profits from its ingenuity in drawing district lines. Gerrymandering, in other words, is effective. Consider the 1984 congressional elections in populous California. Democratic congressional candidates won twenty-seven out of forty-five districts (60 percent), even though collectively Republican candidates out-polled Democratic candidates 4,423,734 to 4,327,237—a margin of 50.5 percent to 49.5 percent. What counted was the geographic distribution of the vote in relation to district lines.

Extreme partisan gerrymandering, however, may be on the way out. In 1986 the Supreme Court refused to invalidate an Indiana reapportionment act that favored the Republican party, stating that this particular gerrymander of state legislative districts was not sufficiently offensive to warrant judicial intervention. At the same time the Court warned that gerrymanders will be held unconstitutional "when the electoral system is arranged in a manner that will consistently degrade a voter's or a group of voters' influence on the political process as a whole." [9] Thus, solutions to the problem of gerrymandering may be found in the courts. The lasting impact of the Supreme Court's opinion should become apparent following the census of 1990. State legislators, who will redraw district lines then, have been served notice that egregious gerrymandering, which entrenches the dominant party, will not pass constitutional muster.

Few, if any, electoral arrangements have had a greater impact on political parties than the direct primary, an innovation of the reform era of the early twentieth century. The primary was introduced to combat the power of those party oligarchs who, insulated from popular influences, dominated the selection of nominees in state and local party conventions. The primary was designed to democratize the nominating process by empowering the voters to choose the party's nominees. Today, all states employ some form of primary system, although mixed convention-primary arrangements are used in a handful of states. In New York, for example, a candidate for a statewide office must receive at least 25 percent of the party convention vote to win a place on the primary ballot. Access to the primary ballot in Colorado requires a candidate to obtain 20 percent of the convention vote, while a 15 percent vote is required by the Massachusetts Democratic party. [10]

The convention method survives for the nomination of presidential and vice-presidential candidates. But convention decisions, as is well known, are heavily influenced by the outcomes of presidential primaries. In 1988 nearly two-thirds of the states selected their delegates in presidential primaries.

The precise impact of the primary on the parties is difficult to establish. Its effects nevertheless appear to be substantial. First, by transferring the choice of nominees from party assemblies to the voters, the primary has increased the probability that candidates with different views on public policy will be brought together in the same party. Whatever their policy orientations, the victors in primary elections become the party's nominees, perhaps to the embarrassment of other party candidates. In 1986, to take an unusual example, two disciples of Lyndon H. LaRouche captured the Democratic nominations for lieutenant governor and secretary of state in Illinois. Citing the views of LaRouche followers as "abhorrent, racist, anti-Semitic, anti-democratic, and irrational," and unwilling to run on the same ticket with them, Adlai E. Stevenson III resigned as the Democratic candidate for governor. After being barred from running as an independent (since he had missed the filing deadline), Stevenson created a third party, the Illinois Solidarity party, for the November election—and lost decisively.

Second, observers contend that primaries have contributed to a decline in party responsibility. Candidates who win office largely on their own, who have their own distinctive followings within local electorates, have less reason to defer to party leaders or to adhere to traditional party positions. Their party membership is simply what they choose to make it. Third, the primary has contributed to numerous intraparty clashes; particularly bitter primary fights sometimes render the party incapable of generating a united campaign in the general election.[11] Finally, primaries apparently contribute to the consolidation of one-party politics. In an area where one party ordinarily dominates, its primaries tend to become the arena for political battles. The growth of the second party is inhibited not only by the lack of voter interest in its primaries but also by its inability to attract strong candidates to its colors. One-party domination reveals little about the party's organizational strength—indeed, one-party political systems likely will be characterized more by factionalism and internecine warfare than by unity, harmony, and ideological agreement.

"The cumulative effect of the direct primary," in the view of David B. Truman,

> is in the direction of organizational atrophy. The direct primary has been the most potent in a complex of forces pushing toward the disintegration of the party. . . . Even in those states using a closed primary and some reasonably restrictive form of enrollment to qualify as a voter in the primary, the thrust of the direct primary is disintegrative. In states that have embraced the full spirit of the direct primary by providing for an open system in one or another of its forms, where in effect anyone can wander in off the street to vote in the primary election of any party or where any organized interest group can colonize any party, the likelihood of any organization controlling nominations on a continuing basis is small.[12]

Such are the arguments developed against the primary. Of course, others can be made on its behalf.[13] In some jurisdictions, moreover, the dominant party organization is sufficiently strong that nonendorsed candidates have little or no chance of upsetting the organization slate. Potential challengers may abandon their campaigns once the party leaders or the organization have made known their choices. Other candidacies may never materialize because the prospects for getting the nod from party leaders appear unpromising. Taking the country as a whole, nevertheless, the evidence is persuasive that the primary weakens party organization. Unable to control its nominations, a party forfeits some portion of its claim to be known as a party, some portion of its raison d'être. The loose, freewheeling character of American parties owes much to the advent, consolidation, and extension of the direct primary.

For an additional illustration of the relationship between the election system and the party system, consider the use and impact of nonpartisan elections. While searching for a formula to improve city government early in the twentieth century, reformers hit upon the idea of the nonpartisan ballot—one in which party labels would not be present. The purpose of the plan was to free local government from the issues and divisiveness of national and state party politics and from the grip of local party bosses, which in turn, it was thought, would contribute to the effectiveness of local units. The nonpartisan ballot immediately gained favor and, once established, has been hard to dislodge; indeed, the plan has grown in popularity over the years. Today, substantially more than half of the American cities with populations of more than five thousand have nonpartisan elections.

A large variety of political patterns is found in nonpartisan election systems. In some cities with nonpartisan ballots, the party presence is nonetheless quite visible, and there is no doubt which candidates are affiliated with which parties. Elections in these cities are partisan in everything but label. In other cities, local party organizations compete against slates of candidates sponsored by various nonparty groups. In still other cities, the local parties are virtually without power, having lost it to interest groups that recruit, sponsor, and finance candidates for office. Finally, in some nonpartisan elections neither party nor nonparty groups slate candidates, thus leaving individual candidates to their own devices. This type is particularly prevalent in small cities.

It is difficult to say how much nonpartisan elections have diminished the vitality of local party organizations. Here and there the answer is plainly, "very little if at all"; elsewhere, the impact appears to have been substantial. Whatever the case, where parties are shut out of the local election process, other kinds of politics enter—possibly centered around interest groups (including the press), celebrity or name politics (the latter favoring incumbents), or the idiosyncratic appeals of individual office seekers. Where party labels are absent, power is up for grabs. Whether the voters in any real sense can hold their representatives accountable, lacking the guidance that party labels furnish, is problematical at best.

Myths to the contrary, election systems are never designed to be neutral and never are neutral. Some election laws and constitutional provisions, such as the single-member district system or the rigorous requirements that minor parties must meet to gain a place on the ballot, provide general support for the two-party system. Of the nearly two dozen minor parties that ran candidates for the presidency in 1980, for example, only the Libertarian party managed to get on the ballot in all fifty states. It did not do as well in 1984, getting on the ballot in only thirty-nine states. No other minor party appeared on the ballot in as many as half the states, and collectively the fourteen minor parties received only 620,582 votes (0.7 percent) out of a total of 92,652,793 cast.

Other laws and constitutional provisions make party government difficult and sometimes impossible—included here are such system features as staggered terms of office, off-year elections, direct primaries, and nonpartisan ballots. The major parties are not always passive witnesses to existing electoral arrangements. At times they simply endure them because it is easier to live with conventional arrangements than to try to change them or because they recognize their benefits. At other times they seek new arrangements because the prospects for party advantage are sufficiently promising to warrant the effort. It is a good bet that no one understands or appreciates American election systems better than those party leaders responsible for defending party interests and winning elections.

The Political Culture and the Parties

A third important element in the environment of American political parties is the political culture—"the system of empirical beliefs, expressive symbols, and values which defines the situation in which political action takes place." [14] As commonly represented, the political culture of a nation is the amalgam of public attitudes toward the political system, its subunits, and the role of the individual within the system. It includes the knowledge and beliefs people have about the political system, their feelings toward it, their identification with it, and their evaluations of it.

Although there is little systematic information on the public's political orientations toward the party system, scattered evidence indicates that large segments of the public do not evaluate parties or party functions in a favorable light. Studies of the Wisconsin electorate between 1964 and 1984 by Jack Dennis bear on this point. [15] The range of public attitudes on a series of propositions about American parties, including those that reveal diffuse or generalized support for the party system as a whole and for the norm of partisanship and those that reveal acceptance of the ideas or practices congruent with a system of responsible parties, is presented

TABLE 1-2   Trends in Popular Support for the Party System, 1964-1984
(Shown as Percent Supportive)

	1964	1966	1970	1972	1974	1976	1984
Diffuse support							
The parties do more to confuse the issues than to provide a clear choice on issues. (disagree)	21	19	21	28	24	19	29
The political parties more often than not create conflicts where none really exists. (disagree)	15	14	19	18	18	17	29
It would be better if, in all elections, we put no party labels on the ballot. (disagree)	67	56	44	42	38	36	45
Support for responsible party government							
A senator or representative should follow his or her party leaders even if he or she doesn't want to.	23					10	19
Contributor support							
People who work for political parties during political campaigns do our nation a great service.	68					53	77
The best rule in voting is to pick the best candidate, regardless of party label.	10				5	6	6
Cleavage function support							
Democracy works best where competition between political parties is strong.	74				73	66	73

SOURCE: Jack Dennis, "Public Support for the Party System, 1964-1984" (Paper delivered at the annual meeting of the American Political Science Association, Washington, D.C., August 28-31, 1986), 19. Also see his earlier study, "Support for the Party System by the Mass Public," *American Political Science Review* 60 (September 1966): 600-615.

in Table 1-2.

The principal conclusion to be drawn from the data provided in the table is that the public is highly skeptical of the parties and their activities. In 1964 90 percent of the Wisconsin electorate endorsed the idea that "the best rule in voting is to pick the best candidate, regardless of party label." By 1984 94 percent accepted this idea. An overwhelming majority of the public believes that the parties do more to confuse issues than to clarify them and that they often provoke unnecessary conflict.

Less than half of the electorate sees any merit to even having party labels on the ballot.

Also of interest, the Wisconsin data reveal that support for cohesive and disciplined parties is extremely limited, even less in 1984 than in 1964. Currently, only about one out of five persons believes that a legislator "should follow his or her party leaders even if he or she doesn't want to." Overall, little in this profile of popular attitudes suggests that the public understands or accepts the tenets of a responsible party system.[16]

Whether the orientations of the Wisconsin voters to the parties are representative of popular attitudes elsewhere is hard to say. But it seems likely that this is the case. Nationwide surveys of voter attitudes toward control of the presidency and Congress by the same party point to popular doubts about the parties (see Table 1-3). Only about one-third of the voters believe that the country is better off when the same party controls both the executive and legislative branches of government. The public sees several advantages of divided party control (see Figure 1-1). Chief among these is the belief that it increases the likelihood that corruption will be detected and that power will not be abused. Most Americans clearly are dubious of government by party.

Popular dissatisfaction with the party system is also reflected in the trends concerning party identification and straight-ticket voting. The number of people who identify themselves as Democrats and Republicans dropped from 80 percent in 1940 to 70 percent in 1986; on several occasions during this period the proportion of party identifiers fell below 70 percent. On the other hand, the number of people who classify themselves as independents has grown; this group now represents about 30 percent of the electorate.

TABLE 1-3   Voter Attitudes toward Party Control of Government

	Total voters 1973	Total voters 1976	Total voters 1980	Total voters 1984
Better	50%	40%	51%	54%
Worse	29	38	36	39
Makes no difference or not sure	21	22	13	7

SOURCE: Louis Harris, "Survey Report," January 1973, *Pittsburgh Post Gazette,* September 27, 1976 (as adapted), and Seymour Martin Lipset, "Feeling Better: Measuring the Nation's Confidence," *Public Opinion* 8 (April/May 1985): 7.

NOTE: Question: "Do you think it is better or worse for the country to have a president of one party and a Congress controlled by the other party, or doesn't it make much difference?"

FIGURE 1-1   The Public's Perceptions of the Advantages of Divided Government

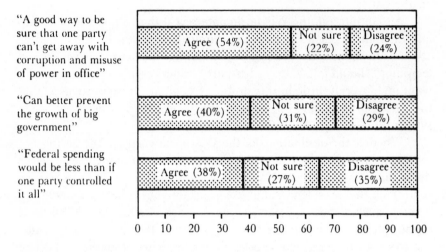

SOURCE: Louis Harris, "Survey Report," *Pittsburgh Post Gazette,* September 27, 1976 (as adapted).

Trends in straight-ticket voting (supporting all the candidates of one party) show a similar erosion of citizen linkage to the parties. The decline in straight-ticket voting has been sharp—dropping from 66 percent of the electorate in 1952 to 37 percent in 1980 (see Figure 1-2). Straight tickets were cast by 43 percent of the voters in 1984, still a modest proportion of the electorate. Straight-ticket voting in off-year elections (not included in the figure) has also declined markedly in recent years. For a great many voters, party loyalty no longer is a matter of much importance.

Ticket splitting is a major explanation for the frequent appearance of a truncated political system, characterized by Republican control of the presidency and Democratic control of Congress. Numerous voters, in other words, regularly support Republican presidential candidates and Democratic congressional candidates. Their preference for Democratic congressional candidates is, in part, simply a preference for incumbents. Of the 232 House Democratic incumbents on the general election ballot in 1986, for example, only one was defeated—a new record for incumbent success, but just barely.

Adding to the party problem, many voters see little or no difference in the effectiveness of the parties in governing. Surveys by the Gallup poll, starting as long ago as the 1940s, have asked voters to identify the most important problem facing the nation and to select the party best able to handle it. The results are illuminating (see Figure 1-3). Over

FIGURE 1-2 Straight-Ticket Voting in Presidential Elections, 1952-1984, in Percentages

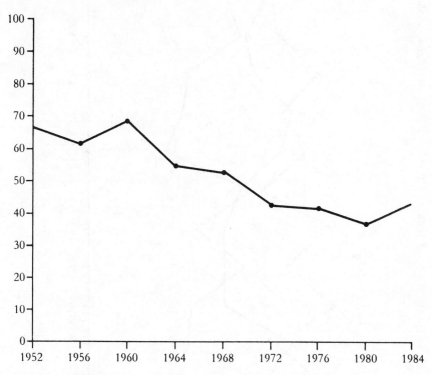

SOURCE: Jack Dennis, "Trends in Public Support for the American Party System" (Paper delivered at the annual meeting of the American Political Science Association, Chicago, August 29-September 2, 1974), 5 (as updated). The data for 1952-1972 were drawn from surveys by the Center for Political Studies and the Survey Research Center of the University of Michigan. The 1976, 1980, and 1984 data were taken from the Gallup poll.

most of the period 1945-1985, the Democratic party received much higher marks than the Republican party. During President Reagan's second term, the public came to view the Republican party as best able to deal with public problems. But the most important fact revealed by the data is that voters who cannot distinguish between the parties' capacity to handle major problems (or who have no opinion) regularly outnumber those who select either party. It is rare for the proportion of uncommitted voters to fall below 35 or 40 percent in these surveys. Perhaps one-third to one-half of all voters take a neutral stance when asked to judge the two parties as agencies for solving major public problems.[17]

The evidence thus indicates that American political parties rest on a relatively narrow and uncertain base of popular support. Scarcely anyone can fail to notice the widespread skepticism of politics and politicians

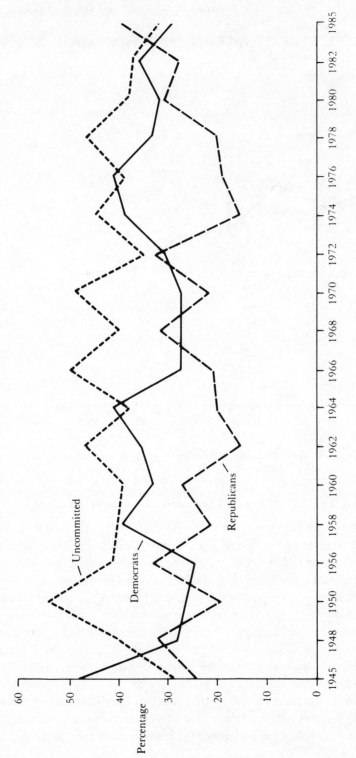

FIGURE 1-3 The Public's Perception of the Party Best Able to Handle the Most Important Problem Facing the Nation, 1945-1985

SOURCE: Developed from data appearing in *Gallup Report*, April 1985, 23.

that pervades popular thought. Few vocations stir so little interest as that of the politician. The language of American politics is itself laced with suspicion and hostility. In the argot of popular appraisal, political organizations turn into "machines," party workers emerge as "hacks," political leaders become "bosses," and campaign appeals degenerate into "empty promises" or "sheer demagoguery." That some politicians have contributed to this state of affairs, by debasing the language of political discourse or by their behavior, as in the Watergate affair, is perhaps beside the point. The critical fact is that the American political culture contains a strong suspicion of the political process and the agencies that try to dominate it, the political parties.

A Heterogeneous Nation

To complete the analysis of the environment of American parties, it is necessary to say something about the characteristics of the nation as a whole. No array of statistics is required to make the point that in the magnitude of its diversity, no nation can lay greater claim than the United States. The American community is composed of an endless variety of economic and social interests, class configurations, ethnic and religious groups, occupations, regional and subregional interests, and loyalties, values, and beliefs. There are citizens who are deeply attached to inherited patterns and those who are impatient advocates of change, those who care intensely about politics and those who can take it or leave it, and those who elude labeling—those who are active on one occasion and passive on another. There are citizens who think mainly in terms of farm policy, some who seek advantage for urban elements, others whose lives and political interests revolve around business or professions. Diversity abounds. Sometimes deep, sometimes shallow, the differences that separate one group from another and one region from another make the formation of public policy that suits everyone all but impossible.

The essential requirement for the major parties is that they accommodate themselves to the vast diversity of the nation. And they have done this remarkably well. Each party attracts a wide range of interests. Voting behavior in the 1984 presidential election (Reagan vs. Mondale) illustrates this point (see Figure 1-4). Most groups divided their vote between the parties in a ratio fairly close to that of the electorate as a whole (41 percent Democratic, 59 percent Republican). The most distinctive vote distributions on the Democratic side were those of blacks and Jews, and on the Republican side, those of white Protestants, white born-again Christians, and persons with incomes over $50,000. The

FIGURE 1-4 The Voting Behavior of Groups in the 1984 Presidential Election, in Percentages

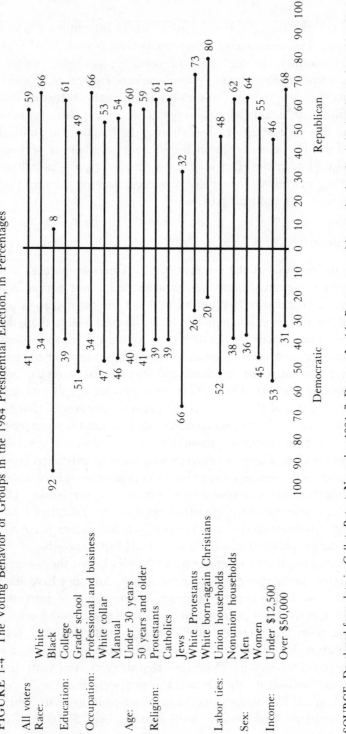

SOURCE: Developed from data in *Gallup Report*, November 1984, 7. Data on Jewish, Protestant, and income-level voting behavior drawn from *New York Times*/CBS News poll, as reported in Gerald M. Pomper, *The Election of 1984* (Chatham, N.J.: Chatham House Publishers, 1985), 67-68.

important point to recognize is that neither party excludes any group from its calculations for winning elections. On the contrary, each party expects to do reasonably well among virtually all groups. And ordinarily they do.

The heterogeneity of the nation is one explanation for the enduring parochial cast of American politics. As Herbert Agar has explained:

> Most politics will be parochial, most politicians will have small horizons, seeking the good of the state or the district rather than of the Union; yet by diplomacy and compromise, never by force, the government must water down the selfish demands of regions, races, classes, business associations, into a national policy which will alienate no major groups and which will contain at least a plum for everybody. This is the price of unity in a continentwide federation.[18]

Party Organization

Party organization has two common features in all parts of the United States. First, parties are organized in a series of committees, reaching from the precinct level to the national committee. Second, party committee organization parallels the arrangement of electoral districts. With the exception of heavily one-party areas, party committees will be found in virtually all jurisdictions within which important government officials are elected. The presence of party committees, of course, reveals little about their activities or their vitality in campaigns.

A familiar description of American parties begins by likening their organizational structure to that of a pyramid. At the top of the pyramid rests the national committee, at the bottom the precinct organizations, with various ward, city, county, and state committees lodged in between. Although it is convenient to view party organization within this pattern, it is misleading if it suggests that power flows steadily from top to bottom, from major national leaders to local leaders and local rank and file. Subnational committees actually have substantial autonomy, particularly in the crucial matters of selecting and slating candidates for public office (including federal office), raising and spending money, and conducting campaigns.

The National Committee

The most prestigious and visible of all party committees is the national committee.[19] The people who serve on the national committee of each party are prominent state politicians, chosen in a variety of ways and under a number of constraints. Their official tenure begins when they are accepted by the national convention of each party.

The selection of national committee members is not a simple matter. The Democratic party, operating under its 1974 charter, has especially elaborate provisions governing the composition of its national committee. Among its membership are the chairperson and the highest ranking official of the opposite sex of each recognized state party, two hundred additional members allotted to the states on the same basis as delegates are apportioned to the national convention, and a number of delegates representing such organizations as the Democratic Governor's Conference, the Congress, the National Finance Council, the Conference of Democratic Mayors, the National Federation of Democratic Women, the Democratic County Officials Conference, the State Legislative Leaders Caucus, and the Young Democrats of America. As in the case of delegates to the party's national convention, members of the national committee must be selected "through processes which assure full, timely, and equal opportunity to participate" and with due attention to "affirmative action" standards.

To know what the national committee is, it is necessary to look at what it does.[20] One of its principal responsibilities is to make arrangements for the national convention every four years. In this capacity it chooses the convention site, prepares a temporary roster of convention delegates, and selects convention speakers and temporary officers who will manage the assembly in its opening phase. The committee is especially active during presidential campaigns in coordinating campaign efforts, publicizing the party and its candidates, and raising money. Following the election, the committee often faces the task of raising the necessary funds to pay off campaign debts.

The influence of the president on his party's national committee is substantial. "I don't think the Republican National Committee can ever really be independent," a longtime committee staff member has said. "[The committee has] a responsibility to the leader. Policy is always made at the White House, not here. We accept it and support it." [21] The same is true for the Democratic National Committee (DNC). "The president likes a party that serves as a supportive tool for the president," observed a state party chairman during the Carter administration. "An independent organization is looked upon as a nuisance. That is inevitable." Or, as a White House aide remarked, President Carter "is turned on to the DNC as a service institution." [22]

The national committees come to life during presidential election years because their major efforts are directed toward the election of their party's presidential candidate. During nonpresidential years most of the national committee's work is carried on by committees or the national chairman. Study groups occasionally are created by the committee (perhaps under instructions from the national convention) to examine certain problems, such as party organization, party policy, or convention management. In 1969, for example, the Democratic National Committee created the Commission on Party Structure and Delegate Selection, known as the McGovern-Fraser Commission, to hold hearings and to suggest proposals for changes in party procedures. Included in its wide-ranging report were recommendations urging state parties (and, in certain cases, state legislatures) to eliminate discrimination of all kinds in party rules, to open party meetings and processes to participation by all members of the party, to remove or moderate restrictive voter registration laws or practices, and to provide for the fair representation of blacks, women, and young persons in state delegations to the national convention.

Four subsequent reform commissions—the Mikulski Commission (1972-1973), the Winograd Commission (1975-1978), the Hunt Commission (1981-1982), and the Fairness Commission (1984-1985)—further refined party rules. The broad thrust of the 1969-1978 reforms was to increase popular participation in the presidential nominating process while at the same time diluting the power of party professionals. In counterpoise, the recommendations of the Hunt Commission were directed toward restoring the influence of party regulars and officeholders in the presidential nominating process and relaxing certain other party rules introduced in the 1970s. Adopted by the Democratic National Committee in 1986, the recommendations of the Fairness Commission largely reaffirmed the system used in 1984, though it made several changes regarding delegate positions for party and elected officials, eligibility for participation in primaries and caucuses, and the allocation of delegates. (See Chapter 3.)

The national committees of the two parties are by no means alike. In recent years, the Republican National Committee (RNC) has been much more effective than its Democratic counterpart in raising campaign funds (especially through direct-mail methods) and in providing services for candidates. Operating with a large field staff, the RNC makes a variety of technical services available to national and state candidates; these services include public opinion surveys and computer analyses of voting patterns. Extending its reach, the RNC even makes financial contributions to party candidates in key state legislative races.[23]

National and state organizations have become more interdependent in the Republican party than they have in the Democratic party.[24] With a less elaborate organization and a much less successful fund-raising operation, the DNC concentrates its efforts on the presidential election. And many Democratic party politicians find fault with its emphasis. "There is no sense that the Democratic state parties are part of a national whole," observed one leader. "The DNC is viewed by the state parties as a foreign power that does not dispense foreign aid." [25]

The National Chairman

The head of the national party is the national chairman.[26] Although the chairman is officially selected by the members of the national committee, in practice he is chosen by the party's presidential candidate shortly after the national convention has adjourned. Very few chairmen in either party have held the position for an extended period—the chairman of the party winning the presidency usually receives a major appointment in the new administration, and the chairman of the losing party is replaced by a new face. When a vacancy in the chairmanship of the out party occurs, selection of the new chairman is made by the national committee. Factional conflicts may come to the surface when the committee is faced with the responsibility of finding a replacement, since the leading candidates will usually be identified with certain wings of the party.

The central problem with which the national chairman must come to terms in presidential years is the direction and coordination of the national campaign. The Republican national organization has far outstripped its Democratic rival in the task. One major reason is that such national chairmen as Ray C. Bliss (1965-1969) and Bill Brock (1977-1981) concentrated their efforts on organizational reform, seeking in particular to strengthen state and local Republican organizations by providing them with all kinds of "electioneering" assistance.[27] A successful fund-raising program, based on more than two million small contributors, makes these efforts possible.[28]

On the Democratic side, the position of the national chairman has been particularly frustrating. No recent Democratic president has made a significant effort to strengthen the national party apparatus; indeed, each has tended to downgrade it.[29] The difficulties that face the national chairman were aptly described by Kenneth M. Curtis, who resigned in 1978 after only one year in office:

> Have you ever tried to meet the payroll every two weeks of a bankrupt organization and deal with 363 bosses [national committee members]

and 50 state chairs? . . . I tried it for a year and simply decided I'd like to do something else with my life. It's not the sort of job that you lay down in the street and bleed to keep. . . .[30]

Congressional and Senatorial Campaign Committees

The other principal units of the national party organization are the congressional and senatorial campaign committees, one committee for each party in each house. These committees, composed of members of Congress, are independent of the national committees. The campaign committees are an outgrowth of the need of members of Congress to have organizations concerned exclusively with their political welfare. As such, the committees raise campaign funds for members, help to develop campaign strategies, conduct research, and otherwise provide assistance to members running for reelection.[31] In addition, the committees may make funds available for party candidates in states or districts where the party has no incumbent. A certain degree of informal cooperation occurs between the party committees of Congress and the national committees, but for the most part they go their separate ways: the former bent on securing reelection of incumbent legislators and on improving the party's prospects for winning or retaining control of Congress, the latter preoccupied with the presidential race.

The Republican campaign committees are the most active and best financed. In 1984 the National Republican Senatorial Committee spent about twice as much money on Republican senatorial candidates as the Democratic Campaign Committee did on its candidates. On the House side, the National Republican Congressional Committee (NRCC) outspent its rival by almost six to one. Nevertheless, the spending gap between the parties was not as large in 1984 as it had been in 1982 or 1980.[32] Occasionally, the NRCC enters congressional primary fights, supporting one Republican over another.[33] Overall, the influence of the national Republican party committees on House and Senate elections has grown substantially in recent years. Democrats have much to learn from them about "party building."

State Committees

Midway between the national party apparatus and local party organizations are the state party committees, often called state central committees. So great are the differences between these committees from state to state—in membership selection, size, and function—that it is difficult to generalize about them. In some states the membership is made up of county chairmen; more commonly, state committee members are chosen in primaries or by local party conventions. Their number ranges from less than a hundred members to several hundred. In some states the state central committee is a genuinely powerful party unit and is charged by custom with drafting the party platform, slating statewide candidates, and waging an intensive fund-raising campaign. In other states the committee's impact on state politics is scarcely perceptible. In a fashion similar to that found at the national level, the state chairman is ordinarily selected by the party's gubernatorial candidate. And like the national chairman, the state chairman is usually a key adviser to the governor on party affairs, particularly on matters involving the distribution of patronage.[34]

Local Party Organization

Below the state committee of the party is the county committee, ordinarily a very large organization composed of all the precinct officials within the county. At the head of this committee is the county chairman, who is usually elected by the members of the county committee. Often a key figure in local party organization, the county chairman is active in the campaign planning, in the recruitment and slating of party candidates, in the supervision of campaign financing, and in the allocation of patronage to the party faithful. In many counties, the county chairman's power is enhanced by the fact that he actively recruits candidates for precinct committee members—the very people who in turn elect him to office. Some states have congressional district party organizations, developed around the office of U.S. representative. Where these committees exist, they function essentially as the member's personal organization, set off from the rest of the party and preoccupied with "errand running" for constituents and the election of the member. Although local party officials, such as the county chairman, may be instrumental in controlling the original congressional nomination, their influence on the representative's policy orientations is virtually nil. Indeed, one of the dominant characteristics of congressional district organization is its autonomy. Further down the line are the city and ward committees, which vary in size and importance throughout the country. Their activities, like those of other committees, are centered around campaigns and elections.

The cornerstone of American party organization is the precinct committee, organized within the tens of thousands of election or voting districts of the nation. In metropolitan areas a precinct is likely to number one thousand or two thousand voters; in open-country areas, perhaps only a dozen. The complexity of party organization at the precinct level is mainly a function of precinct size. The precinct committee member is chosen in one of two ways: by the voters in a primary election or by the vote of party members attending a precinct caucus.

In the lore of American politics, elections are won or lost at the precinct level. A strong precinct organization, the argument runs, is essential to party victory, and the key to a strong organization is a precinct leader bent on carrying his precinct. In attempting to advance their party's fortunes, the committee members engage in four main activities: those associated with the campaign itself, party organizational work (for example, recruitment and organization of workers), promulgation of political information, and identification and recruitment of candidates for local office. For most jurisdictions, it appears, their most important activities are those related to the campaign, such as inducing and helping people to register, contacting voters, raising money, campaigning for votes, and transporting voters to the polls. Undoubtedly there are differences in the role perceptions of party officials. A study of precinct leaders in Massachusetts and North Carolina, for example, found that about 60 percent saw their principal task as that of mobilizing voters.[35] In Connecticut and Michigan the leading activities of precinct officials are fundraising, canvassing, and distributing literature.[36] And in Pittsburgh, about two-thirds of the committee members describe their most important task as electoral—but here they tend to be indifferent to organizational goals and more supportive of particular candidates than of the party slate as a whole.[37] One study has shown that the organizational vitality of local parties (as measured by such things as the presence of officials, allocation of time to party business, regular meetings, the existence of a budget, and participation in various kinds of campaign activities) is highest in the East (for example, New Jersey, New York, Pennsylvania, and Delaware) and Midwest (for example, Indiana, Ohio, and Illinois) and lowest in the South (for example, Louisiana, Georgia, Florida, Kentucky, and Texas).[38]

The Changing Parties: "Old Style" and "New Style" Politics

In the late nineteenth and early twentieth centuries the best examples of strong party organization could be found in the large cities of the Northeast and Midwest—New York City, Boston, Philadelphia, Jersey City, Kansas City, and Chicago. Well-organized and strongly disciplined, the urban machine during this era was well-nigh invincible.

Precinct and ward officials maintained steady contacts with their party constituencies, finding jobs for people out of work, helping those who were in trouble with the law, aiding others to secure government benefits such as welfare payments, assisting neighborhoods to secure government services, helping immigrants to cope with a new society, and facilitating merchants and tradespeople in their efforts to obtain contracts, licenses, and the like. The party organization was at the center of community life, an effective mediator between the people and their government. Party officials were "brokers," exchanging information, access, and influence for loyalty and support at the polls.

Today the picture is much different. Although the party organizations continue to provide social services in certain large cities, the volume of such exchanges has declined sharply. Numerous factors have contributed to this loss of function, including (1) the growth of civil service systems and the corresponding decline in patronage; (2) the relative decline in the value of patronage jobs; (3) the arrival of the welfare state with its various benefits for low-income groups; (4) the steady assimilation of immigrants; (5) the growing disillusionment among better educated voters over many features of machine politics; and (6) the coming of age of the mass media with its potential for contacts between candidates and their publics. Many disadvantaged citizens remain, particularly in large cities, who continue to rely on local party leaders for assistance in solving the problems in their lives. But most Americans scarcely give a thought to using party officials in this way. Where the parties have suffered a loss of functions, it is reasonable to assume that they have also suffered a loss of vitality. The result, undoubtedly, has been a decline in their ability to deliver the vote on election day.

One of the interesting struggles within both national parties over the past couple of decades has been that occurring between "purists" and "professionals"—the distinction drawn by Nelson Polsby and Aaron Wildavsky. Concerning the former group, they observe:

> When party activists seek power primarily over the party, and only secondarily over the government, we refer to them as "purists." Purists wish their views to be put forth by the parties without equivocation or compromise and although they otherwise seek to win elections, they do not care to do this at the expense of self-expression. Where a party politician might promote his own views up to the point where it would cost his party's candidate the election, the purist pursues electoral victory but not past the point where it would impede the expression of his views. In the purist conception of things, instead of a party convention being a place where a party meets to choose

candidates who can win elections by pleasing voters, it becomes a site for finding a candidate who will embody the message delegates seek to express.[39]

By contrast, the professionals set great store by the party itself:

They have served it before the nomination contest and expect to serve it after the election. They regard threats to bolt the party as dirty pool; their morality requires the candidates and factions to compete in good faith and the losers to unite behind the winners—though a particularly unsuitable candidate may incline even the professionals to "go fishing" on election day. Winning the election is the party's prime goal, for it is an indispensable prerequisite for everything else it wants to do. Therefore the professionals seek a candidate whose style they think will appeal to the voters they need to win, not necessarily to party leaders. They judge a candidate by how well or badly he runs in the election and by how much he has helped or hurt the rest of the ticket. And they see negotiation, compromise, and accommodation not as hypocrisy or immorality but as the very essence of what keeps parties—and nations—from disintegrating.[40]

The "new politics" of recent years has changed familiar political terrain. Today, far more activist newcomers are engaged in party activities and political campaigns, particularly in the Democratic party, than in the past. These newcomers, younger, leery of party machines, repelled by patronage and deals, committed to an open political process, often suspicious of the Washington establishment, stimulated by high principle and rectitude appeals, and greatly concerned with issues, have had a dramatic impact on American politics. Enthusiastically committed to Eugene McCarthy, they influenced Lyndon B. Johnson's decision to withdraw from the presidential contest in 1968. In 1972, still held together by opposition to the Vietnam War, they worked ceaselessly to win the nomination for George McGovern, using party rules on delegate selection that gave unprecedented representation to women, blacks, and youth in the national convention. In 1976, as members of the "peanut brigade," amateur activists helped an outsider, a relatively unknown former Georgia governor, Jimmy Carter, to win the Democratic nomination and ultimately the election. In 1984 they were attracted to another "outsider," Gary Hart, who had managed George McGovern's campaign in 1972. They preferred his "new ideas, new generation" theme to the "old politics" of Walter F. Mondale, the consummate "insider." For them, Mondale was the candidate of the party establishment, of "party bosses," and, especially, of such special interest groups as organized labor and teachers.

Another major feature of the new style of politics is the growth of *candidate-centered* campaigns.[41] Nowhere is the campaign apparatus of the parties as important as the personal organizations of individual candidates. Candidates—for minor offices and major ones, incumbents and challengers—all have their own organizations for managing the activities of campaigns. Within these units the key decisions are made on campaign strategies, issues, worker recruitment, voter mobilization, and the raising and spending of funds. Candidates often hire campaign management firms, public relations specialists, and political consultants to assist them. These professionals conduct public opinion surveys, prepare films and advertising, raise money, buy radio and television time, write speeches, provide computer analyses of voting behavior, and develop strategies, issues, and images. Less and less of campaign management is left to chance, hunch, or the party organizations.

Candidate-centered campaigns revolve around candidate-centered fund raising. Although the national parties continue to supply funds to candidates and to spend money on their behalf—especially important on the Republican side—their role in campaign finance is not as decisive as that of political interest groups or of individual contributors. Currently, House candidates obtain about half of their funds from individual contributors while Senate candidates receive almost two-thirds of their funds from this source. Political action committees (PACs) rank next in importance. House incumbents, for example, received 42 percent of all their campaign funds in 1984 from PACs, while Senate incumbents received 23 percent. Interest groups clearly have outpaced the parties in funding campaigns for Congress. Their prominence helps to account for the candidate-centeredness of contemporary American politics.

The role of independent expenditures in campaigns also needs to be understood. Under the Federal Election Campaign Act (FECA) passed in 1971 and amended several times since then, limits are placed on the amount of money an individual or political action committee can give to a federal candidate. In addition, a presidential candidate who accepts federal funds for the general election campaign cannot accept private contributions. But no limit exists on the amount of money that supporters of federal candidates can spend to aid their campaigns as long as the funds are spent *independently*—that is, without contact with the candidates or their campaign organizations. As a result, groups of all kinds now spend heavily, especially in media advertising, opposing as well as supporting presidential and congressional candidates. In the 1984 presidential race, independent expenditures exceeded $17 million, about ten times the amount spent by independent groups in 1976.[42] The

PAC Contributions to Congressional Candidates, 1972-1984

Under the terms of the Federal Election Campaign Act adopted in 1971, corporations and unions are permitted to use funds from their treasuries to establish and administer political action committees (PACs) and to solicit financial contributions to them. Amendments to the act in 1974 further encouraged the development of PACs and their financial participation in partisan campaigns. In 1974 there were about six hundred PACs; by 1987 the number exceeded four thousand. Their contributions to House and Senate candidates have grown apace:

Year	Total contributions to congressional candidates (in millions)	Percent to incumbents
1972	$ 8.5	[a]
1974	12.5	[a]
1976	22.6	[a]
1978	34.1	57
1980	55.2	61
1982	83.6	66
1984	104.9	73

SOURCE: Assorted press releases, Federal Election Commission.

[a] Not available.

intense involvement of groups in campaigns has changed the nation's political ambiance and its political structures, serving, in the main, to promote the independence of candidates and officeholders from party controls, while doubtlessly making them even more reliant on interest groups.

The Activities of Parties

A principal thesis in the scholarship on political parties is that they are indispensable to the functioning of democratic political systems. Scholars have differed sharply in their approaches to the study of parties and in their appraisals of the functions or activities of parties, but they are in striking agreement on the linkage between parties and democracy. Rep-

resentative of a wide band of analysis, the following statements by V. O.
Key, Jr., and E. E. Schattschneider, respectively, sketch the broad out-
lines of the argument:

> Governments operated, of course, long before political parties in the
> modern sense came into existence. . . . The proclamation of the right
> of men to have a hand in their own governing did not create institu-
> tions by which they might exercise that right. Nor did the machinery
> of popular government come into existence overnight. By a tortuous
> process party systems came into being to implement democratic ideas.
> As democratic ideas corroded the old foundations of authority, mem-
> bers of the old governing elite reached out to legitimize their positions
> under the new notions by appealing for popular support. That appeal
> compelled deference to popular views, but it also required the devel-
> opment of organization to communicate with and to manage the
> electorate. . . . In a sense, government, left suspended in mid-air by the
> erosion of the old justifications for its authority, had to build new
> foundations in the new environment of a democratic ideology. In
> short, it had to have machinery to win votes.[43]

> The rise of political parties is indubitably one of the principal distin-
> guishing marks of modern government. The parties, in fact, have
> played a major role as *makers* of governments, more especially they
> have been the makers of democratic government. . . . [Political] parties
> created democracy and . . . modern democracy is unthinkable save in
> terms of the parties. . . . The parties are not . . . merely appendages of
> modern government; they are in the center of it and play a determi-
> native and creative role in it.[44]

The contributions of political parties to the maintenance of democratic politics can be judged in a rough way by examining the principal
activities in which they engage. Of particular importance are those
activities associated with the recruitment and selection of leadership, the
representation and integration of interests, and the control and direction
of government.

Recruitment and Selection of Leaders

The processes by which political leaders are recruited, elected, and
appointed to office form the central core of party activity.[45] The party
interest, moreover, extends to the appointment of administrative and
judicial officers—for example, cabinet members and judges—once the
party has captured the executive branch of government.[46] As observed
earlier, the party organizations do not necessarily dominate the process

by which candidates are recruited or nominated. Increasingly, candidates are self-starters, choosing to enter primaries without waiting for approval from party leaders. With their own personal followings and sources of campaign money, they often pay scant heed to party leaders or party politics. Some candidates are recruited and groomed by political interest groups. Many candidates find interest groups a particularly lucrative source of campaign funds. The looseness of the American party system creates conditions under which party control over the candidates who run under its banner is thin or nonexistent.

Still and all, the political parties play an important role in finding candidates and in electing them to office. It is difficult to see how hundreds of thousands of elective offices could be filled in the absence of parties without turning each election into a free-for-all, conspicuous by the presence of numerous candidates holding all varieties of set, shifting, and undisclosed views. Composing a government out of an odd mélange of officials, especially at the national level, would be very difficult. Any form of collective accountability to the voters would vanish. Hence, whatever their shortcomings, by proposing alternative lists of candidates and campaigning on their behalf, the parties bring certain measures of order, routine, and predictability to the electoral process.

The constant factors in party politics are the pursuit of power, office, and advantage. Yet, in serving their own interest in winning office, parties make other contributions to the public at large and to the political system. For example, they help to educate the voters concerning issues and mobilize them for political action, provide a linkage between the people and the government, and simplify the choices to be made in elections. The parties do what voters cannot do by themselves: from the totality of interests and issues in politics, they choose those that will become "the agenda of formal public discourse." [47] In the process of shaping the agenda, they provide a mechanism by which voters can not only make sense out of what government does but also relate to the government itself. The role of the parties in educating voters and in structuring opinion has been described by Robert MacIver in this way:

> Public opinion is too variant and dispersive to be effective unless it is organized. It must be canalized on the broad lines of some major division of opinion. Party focuses the issues, sharpens the differences between contending sides, eliminates confusing crosscurrents of opinion. . . . The party educates the public while seeking merely to influence it, for it must appeal on grounds of policy. For the same reason it helps to remove the inertia of the public and thus to broaden the range of public opinion. In short the party, in its endeavors to win the public

to its side, however unscrupulous it may be in its modes of appeal, is making the democratic system workable. It is the agency by which public opinion is translated into public policy.[48]

Representation and Integration of Group Interests

The United States is a complex and heterogeneous nation. An extraordinary variety of political interest groups, organized around particularistic objectives, exists within it. Conflicts between one group and another, between coalitions of groups, and between various groups and the government, are inevitable. Since one of the major functions of government is to take sides in private disputes, what it decides and does is of high importance to groups. When at their creative best, parties and their leaders help to keep group conflicts within tolerable limits. Viewed from a wider perspective, the relationship between parties and private organizations is one of bargaining and accommodation—groups need the parties as much as the parties need them. No group can expect to move far toward the attainment of its objectives without coming to terms with the realities of party power; the parties, through their public officeholders, can advance or obstruct the policy objectives of any group. At the same time, no party can expect to receive widespread electoral success without significant group support. Quid pro quo, Latin's most useful political expression, explains this nexus.

Bargaining and compromise are key elements in the strategy of American parties. The doctrinal flexibility of the parties means that almost everything is "up for grabs"—each party can make at least some effort to satisfy virtually any group's demands. Through their public officials, the parties serve as "brokers" among the organized interests of American society, weighing the claims of one group against those of another, accepting some programs, and modifying or rejecting others.[49] The steady bargaining that takes place between interest groups and key party leaders (in the executive and legislative branches) tends to produce settlements the participants can live with for a time, even though these compromises may not be wholly satisfactory to anyone. In addition, of deeper significance, the legitimacy of government itself probably depends in part on the capacity of the parties to represent diverse interests and to integrate the claims of competing groups in a broad program of public policy. Their ability to do this is certain to bear on their electoral success.

The thesis that the major parties are steadily sensitive to the representation of group interests cannot be advanced without a caveat or two. The stubborn fact is that the parties are far more solicitous toward the claims of organized interests than toward those of unorganized interests. The groups that regularly engage the attention of parties and their representatives in government are those whose support (or opposition) can make a difference at the polls. Organized labor, organized business, organized agriculture, organized medicine—all have multiple channels for gaining access to decision makers. Indeed, party politicians are about as likely to search out the views of these interests as to wait to hear from them. In recent years, special "cause" groups—those passionate and uncompromising lobbies concerned with single issues such as gun control, abortion, tax rollbacks, equal rights, nuclear power, and the environment—have kept legislators' feet to the fire, exerting extraordinary influence as they judge members on the "correctness" of their positions. By contrast, many millions of Americans are all but shut out of the political system. The political power of such groups as agricultural workers, sharecroppers, migrants, and unorganized labor has never been commensurate with their numbers or, for that matter, with their contribution to society. With low participation in elections, weak organizations, low status, and poor access to political communications, their voices are often drowned out in the din produced by organized interests.[50]

No problem of representation in America is more important than that of finding ways to move the claims of the unorganized public onto the agenda of politics. But the task is formidable: "All power is organization and all organization is power. . . . A man who has no share in any form of organized power is not independent of organized power. He is at the mercy of it. . . ."[51]

Control and Direction of Government

A third major activity of the parties involves the control and direction of government. Parties recruit candidates and organize campaigns to win political power, gain public office, and take control of government. Given the character of the political system and the parties themselves, it is unrealistic to suppose that party management of government will be altogether successful. In the first place, the separate branches of government may not be captured by the same party. In about two-thirds of the elections from 1950 to 1988, the party that won the presidency was unable to win control of both houses of Congress. Every Republican president since Dwight D. Eisenhower has faced this problem. Division of party control complicates the process of governing, forcing the president not only to work with his own party in Congress but also with elements of the other party. The legislative success of Republican presidents depends on their relations with conservative southern Democrats. The result is that party achievements in majority building tend to be blurred in the mix of coalition votes, and party accountability to the voters suffers. In the second place, even though one party may control both the legislative and executive branches, its margin of seats in the legislature may be too thin to permit it to govern effectively. Disagreement within the majority party, moreover, may be so great on certain issues that the party finds it virtually impossible to pull its ranks together to develop coherent positions. When majority party lines are shattered, opportunities arise for the minority party to assert itself in the policy-making process. In the third place, midterm (or off-year) elections invariably complicate the plans of the administration party. The president's party almost always loses seats in both houses. The Republican party lost five House seats and eight Senate seats in 1986, after losing twenty-six House seats and breaking even in the Senate in 1982. Since 1946 the administration party at midterm has suffered an average loss of twenty-seven seats in the House and four in the Senate (see Table 1-4). Very few events are as predictable in American elections or as dispiriting for administrations as the chilly midterm verdict of the voters. And finally, the problems the majority party has in managing the federal government about equal the problems it has in managing most state governments.

The upshot is that although the parties organize governments, they do not wholly control decision-making activities. In some measure they compete with political interest groups bent on securing public policies advantageous to their clienteles, and there are times when certain groups have fully as much influence on the behavior of legislators and bureaucrats as legislative party leaders, national and subnational party leaders, or the president. Yet, to point out the difficulties that confront the parties in seeking to manage the government is not to suggest that the parties' impact on public policy is insubstantial. Not even a casual examination of party platforms, candidates' and officeholders' speeches, or legislative voting can fail to detect the contributions of the parties to shaping the direction of government or can ignore the differences that separate the parties on public policy matters.

An understanding of American parties begins with recognizing that party politicians are more likely to set great store in the notion of winning elections than in using election outcomes to achieve a broad range of policy goals. To be sure, candidates have interests and commitments in policy questions, but rarely to the point that they rule out

TABLE 1-4   Off-year Gains and Losses in Congress by the President's Party, 1946-1986

Year	House		Senate	
1986	R	-5	R	-8
1982	R	-26	R	0
1978	D	-15	D	-3
1974	R	-48	R	-5
1970	R	-12	R	+2
1966	D	-47	D	-3
1962	D	-4	D	+4
1958	R	-47	R	-13
1954	R	-18	R	-1
1950	D	-29	D	-6
1946	D	-55	D	-12

NOTE: R = Republican; D = Democrat.

bargaining and compromise in the interest of achieving half a "party loaf." Politicians tend to be intensely pragmatic and adaptable persons. For the most part, they are attracted to a particular party more because of its promise as a mechanism for moving into government than as a mechanism for governing itself. Party is a way of organizing activists and supporters in order to make a bid for office.[52] This is the elemental truth of party politics. That the election of one aggregation of politicians as against another has policy significance, as indeed it does, comes closer to representing an unanticipated dividend than a triumph for the idea of responsible party government.

Notes

1. Alexander Hamilton, John Jay, and James Madison, *The Federalist* (New York: Modern Library, 1937), 55.
2. E. E. Schattschneider, *Party Government* (New York: Holt, Rinehart and Winston, 1942), 1.
3. This proposition is debatable. For the counterposition—one that stresses the capacity of parties to shape themselves—see Austin Ranney, *Curing the Mischiefs of Faction: Party Reform in America* (Berkeley: University of California Press, 1975), especially Chapter 1, and Jeane Jordan Kirkpatrick, *Dismantling the Parties: Reflections on Party Reform and Party Decomposition* (Washington, D.C.: American Enterprise Institute for Public Policy Research, 1978). For a wide-ranging analysis of the proposition presented in the text, see Robert Harmel and Kenneth Janda, *Parties and Their Environments* (New York: Longmans, 1982).
4. From *Party Government* by E. E. Schattschneider. Copyright 1942 by E. E. Schattschneider. Reprinted by permission of Holt, Rinehart and Winston, 6-7.
5. David R. Mayhew, *Placing Parties in American Politics* (Princeton, N.J.:

Princeton University Press, 1986).

6. David E. Price, *Bringing Back the Parties* (Washington, D.C.: CQ Press, 1984), particularly Chapter 5.

7. Mayhew, *Placing Parties in American Politics,* particularly Chapters 2 and 7.

8. For a careful exposition of this argument, see Schattschneider, *Party Government,* 67-84.

9. *Davis v. Bandemer,* 106 S. Ct. 2810 (1986). For a comprehensive examination of legislative reapportionment, see Bernard Grofman, "Criteria for Districting: A Social Science Perspective," *UCLA Law Review* 33 (October 1985): 77-184. The political considerations in reapportionment are explored in Q. Whitfield Ayres and David Whiteman, "Congressional Reapportionment in the 1980s: Types and Determinants of Policy Outcomes," *Political Science Quarterly* 99 (Summer 1984): 303-314.

10. Price, *Bringing Back the Parties,* 126.

11. For evidence on the disruptive impact of primaries on campaign workers, see the instructive article by Donald B. Johnson and James R. Gibson, "The Divisive Primary Revisited: Party Activists in Iowa," *American Political Science Review* 68 (March 1974): 67-77. The authors find that campaign workers for candidates who are defeated in contested primaries are typically less active in the general election campaign and, not infrequently, decide not to vote for either candidate or decide to work and vote for the opposition party.

12. David B. Truman, "Party Reform, Party Atrophy, and Constitutional Change: Some Reflections," *Political Science Quarterly* 99 (Winter 1984-1985): 649-650.

13. For a more extensive analysis of the primary, see Chapter 3.

14. Lucian W. Pye and Sidney Verba, eds., *Political Culture and Political Development* (Princeton, N.J.: Princeton University Press, 1965), 513.

15. The data and general line of argument developed in these paragraphs are derived from Jack Dennis, "Support for the Party System by the Mass Public," *American Political Science Review* 60 (September 1966): 600-615; Dennis, "Changing Support for the American Party System," in *Paths to Political Reform,* ed. William J. Crotty (Lexington, Mass.: Heath, 1980), 35-66; and Dennis, "Public Support for the Party Sysem, 1964-1984" (Paper delivered at the annual meeting of the American Political Science Association, Washington, D.C., August 28-31, 1986), 19.

16. A system of "responsible parties" would be characterized by centralized, unified, and disciplined parties committed to the execution of programs and promises offered at elections and held accountable by the voters for their performance.

17. For a careful analysis of the meaning of data such as presented here, see Martin P. Wattenberg, *The Decline of American Political Parties, 1952-1984* (Cambridge, Mass.: Harvard University Press, 1986), especially Chapter 4, and his earlier study, "The Decline of Political Partisanship in the United States: Negativity or Neutrality?" *American Political Science Review* 75 (December 1981): 941-950. Wattenberg finds that negative attitudes toward the parties have not increased significantly since the 1950s. Rather, the public has become more *neutral* in its evaluation of them. For a challenge to the "neutrality hypothesis," see Stephen C. Craig, "The Decline of Partisanship in the United States: A Reexamination of the Neutrality Hypothesis," *Political Behavior* 7, no. 1 (1985): 57-78.

18. Herbert Agar, *The Price of Union* (Boston: Houghton Mifflin, 1950), xiv.

19. For an instructive study of the national committee and the national chairman, see Cornelius P. Cotter and Bernard C. Hennessy, *Politics without Power: The*

National Party Committees (New York: Atherton Press, 1964).

20. See two studies that trace the growing importance of the national party: Charles H. Longley, "National Party Renewal," and John F. Bibby, "Party Renewal in the National Republican Party," in *Party Renewal in America: Theory and Practice,* ed. Gerald M. Pomper (New York: Praeger Special Studies, 1980), 69-86 and 102-115.

21. *Congressional Quarterly Weekly Report,* February 16, 1974, 352.

22. *Congressional Quarterly Weekly Report,* January 14, 1978, 61.

23. *Congressional Quarterly Weekly Report,* October 25, 1982, 3188-3192.

24. See an excellent study of the institutionalization of the parties by Cornelius P. Cotter and John F. Bibby, "Institutional Development of Parties and the Thesis of Party Decline," *Political Science Quarterly* 95 (Spring 1980): 1-27.

25. *Congressional Quarterly Weekly Report,* January 17, 1982, 140.

26. See Cotter and Hennessy, *Politics without Power,* 67-80. They see the roles of the national chairman as "image-maker, hell-raiser, fund-raiser, campaign manager, and administrator."

27. Robert J. Huckshorn and John F. Bibby, "State Parties in an Era of Political Change," in *The Future of American Political Parties,* ed. Joel L. Fleishman (Englewood Cliffs, N.J.: Prentice-Hall, 1982), 82.

28. F. Christopher Arterton, "Political Money and Party Strength," in *The Future of American Political Parties,* ed. Joel L. Fleishman, 105.

29. Huckshorn and Bibby, "State Parties in an Era of Political Change," 83.

30. *Congressional Quarterly Weekly Report,* January 14, 1978, 58.

31. The chairmanship of a congressional campaign committee is a major political plum. The chairman has numerous opportunities to help party candidates be elected and, more important, to help incumbents be reelected. The chairman concentrates on fund raising, "signs the checks" for the party's candidates, and inevitably gains the gratitude of winners. The election of Tony Coelho (D-Calif.) as House majority whip for the One-hundredth Congress (1987-1988) was widely attributed to the support of members he assisted during his six years as chairman of the Democratic Congressional Campaign Committee. (As provided by the Constitution, each of the two regular sessions that make up a Congress convenes at noon on January 3, unless a different day is appointed. Thus, the One-hundredth Congress actually runs from 1987 to 1989; the first session from 1987 to 1988, the second session from 1988 to 1989. For the sake of clarity, however, this technicality will be sidestepped. Congress usually adjourns some time before the new year. So, in effect, the life of the One-hundredth Congress, for example, is from 1987 to 1988; the first session covering the year 1987, the second session 1988.) See an account in *Congressional Quarterly Weekly Report,* December 13, 1986, 3068-3069.

32. Press release, Federal Election Commission, May 7, 1985.

33. *Congressional Quarterly Weekly Report,* November 1, 1980, 3234-3239.

34. For an examination of the strength of party organizations at the state level, see John F. Bibby, Cornelius P. Cotter, James L. Gibson, and Robert J. Huckshorn, "Trends in Party Organizational Strength, 1960-1980," *International Political Science Review* 4 (January 1983): 21-27, and "Assessing Party Organizational Strength," *American Journal of Political Science* 27 (May 1983): 193-222.

35. Lewis Bowman and G. R. Boynton, "Activities and Role Definitions of Grassroots Party Officials," *Journal of Politics* 28 (February 1966): 121-143. Also see Lee S. Weinberg, "Stability and Change among Pittsburgh Precinct Politicians," *Social Science* (Winter 1975): 10-16.

36. Barbara C. Burrell, "Local Political Party Committees, Task Performance and

Organizational Vitality," *Western Political Quarterly* 39 (March 1986): 48-66.

37. Michael Margolis and Raymond E. Owen, "From Organization to Personalism: A Note on the Transmogrification of the Local Political Party," *Polity* 18 (Winter 1985): 313-328.

38. James L. Gibson, Cornelius P. Cotter, John F. Bibby, and Robert J. Huckshorn, "Whither the Local Parties?: A Cross-Sectional and Longitudinal Analysis of the Strength of Party Organizations," *American Journal of Political Science* 29 (February 1985): 139-160.

39. Nelson W. Polsby and Aaron Wildavsky, *Presidential Elections: Strategies of American Electoral Politics* (New York: Charles Scribner's Sons, 1980), 22-23. For a study of "amateur" and "professional" county party chairpersons, see Michael A. Maggiotto and Ronald E. Weber, "The Impact of Organizational Incentives on County Party Chairpersons," *American Politics Quarterly* 14 (July 1986): 201-218.

40. Ranney, *Curing the Mischiefs of Faction,* 141. Like Polsby and Wildavsky, Ranney recognizes that few politicians are completely "unsullied purists or unprincipled professionals." See an analysis of the positions of Democratic party regulars and party reformers on the question of intraparty democracy in William J. Crotty, "The Philosophies of Party Reform" in *Party Renewal in America: Theory and Practice,* ed. Gerald M. Pomper, 31-50.

41. See an analysis of President Reagan's popularity and an accompanying argument regarding the decline of partisanship and the growing candidate-centeredness of presidential elections in Martin P. Wattenberg, "The Reagan Polarization Phenomenon and the Continuing Downward Slide in Presidential Candidate Popularity," *American Politics Quarterly* 14 (July 1986): 219-245.

42. Press release, Federal Election Commission, May 19, 1985.

43. V. O. Key, Jr., *Politics, Parties, and Pressure Groups* (New York: Crowell, 1964), 200-201.

44. From *Party Government* by E. E. Schattschneider. Copyright 1942 by E. E. Schattschneider. Reprinted by permission of Holt, Rinehart and Winston, 1.

45. Agreement among students of political parties on the nature of party functions, their relative significance, and the consequences of functional performance for the political system is far from complete. Frank J. Sorauf points out that among the functions that have been attributed to American parties have been those of simplifying political issues and alternatives, producing automatic majorities, recruiting political leadership and personnel, organizing minorities and opposition, moderating and compromising political conflict, organizing the machinery of government, promoting political consensus and legitimacy, and bridging the separation of powers. The principal difficulty with listings of this sort, according to Sorauf, is that "it involves making functional statements about party activity without necessarily relating them to functional requisites or needs of the system." He suggests that at this stage of research on parties, emphasis should be given to the activities performed by parties, thus avoiding the confusion arising from the lack of clarity about the meaning of function, the absence of consensus on functional categories, and the problem of measuring the performance of functions. See his instructive essay, "Political Parties and Political Analysis," in *The American Party Systems: Stages of Political Development,* ed. William Nisbet Chambers and Walter Dean Burnham (New York: Oxford, 1967), 33-53.

46. In about four-fifths of the states, judges are chosen in some form of partisan or nonpartisan election. In the remaining states they come to office through appointment. A few states employ the so-called Missouri Plan of judge selection, under which the governor makes judicial appointments from a list of

names supplied by a nonpartisan judicial commission composed of judges, lawyers, and laymen. Under this plan, designed to take judges "out of politics," each judge, after a trial period, runs for reelection without opposition; voters may vote either to retain or to remove him from office. If a majority of voters cast affirmative ballots, the judge is continued in office for a full term; if the vote is negative, the judge loses office and the governor makes another appointment in the same manner. Even under this plan, of course, the governor may give preference to aspirants of his own party. Irrespective of the system used to choose judges, party leaders and party interest will nearly always be involved.

47. Theodore J. Lowi, "Party, Policy, and Constitution in America," in *The American Party Systems,* ed. William Nisbet Chambers and Walter Dean Burnham, 263.
48. Robert MacIver, *The Web of Government* (New York: Macmillan, 1947), 213.
49. See a discussion of the party role in "the aggregation of interests" in Gerald M. Pomper, "The Contributions of Political Parties to American Democracy," in *Party Renewal in America: Theory and Practice,* ed. Gerald M. Pomper, 5-7.
50. Few facts about the political participation of Americans are of greater significance than those that reveal its social class bias. A disproportionate number of the people who are highly active in politics are drawn from the upper reaches of the social order, from among those who hold higher status occupations, are more affluent, and are better educated. Citizens from lower socioeconomic levels constitute only about 10 percent of the participants who are highly active in politics. See Sidney Verba and Norman H. Nie, *Participation in America: Political Democracy and Social Equality* (New York: Harper and Row, 1972), especially Chapter 20.
51. Harvey Fergusson, *People and Power* (New York: Morrow, 1947), 101-102.
52. Consider the development and components of a party model based on the idea that the only standard useful in evaluating the vitality of American parties is simply the ability of the party to win office. Using this standard, Joseph Schlesinger argues that the major parties are healthier now than ever in the past. See his "On the Theory of Party Organization," *Journal of Politics* 46 (May 1984): 369-400.

c h a p t e r   t w o

The Characteristics
of American Parties

THE MAJOR parties are firm landmarks on the American political
scene. In existence for more than a century, the parties have made
important contributions to the development and maintenance of a democratic political culture and to democratic institutions and practices. In
essence, the parties form the principal institution for popular control of
government, and this achievement is remarkable given the limitations
under which they function. This chapter examines the chief characteristics of the American party system.

The Primary Characteristic: Dispersed Power

Viewed at some distance, the party organizations may appear to be
neatly ordered and hierarchical—committees are piled, one atop another,
from the precinct to the national level, conveying the impression that
power flows from the top to the bottom. In reality, however, the
American party is not nearly so hierarchical. State and local organizations have substantial independence on most party matters. The practices
that state and local parties follow, the candidates they recruit or help to
recruit, the campaign money they raise, the auxiliary groups they form
and reform, the innovations they introduce, the organized interests to
which they respond, the campaign strategies and issues they create, and,
most important, the policy orientations of the candidates who run under
their label—all bear the distinctive imprints of local and state political
cultures, leaders, traditions, and interests.[1]

Although there is no mistaking the overall decentralization of American parties, the power of the national party to control the presidential nominating process has grown immensely—particularly for the Democratic party. The Democratic reform movement, begun in the late 1960s, drastically altered the rules and practices of state parties in matters related to the selection of national convention delegates. In 1974 the Democratic party held a midterm convention to draft a charter—the first in the history of either major party—to provide for the governance of the party. The charter formally establishes the Democratic national convention as the highest authority of the party and requires state parties to observe numerous standards in the selection of convention delegates. Moreover, as a result of a 1975 Supreme Court decision, national party rules must govern if a conflict arises between national and state party rules concerning the selection of delegates. "The convention serves the pervasive national interest in the selection of candidates for national office," the Supreme Court ruled, "and this national interest is greater than any interest of an individual state." [2]

The centralizing reforms of the Democratic party, however, need to be kept in perspective. On the whole, they have contributed more to the devitalization of the national party organizations than to their strengthening. The reforms certainly have not increased the probability that candidates who can win the presidency will be nominated. Furthermore, the spread of presidential primaries and the opening up of party caucuses have transformed the national convention, diminishing its independent role in choosing the presidential nominee. In recent conventions the delegates have done little more than ratify the choices made earlier in party primaries and caucuses. In effect, the "average party voter," joined by "candidate enthusiasts," not the convention, picks the nominee. And in reality the choice may be limited simply to the candidates who have somehow survived the Iowa caucuses and the New Hampshire primary. The party conventions themselves are less and less party gatherings. Rather, they are assemblies dominated by the leading candidate, his organization, his entourage of advisers, and the activists drawn to his preconvention campaign. Public officials and party leaders draw power from their relationship to the candidate whose nomination the convention will confirm. Those aligned with candidates rejected in the preconvention period are of minimal interest, even to television reporters in search of an angle that can be parlayed into a story. All recent conventions have been dominated by the leading candidate and his organization. The same can be said for state delegations—where all the action takes place in candidate caucuses. When the preconvention struggle produces a nominee, the party presence in the convention is scarcely more than a backdrop.

In the Democratic party, the influence of national party agencies on state and local organizations is confined mainly to the presidential nominating process.[3] National party rules thoroughly regulate the processes by which national convention delegates are chosen. The influence of Republican national party agencies on subnational parties, by contrast, shows up most clearly in matters of campaign finance. In 1984, for example, Republican party committees' contributions to House and Senate candidates and expenditures on their behalf totaled nearly $20 million; comparable Democratic committees provided less than half that amount. Republican congressional nominees now count on substantial financial support from the national party. In addition, Republican national committees spend vastly more money than their rivals in national advertising campaigns and in the provision of other services (for example, polls, registration drives) beneficial to all the party's candidates.[4]

National party leaders do not have a great impact on the nomination of candidates for Congress. Ordinarily, these nominations are treated as local matters, even though members of Congress are national officials. Furthermore, congressional party leaders rarely attempt to discipline fellow party members who stray from the "reservation"—who vote with the other party on key legislative issues or otherwise fail to come to the aid of their party. (In an unusual action in 1983, the House Democratic Caucus removed a Texas representative, Phil Gramm, from the Budget Committee because he had played a major role in shaping President Reagan's budget strategy in the previous Congress. In response, Gramm resigned his seat, switched parties, and was reelected as a Republican. Other conservative "Boll Weevil" Democrats who had supported Reagan's economic program suffered no penalties, however.) Members who ignore their party typically escape sanctions and, by dramatizing their capacity to resist party claims, sometimes improve their standing with the voters.

The position of the national party apparatus is also revealed in the character and activities of the national committee. For the party in power, the national committee is predominantly an arm of the president. Neither national committee has significant influence on fellow party members in Congress, on the party's governors, or on the party's public officials further down the line. The shaping of party positions on major questions of public policy is thus well beyond the capacity of the committee.

Factors Contributing to the Dispersal of Party Power

The position of the national party is strongly affected by the legal and constitutional characteristics of the American political system. American parties must find their place within a federal system where powers and responsibilities lie with fifty states as well as with the national government. The basic responsibility for the design of the electoral system in which the parties compete is given to the states, not to the nation. Not suprisingly, party organizations have been molded by the electoral laws under which they contest for power. State and local power centers have naturally developed around the thousands of governmental units and elective offices found in the states and the localities. With his distinctive constituency (frequently a "safe" district), his own coterie of supporters, and his own channels to campaign money, the typical officeholder has a remarkable amount of freedom in defining his relationship to his party. His well-being and the organization's well-being are not identical. To press this point, it is not too much to say that officeholders are continuously evaluating party claims and objectives in the light of their own career aspirations. When the party's claims and the officeholder's aspirations diverge, the party ordinarily loses out. A federal system, with numerous elective offices, opens up an extraordinary range of political choices to subnational parties and, especially, to individual candidates.

For all of its significance for the party system and the distinctiveness of American politics, however, federalism is but one of several explanations for the fragmentation of party power. Another constitutional provision, separation of powers, also contributes to this condition. A frequent by-product of separation of powers is a truncated party majority—when one party controls one or both houses of the legislature and the other party controls the executive. At worst, the result is a dreary succession of narrow partisan clashes between the branches; at best, a clarification of differences between the parties occasionally may come about. At no time, however, does a truncated majority help in the development and maintenance of party responsibility for a program of public policy. The dimensions of this party problem in the states are revealed by the data provided in Table 2-1. Currently, more than half of all gubernatorial-legislative elections lead to divided party control of the branches. Republican governors in particular are likely to confront this situation. The pattern at the national level is just about the same.

A third factor helping to disperse party power is the method used to make nominations. It was noted earlier that nominations for national office are sorted out and settled at the local level, ordinarily without

TABLE 2-1   Incidence of Party Division (Governor versus Legislature) Following 1982, 1984, and 1986 Elections

Relation between governor and legislature	Following 1982 election		Following 1984 election		Following 1986 election	
	Number	Percent	Number	Percent	Number	Percent
Governor opposed	21	43	27	55	29 [a]	59
Governor unopposed	28	57	22	45	20	41

SOURCE: Developed from data in *Congressional Quarterly Weekly Report*, November 13, 1982, 2848-2849; November 17, 1984, 2944-2945; and November 15, 1986, 2894-2895.

NOTE: Nebraska is excluded because it has a nonpartisan legislature.

[a] As a result of the 1986 election, 18 of these 29 governors faced opposition party majorities in both houses. Fourteen of the 18 were Republicans.

interference from national party functionaries. One of the principal supports of local control over nominations is the direct primary. Its use virtually guarantees that candidates for national office will be tailored to the measure of local specifications. Consider this analysis by Austin Ranney and Willmoore Kendall:

> A party's *national* leaders can affect the kind of representatives and senators who come to Washington bearing the party's label only by enlisting the support of the state and local party organizations concerned; and they cannot be sure of doing so even then. Assume, for example, that the local leaders have decided to support the national leaders in an attempt to block the renomination of a maverick congressman, and are doing all they can. There is still nothing to prevent the rank and file, who may admire the incumbent's "independence," from ignoring the leaders' wishes and renominating him. The direct primary, in other words, is *par excellence* a system for maintaining *local* control of nominations; and as long as American localities continue to be so different from one another in economic interests, culture, and political attitudes, the national parties are likely to retain their present ideological heterogeneity and their tendency to show differing degrees of cohesion from issue to issue.[5]

Fourth, the distribution of power within the parties is affected by patterns of campaign finance. Few, if any, campaign resources are more important than money. A large proportion of the political money donated in any year is given directly to the campaign organizations of individual candidates rather than to the party organizations. Candidates with access to campaign money are automatically in a strong position vis-à-vis the party organization. Not having to rely heavily on the party for campaign funds, candidates can stake out their independence from it. Whether candidates can remain independent from the interest groups that pour money into their campaigns is another question.

Fifth, a pervasive spirit of localism dominates American politics and adds to the decentralization of political power. Local interests find expression in national politics in countless ways. Even the presidential nominating process may become critical for the settlement of local and state political struggles. A prominent political leader who aligns with the candidate who eventually wins the presidential nomination, particularly if his support comes early in the race, can put new life into his own career. He gains access to the nominee and increased visibility. If his party wins the presidency, an appointment in the new administration may be offered to him. Or if he chooses to run for a major public office, he is likely to secure the support of the president. National conventions settle more than national matters.

Congress has always shown a remarkable hospitality to the idea that governmental power should be decentralized. A great deal of the major legislation that has been passed in recent decades, for example, has been designed to make state and local governments participants in the development and implementation of public policies. Locally based political organizations profit from these arrangements. A basic explanation for Congress's defense of state and local governments lies in the backgrounds of the members themselves. Many of them were elected to state or local office prior to their election to Congress. They are steeped in local lore, think in local terms, meet frequently with local representatives, and work for local advantage. Their steady attention to the local dimensions of national policy helps to safeguard their own careers and to promote the interests of those local politicians who look to Washington for assistance in solving community problems.

Finally, the fragmentation of party power owes much to the growing importance of outsiders in the political process. Chief among them are the media, campaign management firms, and political interest groups. Increasingly, candidates hire expert consultants to organize their campaigns, to shape their strategies, and to mold their images. And they use the media to present themselves to the voters—what counts, modern candidates know, is how they are perceived by the voters. As for political interest groups, their role in campaigns, particularly in their financing, probably has never been more important than it is right now. In 1986 PACs contributed about $85 million to the campaigns of U.S. House candidates—roughly three and one-half times as much as they gave in 1978. Interest group money clearly has become a major force—some would say an overwhelming force—in American politics, particularly in congressional elections. The heightened prominence of interest groups in election campaigns undoubtedly has increased their influence on officeholders.[6]

The Power of Officeholders

The structure, tone, and mood of American parties bear the heavy imprint of decentralization. This concept, more than any other, brings into focus the essential weakness of national party leaders and institutions. But to stress this point is perhaps to create an illusion of great organizational strength among state and local party units. Only a few state and local party organizations, *qua* organizations, actually have any real strength. James M. Burns makes the argument this way:

> At no level, except in a handful of industrial states, do state parties have the attributes of organization. They lack extensive dues-paying memberships; hence they number many captains and sergeants but few foot soldiers. They do a poor job of raising money for themselves as organizations, or even for their candidates. They lack strong and imaginative leadership of their own. They cannot control their most vital function—the nomination of their candidates. Except in a few states, such as Ohio, Connecticut, and Michigan, our parties are essentially collections of small cliques and they are often shunted aside by the politicians who understand political power. Most of the state parties are at best mere jousting grounds for embattled politicians; at worst they simply do not exist, as in the case of Republicans in the rural South or Democrats in the rural Midwest.[7]

The malaise that characterizes party organizations in many jurisdictions results in a concentration of power in the hands of public officeholders and candidates for public office. Sometimes in their own names and sometimes in the name of their party, they assume the critical functions associated with campaigns and elections. In most jurisdictions the officeholders or aspirants develop issues and strategies, recruit the corps of campaign workers, raise the necessary political money, mobilize the voters, and carry the party banner. Their power comes not as the result of wresting leadership from party officials but from taking over campaign responsibilities that otherwise would be met inadequately, or perhaps not at all, by the formal party organization. Candidates and officeholders are plainly the life of the party.

Law and the Parties

One of the major features of American parties is that their organization and activities are extensively regulated by law—state law in particular. David E. Price has distinguished two general bodies of state law: statutes that relate to *nominations and elections* and statutes that affect *party cohesion in government.*[8]

Laws affecting nominations and elections differ from state to state. A few examples will help to illustrate their diversity. Although the direct primary system is used everywhere, some states still permit party conventions to participate in the choice of nominees. For example, state law or party rules may stipulate that a candidate for a statewide office must receive a certain percentage of the party's state convention vote to qualify for a place on the primary ballot. In some states, law or practice encourages the parties to make preprimary endorsements; in other states such "gatekeeping" action is prohibited. States vary sharply in the extent to which they seek to protect the integrity of the parties by limiting primary voting to persons preregistered by party. The best (or at least most benign) arrangement, from the standpoint of the parties, is the closed primary. (See Table 2-2 for data on regional differences in party influence on nominations as promoted by state laws or practices.) States also differ significantly in how their laws protect the parties from independent candidates and "sore losers" (candidates who lose their party's nomination and then run under another banner in the general election). As a final example, law in eight states helps to promote the parties through public funding of campaigns, channeled through the parties.

The impact of state law on party cohesion in government is sizable. Laws may make it easy for the parties to function as collectivities or they may make it difficult. Where ballots facilitate straight-ticket voting, for example, as they do in twenty-one states, the probability increases for gubernatorial-legislative coattailing and thus for the election of candidates who share the same party label. The election calendar may also affect party control of government. Election of the governor and the legislature at the same time promotes party control, while elections held at different times encourage divided control of government. Finally, states differ in the degree to which they consolidate executive power. Short terms for the governor, prohibition against reelection, and provision for a multiplicity of statewide elective offices all contribute to the weakness of executive authority and, ultimately, to the fragmentation of party power.

TABLE 2-2   Party Capacity for Influencing Nominations, as Reflected in State Laws and Practices

	Party-strengthening laws and practices					
	Party conventions help choose major state-level nominees	Parties regularly make preprimary endorsements	Primary voting limited to persons preregistered by party			
Region	Number of states	Number of states	Number of states	Number of states	Total	Average per state
Northeast	10	3	6	8	17	1.7
Border	4	0	0	4	4	1.0
South	11	0	0	2	2	0.2
Midwest	12	1	7	4	12	1.0
West	13	3	3	7	13	1.0
Regular party organization states	8	2	6	5	13	1.6

SOURCE: Developed from data in David E. Price, *Bringing Back the Parties* (Washington, D.C.: CQ Press, 1984), 128-129 (as adapted). Price examines eleven party-strengthening laws and practices in the states, three of which, shown here, are central to party influence on nominations. The table also reflects the presence of party-strengthening laws and practices in states where local parties traditionally have been strongest. As identified by David R. Mayhew, who examined the structure of American parties at the local level, these "regular party organization states" are Connecticut, Delaware, Illinois, New Jersey, New York, Ohio, Pennsylvania, and Rhode Island. Local party organizations in these states have been distinguished by hierarchy, substantial autonomy, lasting power, an active role in the nominating process, significant patronage, and an absence of factional conflict. See Mayhew, *Placing Parties in American Politics* (Princeton, N.J.: Princeton University Press, 1986), Chapter 2.

State laws can be either a boon or a barrier to strong parties. Party strengthening laws are most likely to be found in the northeastern states. Southern states are least likely to have laws favorable to the parties, their leaders, and their organizations. Intraregional variation is particularly noticeable in the Midwest and West. In the Midwest, Kansas and Nebraska do not have nearly as many proparty laws as Michigan and North Dakota. In the West, California is largely antiparty in its statutes, while Utah is considerably more proparty. On the whole, state law is more likely to have a negative than positive impact on the strength of the parties. Can the parties be trusted? Are they worth preserving? In most states the law seems to say no, probably not, or, at best, perhaps.

Variations in Party Competition from State to State and from Office to Office

Familiar and conventional interpretations in American politics are never easy to abandon. Old labels persist even though their descriptive power has been sharply eroded. Such is the case in the designation of the American two-party system. Vigorous two-party competition in all jurisdictions is clearly unattainable. Surprisingly little two-party competition is found, however, in certain electoral districts of the nation. The American party system is in some places and at some times strongly two-party, and in other places and at other times, dominantly one-party. In some states and localities factional politics within one or both major parties is so pervasive and persistent as to suggest the presence of a multiple-party system. Competition between the parties is a condition not to be taken for granted, despite the popular tendency to bestow the two-party label on American politics.

Competitiveness in Presidential and Congressional Elections

Although in many states and localities there is little more than a veneer of competitiveness between the parties, this is not the case in presidential elections. Contests for the presidency provide the best single example of authentic two-party competition, particularly in recent decades.[9] With but three exceptions in all two-party presidential contests since 1940, the losing presidential candidate has received at least 45 percent of the popular vote; the exceptions occurred in 1964 (Barry Goldwater received 39 percent of the vote), 1972 (George McGovern, 38 percent), and 1984 (Walter F. Mondale, 41 percent). Several elections in the modern era have been extraordinarily close: in 1960 John F. Kennedy received 49.7 percent of the popular vote to Richard Nixon's 49.5 percent, and in 1968 Nixon obtained 43.4 percent to Hubert H. Humphrey's 42.7 percent (with George C. Wallace receiving 13.5 percent). In another extremely close race in 1976, Jimmy Carter received 50.1 percent of the vote, while Gerald R. Ford received 48.0 percent. The two major parties are now so evenly matched in presidential contests that the losing party has excellent reason to expect that it can win the office within an election or two.

A view of presidential elections from the states is worth examining. In the last two decades the number of one-party states and regions in presidential elections has declined precipitously. The tempo of Republican growth in the once-solid Democratic South has quickened (see Figure 2-1). The watershed in southern political history appears to have

FIGURE 2-1 Republican Percentage of Two-Party Presidential Vote in
Eleven Southern States, 1940-1984

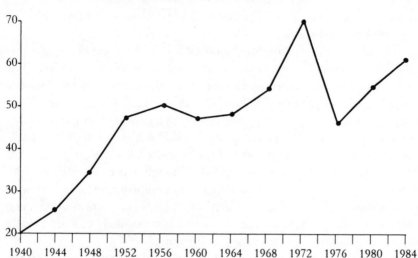

been 1952. Dwight D. Eisenhower carred four southern states (Florida, Tennessee, Texas, and Virginia), narrowly missing victories in several others, while receiving more than 48 percent of the popular vote throughout the South. Nixon's victory in 1968 was similarly impressive. In the District of Columbia and in thirty-nine states outside the South, Humphrey led Nixon by about 30,000 votes; in the eleven southern states Nixon led Humphrey by more than 500,000 votes. The high point of Republican appeal was reached in 1972, when Nixon received 70 percent of the southern vote, a much larger proportion than he received in 1968. One result of the 1976 nomination by the Democrats of Jimmy Carter, a native of Georgia, was that the Republican surge in the South was arrested; although Gerald Ford ran well in nearly all states of the Confederacy, he carried only Virginia. In 1980 the Republicans again did well in the South. Reagan received 53.6 percent of the major party vote in the South, winning all of this region's states except Georgia. In 1984 his percentage jumped to 62.6, a level well above his national average of 58.8.

At the other end of the scale, certain traditionally Republican strongholds have become more competitive. At one time immoderately Republican, such states as Maine, New Hampshire, and Vermont are no longer in the bag. Each election puts a further strain on old party loyalties. Landslide elections occur from time to time, as in 1964 (Johnson over Goldwater), 1972 (Nixon over McGovern), and 1984 (Reagan over Mondale), but they are often followed by cliffhangers, as in 1968

(Nixon over Humphrey) and 1976 (Carter over Ford). It is a good guess that most future presidential elections will be closely competitive—decided by thin margins in a handful of states—especially when no incumbent is in the race.

Congressional elections are another story. Many congressional districts have a long history of one-party or incumbent domination. The diversion of House and Senate elections from the mainstream of competitive politics is obvious (see Table 2-3). In no election during the 1980s have as many as 20 percent of the House elections been in the marginal (or competitive) category—that is, elections in which the winning candidate receives less than 55 percent of the vote. In 1986 a mere 9.3 percent of all House elections were marginal. Though more competitive than those of the House, Senate elections usually result in control by the same party. Incumbency is the key factor in limiting turnover of congressional seats. As would be expected, party control is most likely to shift when a seat is open—when no incumbent is running.

Decisive party victories are not confined to any region of the country. More than 90 percent of the House elections in the South, East, and West were won by 55 percent or more of the vote in 1986 (see Table 2-4). The Midwest was not far behind. Many elections in southern and eastern states were uncontested. This analysis, of course, is after the fact.

TABLE 2-3　Marginal, Safer, and Uncontested Seats in House and Senate Elections, 1980-1986, by Percentage of Total Seats

Election margin	House				Senate			
	1980	1982	1984	1986	1980	1982	1984	1986
Seats won by Democrats by less than 55 percent of the vote ⌉ Marginal	8.3	9.2	7.4	4.3	8.8	9.1	12.1	29.4
Seats won by Republicans by less than 55 percent of the vote ⌋	10.1	8.3	5.7	5.0	47.1	27.3	6.1	11.8
Seats won by Democrats by 55 percent or more of the vote ⌉ Safer	39.1	42.8	38.9	42.6	23.5	51.5	33.3	29.4
Seats won by Republicans by 55 percent or more of the vote ⌋	30.8	27.3	33.6	31.5	17.7	12.1	45.5	29.4
Uncontested seats	11.7	12.4	14.4	16.6	2.9	0.0	3.0	0.0

SOURCE: Data drawn from various issues of *Congressional Quarterly Weekly Report.*

TABLE 2-4   House and Senate Electoral Margins by Region, 1986

Chamber and region	Seats won by less than 55 percent of the vote	Seats won by 55 percent or more of the vote		
		Contested	Uncontested[a]	Total
House				
South	10%	57%	33%	90%
East	7	74	19	93
Midwest	13	81	6	87
West	8	90	2	92
Senate				
South	56	44	0	44
East	0	100	0	100
Midwest	44	56	0	56
West	50	50	0	50

SOURCE: Developed from data in *Congressional Quarterly Weekly Report,* November 8, 1986, 2864-2871.

NOTE: South: Ala., Ark., Fla., Ga., Ky., La., Miss., N.C., Okla., S.C., Tenn., Texas, and Va.; East: Conn., Del., Maine, Md., Mass., N.H., N.J., N.Y., Pa., R.I., Vt., and W.Va.; Midwest: Ill., Ind., Iowa, Kan., Mich., Minn., Mo., Neb., N.D., Ohio, S.D., and Wis.; West: Alaska, Ariz., Calif., Colo., Hawaii, Idaho, Mont., Nev., N.M., Ore., Utah, Wash., and Wyo.

[a] Includes some elections in which the only opposition was that of a minor party candidate.

Many members of Congress view each election with trepidation, feeling that their constituencies are never as secure as postelection analyses usually stamp them.[10] In view of the hard evidence on one-sided House elections, however, one really has to wonder whether their anxiety is well founded.

Filling out this account of noncompetitiveness at the congressional level is evidence on the advantage of incumbency (see Table 2-5). In the usual election, more than 90 percent of the House incumbents on the ballot are returned to Washington. A record for House incumbents was established in 1986 when more than 98 percent were reelected. Senate incumbents face stiffer opposition, but they also ordinarily do well. Very few incumbents fall by the wayside in the primaries. So overwhelming is the advantage of incumbents that it is rare for more than 1 percent to lose in their bids for renomination. The fact of the matter is that Congress is an arena for two-party politics not because its members are produced by competitive environments but because both parties have managed to develop and maintain large blocs of noncompetitive seats. Incumbency is a major factor in each party's success in reducing competition.[11]

TABLE 2-5   The Advantage of Incumbency in House and Senate Elections, 1968-1986

| Year | Defeated in primary | Total number of incumbents | | | Percentage of incumbents running in general election elected |
		Running in general election	Elected in general election	Defeated in general election	
1968					
House	3	401	396	5	98.75
Senate	4	24	20	4	83.33
1970					
House	7	391	379	12	96.93
Senate	1	29	23	6	79.31
1972					
House	13	380	367	13	96.58
Senate	2	25	20	5	80.00
1974					
House	8	383	343	40	89.56
Senate	2	25	23	2	92.00
1976					
House	3	381	368	13	96.59
Senate	0	25	16	9	64.00
1978					
House	5	377	358	19	94.96
Senate	3	22	15	7	68.18
1980					
House	6	392	361	31	92.09
Senate	4	25	16	9	64.00
1982					
House	4	383	354	29	92.42
Senate	0	30	28	2	93.33
1984					
House	3	408	392	16	96.07
Senate	0	29	26	3	89.65
1986					
House	2	391	385	6	98.46
Senate	0	28	21	7	75.00

SOURCE: *Congressional Quarterly Weekly Report,* November 15, 1986, 2891; and March 25, 1978, 755.

Competitiveness at the State Level

A wide range of competitiveness exists in the fifty states. The degree of interparty competition was calculated (see Figure 2-2) for each state by blending four separate state scores: the average percentage of the popular vote received by Democratic gubernatorial candidates, the average percentage of Democratic seats in the state senate, the average percentage of

FIGURE 2-2   The Fifty States Classified According to Degree of Interparty Competition, 1974-1980

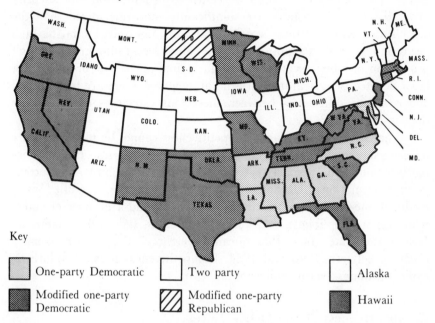

Key

One-party Democratic   Two party   Alaska

Modified one-party Democratic   Modified one-party Republican   Hawaii

SOURCE: Based on data in John F. Bibby, Cornelius P. Cotter, James L. Gibson, and Robert J. Huckshorn, "Parties in State Politics," in *Politics in the American States*, ed. Herbert Jacob and Virginia Gray (Boston: Little, Brown, 1983), 66. The classification scheme was developed by Austin Ranney.

Democratic seats in the state house of representatives, and the percentage of all terms for governor, senate, and house in which the Democrats were in control. Taken together, these percentages constitute an "index of competitiveness" for each state.

In more than one-half of the states, party competition for state offices lacks an authentic ring. Over the period of this study, 1974-1980, eight states (six southern plus Maryland and Rhode Island) were classified as one-party Democratic; another twenty states were designated as either modified one-party Democratic or modified one-party Republican (only North Dakota). Twenty-two states met the test of two-party competition.

Two particularly interesting correlations with competitiveness appear. One concerns the relationship between one-party domination and membership in the Confederacy—all of the southern one-party Democratic states withdrew from the Union, as did South Carolina, Texas, Florida, Tennessee, and Virginia (all modified one-party Democratic states). For many of the states that today have a low level of party competition (in particular for state offices), the Civil War was the great divide. The second correlation is related to urbanization: not surprisingly, the two-party states are significantly more urbanized than the other states. Many of these states are also distinguished by having high per capita incomes, a significant proportion of recent immigrants, a high proportion of labor devoted to manufacturing, and a low proportion of labor devoted to agriculture. In general, however, there are fewer social and economic differences between these four categories of states now than in the past.[12]

The degree of interparty competitiveness cannot be measured only in terms of the struggle for state offices. Some of the states in the one-party or modified one-party categories exhibit vigorous two-party competition in national elections. Virginia, for example, classified as a modified one-party Democratic state, has long had a number of voters who support Republican presidential candidates. Indeed this nominally Democratic state voted Republican in eight of the ten presidential elections between 1948 and 1984. Competitiveness must therefore be explored along several dimensions.

Competitiveness at the Office Level

Party competition differs greatly not only between states but also between offices in the same state.[13] The complexity inherent in the concept of competitiveness is revealed in Figure 2-3. To unravel the figure, examine the location of each state office on the horizontal and vertical axes. The horizontal axis shows the extent to which the parties have controlled each office over the period of the study; the vertical axis shows the rate of turnover in control of the office between the parties. Some offices are steadfastly held by one party and other offices are genuinely competitive. Wide variations exist within each state. Taking the northern states as a group, there is less competition for seats in the House than for any other office. By contrast, the offices of governor and senator are the most competitive—even these offices, however, are not significantly competitive.

Overall, the pattern of competition depicted by the data in Figure 2-3 testifies to the inability of state parties to compete for and to control a range of offices. To emphasize a point made earlier, the figure suggests, albeit subtly, that the successful officeholder is one who develops and maintains his own campaign resources, knowing that the party organization is about as likely to be a spectator to his career as a guardian of it.

FIGURE 2-3   Party Competition for Individual Offices (Selected States)

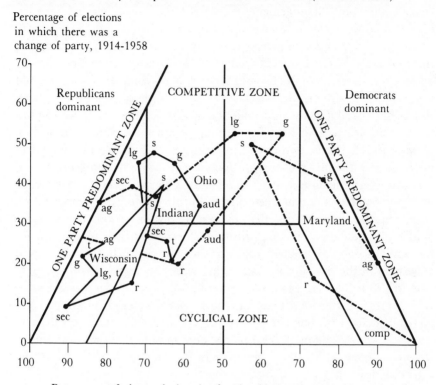

Percentage of elections
in which there was a
change of party, 1914-1958

Percentage of electoral victories for the dominant party, 1914-1958

SOURCE: Joseph A. Schlesinger, "The Structure of Competition for Office in the American States," *Behavioral Science* 5 (July 1960): 203. "The more centrally located on the horizontal axis the more competitive an office was in overall terms; the higher on the diagram the more rapid the rate of turnover; and correspondingly, the lower on the diagram an office falls, the longer the cycles of one-party control, regardless of the degree of overall competition."

NOTE: g = governor; s = senator; r = congressman; lg = lieutenant governor; sec = secretary of state; ag = attorney general; aud = auditor; t = treasurer; comp = comptroller.

The Persistent Two-Party System in America

Despite the existence of one-party systems here and there, political competition in the United States usually comes down to competition between the two major parties, Democratic and Republican. The reason American politics has been receptive to a two-party rather than a multiple-party system, as in many European democracies, is not plain. What follows is a summary of the principal hypotheses, less than "laws" and more than hunches, that have been offered as explanations.

A familiar explanation is that electing House members from single-member districts by plurality vote helps to support the two-party pattern. Under this arrangement a single candidate is elected in each district, and he needs to receive only a plurality of the vote. Third-party candidates have slight inducement to run, since the prospects are poor that they could defeat the candidates of the two major parties. On the other hand, if members of Congress were elected under a proportional representation scheme, with several members chosen in each district, third-party candidates would undoubtedly have a better chance of winning some seats. Third parties are up against the same obstacle in presidential elections as they are in congressional races: only one party can win. For the office of the presidency, the entire nation takes on the cast of a single-member district. Each state's electoral votes are awarded as a unit to the candidate receiving a plurality of the popular vote; all other popular votes are in effect wasted. In 1968, for example, George Wallace, candidate of the American Independent party, received about five million popular votes in states outside the South but won electoral votes only in the five southern states he carried. Running as an independent in 1980, John B. Anderson received nearly six million popular votes (6.6 percent of the total vote) but no electoral votes. If electoral votes were divided in proportion to popular votes in each state, third-party candidates would likely make a bigger dent in the electoral vote totals of the major parties. Electoral practices in the United States are hard on third parties.

The diversity and flexibility that characterize the two major parties also contribute to the preservation of the two-party system. The policy orientations of the parties are rarely so firmly fixed as to preclude a shift in emphasis or direction to attract emerging interests within the electorate. Moreover, each party is made up of officeholders with different views. Almost any political group, as a result, can discover some officials who share its values and predilections and who are willing to represent its point of view. The adaptability of the parties and the officeholders not only permits them to siphon off support that otherwise might contribute to the development of third parties but also creates a great deal of slack in the political system. Groups pressing for change know that there is always some chance that they can win acceptance for their positions within the existing party framework.

Another central explanation for the durability of the two-party system in America is found in a tradition of dualism.[14] Early political conflict occurred between those who favored adoption of the Constitution and those who opposed it. Subsequently, dualism was reflected in struggles between Federalists and Anti-Federalists and, later still, be-

Single-Member Districts and Party Representation One-hundredth Congress (1987-1988)

Members of the U.S. House of Representatives (and of most state legislatures) are elected from single-member districts. (For the small states of Alaska, Delaware, North Dakota, South Dakota, Vermont, and Wyoming—each of which elects one U.S. representative—the entire state is a single-member district.) The single-member district system is a distorting mirror for popular preferences. It inflates the number of seats won by the majority party while reducing the number won by the minority party. Since only one candidate can win in each district, all votes for the losing candidate are wasted. The relationship between votes (statewide congressional vote for each party) and seats won in a variety of states in 1986 is reflected in the table below.

	Democratic		Republican	
State	Statewide congressional vote	Seats won	Statewide congressional vote	Seats won
West Virginia (4)	68%	100%	32%	0%
Massachusetts (11)	58	91	42	9
North Carolina (11)	57	73	43	27
Iowa (6)	48	33	52	67
Utah (3)	46	33	54	67
Maryland (8)	63	75	37	25
California (45)	53	60	47	40
Oklahoma (6)	61	67	39	33
Minnesota (8)	59	63	41	37
Michigan (18)	58	61	42	39
Illinois (22)	56	59	44	41

SOURCE: Developed from data in *Congressional Quarterly Weekly Report,* November 8, 1986, 2864-2871.

NOTE: Number of House members for each state shown in parentheses.

tween Democrats and Whigs. Since the Civil War, the main party battle has been fought between Democrats and Republicans. In sum, the main elements of conflict within the American political system have ordinarily found expression in competition between two dominant groups of politicians and their followings. This, in a nutshell, is the essence of American party history. Third parties have cropped up from time to time to challenge the major parties, but their lives ordinarily have been short and uneventful—so deep-seated is the attachment of a majority of Americans to inherited institutions and practices. Third parties or independent candidates rarely receive as much as 5 percent of the popular vote; this has occurred only eleven times since 1832 (see Table 2-6).

A profusion of other themes might be explored in seeking to account for the two-party character of American politics. Election law, for example, makes it difficult for all but the most well-organized and well-financed third parties to gain a place on the ballot. In presidential elections they must struggle in state after state to recruit campaign workers and funds and to collect signatures for their nominating petitions.[15] Even audiences may be hard to come by. In addition, because the risk of failure looms so large, new political organizations must strain to find acceptable candidates to run under their banner. Aspiring politicians are not notable for their willingness to take quixotic risks for the sake of ideology or principle, particularly if there is some chance that a career in one of the major parties is available. The extraordinary costs of organizing and conducting major campaigns, the difficulties that attend the search for men and women to assume party outposts, and the frustrations that plague efforts to cut the cords that bind American voters to the traditional parties all serve to inhibit the formation and maintenance of third parties. It also appears that the restless impulse for new alternatives that often dominates other nations, thus leading to the formation of new political parties, is found less commonly in the United States.

Finally, strange as it may seem, one-partyism enhances the two-party system. Each party has a number of areas (states or districts) that vote consistently and heavily for its candidates, irrespective of the intensity of forces that play upon voters there and elsewhere. Even when one of the major parties has a particularly bad election year, it is never threatened with extinction. Republicans may "clean up" in outstate and downstate Illinois, but Chicago will remain safely Democratic. Most of the rural, less-populous counties of Pennsylvania will vote Republican "til the cows come home," but Pittsburgh, Philadelphia, and other industrial areas will vote to elect Democratic candidates. Year in and year out, for most offices, Maryland and Rhode Island turn to the Democrats, while Utah and South Dakota faithfully vote Republican. One-party areas remove some of the mystery that surrounds American elections. Each major party owes something to them, counts on them, and is not often disappointed.

TABLE 2-6 Third-Party and Independent Presidential Candidates Receiving
5 Percent or More of Popular Vote

Candidate (party)	Year	Percent of popular vote	Electoral votes
John B. Anderson (Independent)	1980	6.6	0
George C. Wallace (American Independent)	1968	13.5	46
Robert M. LaFollette (Progressive)	1924	16.6	13
Theodore Roosevelt (Progressive)	1912	27.4	88
Eugene V. Debs (Socialist)	1912	6.0	0
James B. Weaver (Populist)	1892	8.5	22
John C. Breckinridge (Southern Democrat)	1860	18.1	72
John Bell (Constitutional Union)	1860	12.6	39
Millard Fillmore (Whig-American)	1856	21.5	8
Martin Van Buren (Free Soil)	1848	10.1	0
William Wirt (Anti-Masonic)	1832	7.8	7

SOURCE: *Congressional Quarterly Weekly Report,* October 18, 1980, 3147 (as adapted).

Parties as Coalitions

Viewed from afar, the American major party is likely to appear as a
miscellaneous collection of individual activists and voters, banded together in some fashion to attempt to gain control of government. But
there is more shadow than substance in that view; when the party is
brought into focus, its basic coalitional character is revealed. The point is
simple but important: the party is much less a collection of individuals
than it is a collection of social interests and groups. In the words of
Maurice Duverger, "A party is not a community but a collection of
communities, a union of small groups dispersed throughout the country. . . ." [16]

Functioning within a vastly heterogeneous society, the major parties
have naturally assumed a coalitional form. Groups of all kinds—social,
economic, religious, and ethnic—are organized to press demands on the
political order. In the course of defending or advancing their interests,

The Voting Behavior of Southern Whites ...

	1976		1980		1984	
	D	R	D	R	D	R
Vote for president	47%	53%	35%	62%	28%	72%
Vote for representative	60	40	48	52	34	66

SOURCE: Developed from data in *Public Opinion*, December/January 1985, 4.

NOTE: D = Democrat; R = Republican.

From shortly after the Civil War to mid-twentieth century, the Democratic party maintained a virtual monopoly of power in the states of the Confederacy. In party language, the confederate states were the "Solid South," since in election after election citizens voted overwhelmingly for Democratic candidates. The cohesion of the South stemmed from the experience of secession and the collective bitterness over the loss of the war, from the durable economic interests of an agricultural society, and, most important, from a widespread desire to maintain segregation and white supremacy by excluding blacks from the political system.

But historical cohesion has its limits. The Solid South was destined for destruction when the national Democratic party became active in the 1940s in promoting policies, economic as well as racial, that were

they contribute substantial energy to the political process—through generating innovations, posing alternative policies, recruiting and endorsing candidates, conducting campaigns, and so on. No party seriously contesting for office could ignore the constellation of groups in American political life.

Traditionally, each party has had relatively distinct followings in the electorate. The urban working classes, union families, blacks, Catholics, Jews, persons at the lower end of the educational scale, and the poor have been mainstays of the Democratic party since the early days of the New Deal. Southerners and various nationality groups have also played major roles in the Democratic party. In counterpoise, the Republican coalition has had a disproportionate number of supporters from such groups as big business, industry, farmers, small-town and rural dwellers, whites, Protestants, upper-income and better-educated persons, non-union families, and "old stock" Americans. Coalition politics has been a major feature of successful election campaigns.

... *in Presidential and Congressional Elections*

anathema to the party's conservative southern wing. In 1948 southern Democrats rebelled and created a "bolter" party, the "Dixiecrats." Although this insurgent party failed—the Dixiecratic candidates carried only four states—it served as an instrument of transition for many southern whites disillusioned with the liberal thrust of the national Democratic party. Thus southern whites who had voted for the Dixiecrats in 1948 found it possible in 1952 to do the unthinkable, to vote for a Republican, Dwight D. Eisenhower. And as a result of the support of these "Presidential Republicans," Eisenhower carried four southern states and only narrowly lost several others.

Throughout the 1950s and 1960s, Republican strength in the South was largely confined to presidential elections. Republican congressional candidates generally fared poorly. The pattern of southern politics is sharply different today. Southern whites are almost as likely to vote for Republican congressional candidates as they are for Republican presidential candidates (see table above). The South has moved a long way toward development of a genuine two-party system for national offices. State and local offices continue to be dominated by the Democratic party. (The South's last fling with a minor party candidate was in 1968, when Alabama's George C. Wallace ran for the presidency.) Today's two-party competition in the South is the natural extension of a secular trend begun some four decades ago.

Today, these coalitions are clearly in flux, particularly on the Democratic side. For example, although the vast majority of state and local offices in the South continue to be controlled by the Democratic party, the Republicans have made major gains at the national level and especially in presidential elections. Consider recent history. Disillusioned over the liberal thrust of the party, many lifelong southern Democrats bolted in 1964 to support Barry Goldwater, the Republican nominee. In even greater number they moved into the ranks of the American Independent party in 1968, voting for George Wallace in preference to the Democratic and Republican nominees, Hubert Humphrey and Richard Nixon. In 1972 they switched to Nixon. With a Georgian, Jimmy Carter, at the head of the Democratic ticket in 1976, southern voters abandoned their newly found Republicanism and returned to the Democratic fold. But their stay was brief. In 1980 and 1984 they voted decisively for Ronald Reagan, and he swept the region (losing only Georgia in his first election).

FIGURE 2-4   The Growing Similarity in Voting Behavior of Catholics and Protestants in Presidential Elections

1960 Kennedy (D) Nixon (R)	-28 ●━━━━━━━━━━━━━━━━━━━━━━━● +12
1964 Johnson (D) Goldwater (R)	-15 ●━━━━━━━━━━━● +6
1968 Humphrey (D) Nixon (R)	-10 ●━━━━━● +6
1972 McGovern (D) Nixon (R)	-10 ●━━━━━● +8
1976 Carter (D) Ford (R)	-6 ●━━━● +5
1980 Carter (D) Reagan (R)	-3 ●━● +3
1984 Mondale (D) Reagan (R)	0 ●● +2

-30   -25   -20   -15   -10   -5   0   +5   +10   +15

Percentage less Republican   Percentage more Republican
than all voters   than all voters

Catholics   Protestants

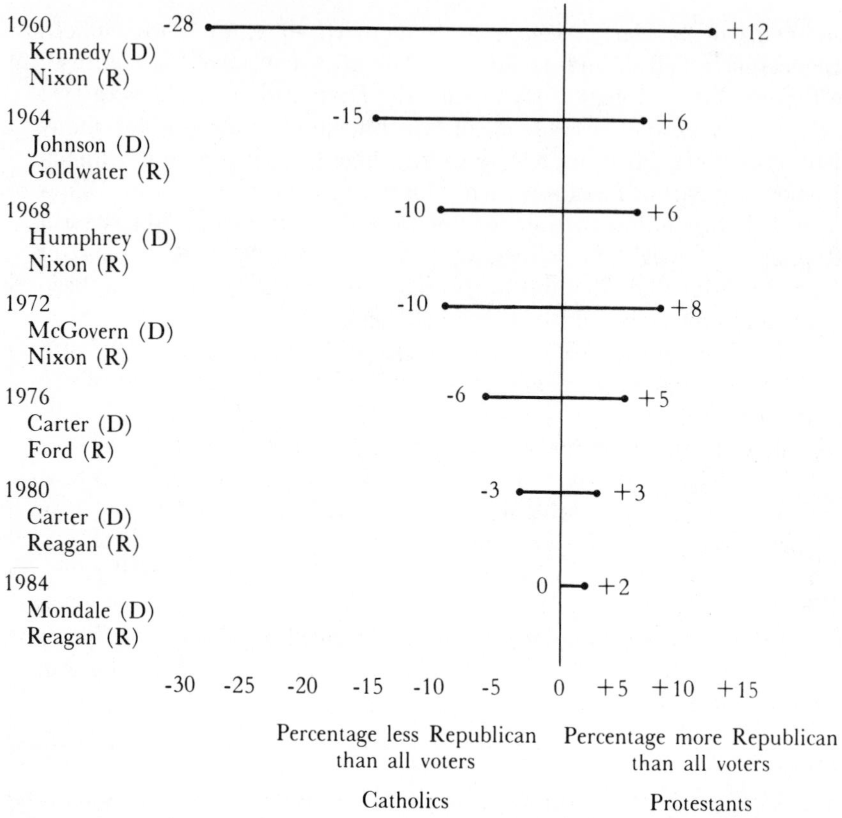

SOURCE: For 1960-1980 data, Everett Carll Ladd, "The Brittle Mandate: Electoral Dealignment and the 1980 Presidential Election," *Political Science Quarterly* 96 (Spring 1981): 13. For 1984, the exit poll of the *Los Angeles Times* (November 6, 1984) reported the Catholic vote at 59 percent Republican, the same as the national Republican average, and the Protestant vote at 61 percent Republican. The Gallup poll showed the groups at 61 percent Republican and 39 percent Democratic, respectively. *Gallup Report,* November 1984, 13.

NOTE: D = Democrat; R = Republican.

Distinctiveness in the voting behavior of religious groups in presidential elections has also eroded in recent years (see Figure 2-4). In 1960 Catholics voted 28 percent less Republican than the entire electorate. Protestants, in contrast, voted 12 percent more Republican than the national average. Since then, Catholic support for Democratic presidential candidates has steadily declined. In 1984, according to most surveys, the Catholic vote closely paralleled the national vote. At the same time,

The Most Loyal Groups in the Traditional Party Coalitions

| | Percent more Democratic than the nation as a whole | | | | Percent more Republican than the nation as a whole | | |
Presidential election year	Black	Poor	Central cities	Union family	White	Nonunion family	Protes- tant
1976	38	17	10	13	5	4	5
1980	47	30	28	9	5	4	3
1984	40	25	29	14	7	4	3

SOURCE: Developed from data in Robert Axelrod, "Presidential Election Coalitions in 1984," *American Political Science Review* 80 (March 1986): 282-283. The survey data are from the Survey Research Center of the University of Michigan.

the overall Protestant vote has become less firmly tied to the Republican party. (But is should be noted that white Protestants voted overwhelmingly for Reagan, especially in 1984.)

Union members have become a somewhat less reliable element in the Democratic coalition than they were in the past, particularly during the Kennedy and Johnson years. In 1984 union families favored Walter Mondale over Ronald Reagan by a margin of only 52 to 48 percent. Overall, the voting behavior of group members is more volatile today, especially in presidential elections—a fact consistent with a period of *dealignment* in which group attachments to the parties become weaker.

American parties are fragile because they are coalitions. At times they seem to be held together by nothing more than generality, personality, and promise. Perhaps what is surprising, all things considered, is that they hold together as well as they do.

The chief threat to party cohesion develops once the election is over and the party is placed in government. It is at this point that coalitions split apart. The behavior of the Democratic party in Congress illustrates this phenomenon. The party unity data in Table 2-7 show how often northern and southern House Democrats voted in agreement with a majority of their party in the second session of the Ninety-ninth Congress (1986). For northern Democrats, party unity was highly important. About three-fourths of this large bloc voted with a majority of their party 80 percent or more of the time. But only 28 percent of all southern Democrats met this standard. At the other pole, roughly one-fourth of all

TABLE 2-7   Intraparty Conflict in House Roll-Call Voting, Ninety-ninth
Congress, Second Session

	Percentage of northern and southern Democrats voting with a majority of their own party					
Region	90 percent or more	80-89.9 percent	70-79.9 percent	60-69.9 percent	50-59.9 percent	Under 50 percent
Northern Democrats	27	49	16	6	2	0
Southern Democrats	2	26	28	20	13	11

SOURCE: Developed from party unity data compiled in *Congressional Quarterly Weekly Report*, November 15, 1986, 2901-2906.

NOTE: Failures to vote lower party unity scores.

southern Democrats voted with their party majority less than 60 percent of the time. Intraparty divisiveness is obviously a major feature of congressional voting. Despite the differences, southern Democrats are somewhat less likely to bolt from their northern colleagues today than in the 1970s or early 1980s (when they steadily supported the Reagan administration).

The facts presented in Table 2-7 are evidence that significant disagreement hides behind the party label, especially in the case of congressional Democrats. When party coalitions come apart in Congress, biparty coalitions are often brought to life. The most persistent and successful biparty coalition in the history of Congress has been the "conservative coalition," formed by a majority of southern Democrats and a majority of Republicans. In existence in one form or another since the late 1930s, this coalition comes together on essentially the same policy issues that divide northern from southern Democrats. The most effective majority in some recent sessions of Congress has been the southern Democrat-Republican coalition. For example, working closely with the Reagan administration in the first session of the Ninety-seventh Congress (1981), the coalition won 92 percent of the time that it formed. Between 1982 and 1986, the conservative coalition won, on average, 84 percent of the time it appeared.[17] About the only modern Congress in which a lid was placed on the coalition's power was the Eighty-ninth (1965-1966), when the Democratic majority under President Johnson was so overpowering that even the defection of many southerners could not ordinarily bring down the party. (See Chapter 5 for additional discussion on the effectiveness of the conservative coalition.)

Parties of Ideological Heterogeneity

To win elections and gain power is the unabashedly practical aim of the major party. As suggested previously, this calls for a strategy of coalition building in which the policy goals of the groups and candidates brought under the party umbrella are subordinated to their capacity to contribute to party victory. The key to party success is its adaptability, its willingness to do business with groups and individuals holding all manner of views on public policy questions. The natural outcome of a campaign strategy designed to attract all groups (and to repel none) is that the party's ideology is not easily brought into sharp focus. It is, in a sense, up for grabs, to be interpreted as individual party members and officeholders see fit.

The data provided in Figure 2-5 illuminate the ideological distance that separates Senate members of the same party on proposals of key interest to the Americans for Democratic Action (ADA)—a group well known for its identification with liberal causes and policies. Those senators voting in harmony with ADA objectives in the Ninety-ninth Congress supported such policies as liberalized benefits for the long-term unemployed, restoration of funding for Head Start and various other education programs, restoration of Medicare and Medicaid funding, higher taxes for corporations, retention of the ban on interstate handgun sales, payment of certain medical expenses for victims of hazardous-waste dumping, elimination of funding for MX missiles, reduced funding for research on antimissile defenses, and economic sanctions against South Africa. In addition, members voting in line with the ADA opposed reductions in Social Security benefits, funding for binary chemical weapons, funding for humanitarian assistance to Nicaraguan rebels, aid to antigovernment Angolan rebels, the line-item veto, and curtailment of federal court jurisdiction over cases involving prayer in public schools. A sketch of ideological conflict in the Senate, presented in Figure 2-5, shows clearly that each party is a mass of tensions and contradictions, with party members marching to different drums.

The divisions within each major party can be easily identified. Southern Democrats do not view the world in the same light as northern Democrats, nor do they respond to the same cues and constituency clienteles as their northern colleagues. Some eastern Republicans have more in common with northern Democrats than they do with fellow party members from the South or the Midwest.[18] But tempting as it is to fasten on intraparty differences as a way of explaining the performance of the parties in policy-making arenas, the argument can easily get out of

FIGURE 2-5   Democratic and Republican Support of Americans for Democratic
Action (ADA) Positions, by Region and Individual Senate
Members, Ninety-ninth Congress, Second Session

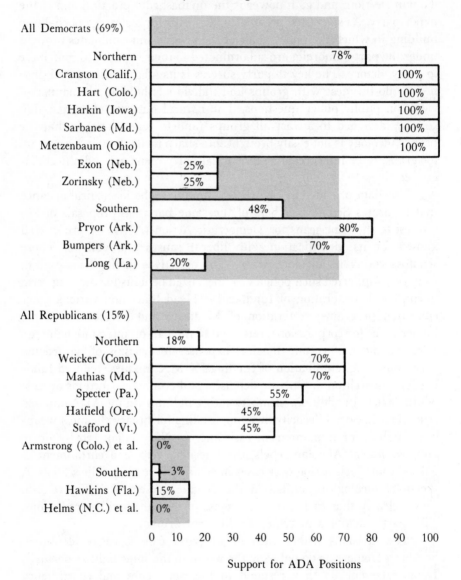

Support for ADA Positions

SOURCE: Developed from data gathered in *Congressional Quarterly Weekly Report*, November 22, 1986, 2966.

NOTE: The eleven states of the Confederacy plus Kentucky and Oklahoma are classified as southern; all others are classified as northern. Eighteen Republican senators had ratings of 0.

hand. In truth, the parties are far from identical, and each has more unity than is commonly supposed.

Although the structure of voting in Congress does not exhibit a high degree of ideological coherence within each party, it nevertheless does show important and continuing policy differences between the parties—at least, between majorities of each party. Democratic members of Congress[19] and Democratic congressional candidates[20] are much more likely to support social welfare legislation and an expanded role for federal government, for example, than are Republican officeholders and Republican candidates. Programs to advance minority rights, to assist public education, to improve the lot of the poverty stricken, to provide medical care for the elderly, or to promote the interests of organized labor typically produce substantial disagreement between the parties, with most Democrats aligned on the liberal side and most Republicans aligned on the conservative side. General differences between party majorities also exist on defense policy and on aid to anticommunist rebels. Hence, to return to the metaphor used earlier, even though party members may be marching to different drums, most of them are playing the same tune.

Parties of Moderation and Inclusivity

Another way to view American parties emphasizes their moderation and inclusivity. They are, in fact, "catchall" parties in which all but the most extreme and intractable elements in society can find a place and, in the process, stake a claim to a "piece of the action."

The American party is anything but clannish. It will devote a friendly ear to just about any request. All groups are invited to support the party, and in some measure all do. Almost everything about the major party at election time represents a triumph for those who press for accommodation in American politics. Platforms and candidate speeches, offering something to virtually everyone, provide the hard evidence that the parties attempt to be inclusive rather than exclusive in their appeals and to draw in a wide rather than a narrow band of voters. "No matter how devoted a party leadership may be to its bedrock elements," V. O. Key, Jr., observed, "it attempts to picture itself as a gifted synthesizer of concord among the elements of society. A party must act as if it were all the people rather than some of them; it must fiercely deny that it speaks for a single interest." [21]

The inclusivity of American parties means that they occupy virtually all of the political space in the political system. Minor parties are forced to search for distinctiveness. Some fashion narrow appeals. Others press bizarre or hopeless causes. Still others maneuver only at the ideological fringes, seeking to address extreme "left wing" or "right wing" audiences. Their dilemma is that only a relative handful of voters are at each ideological pole and only a few will be attracted to a narrow or single-issue appeal.

The founders established an intricate system of divided powers, checks and balances, and auxiliary precautions to reduce the government's vulnerability to factions. The "Madisonian System"—separation of powers, staggered terms of office, bicameralism, federalism, life appointments for federal judges, fixed terms of office for the president and members of Congress, among other things—makes it difficult for any group (faction or party) to gain firm control of the political system. Today's parties qualify as Madison's factions, but with an unexpected twist. They are in no way a factional threat. Their inclusivity and moderation represent at least as great an obstacle to factional domination of government as formal constitutional arrangements. Because the major parties include all kinds of interests, they are not free to favor a single interest or a small cluster of interests to the exclusion of others. Standing party policies are an expression of earlier settlements among divergent interests. Virtually every new policy can be contested by interested party elements. Every affected interest expects a hearing, bargaining occurs as a matter of course, and accommodation typically takes place. The broad consequences, ordinarily, are, first, that policymaking is a slow process and, second, that policy changes are introduced incrementally. The parties' moderation ordinarily means that no one wins completely, no one loses completely. This argument is sketched in Figure 2-6.

The Party as an Interest Group

Although American parties are sometimes criticized for their cool detachment from important social and economic issues, the same cannot be said for their attitude toward a band of issues having high relevance for the party, *qua* party. Certain kinds of issues, or policy questions, that come before legislatures present the party with an opportunity to advance its interests as an organization—in much the same fashion as political interest groups attempt to secure or block legislation that would improve or impair their fortunes. There is, E. E. Schattschneider wrote some years ago, both a "public" and a "private" personality within each

FIGURE 2-6 Moderate Parties and Policy Making

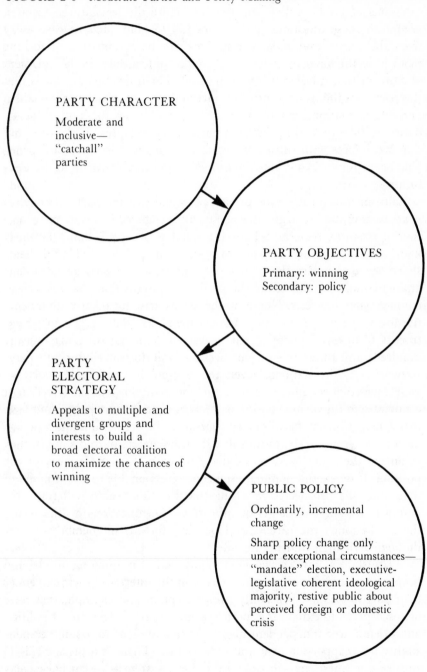

PARTY CHARACTER

Moderate and
inclusive—
"catchall"
parties

PARTY OBJECTIVES

Primary: winning
Secondary: policy

PARTY
ELECTORAL
STRATEGY

Appeals to multiple and
divergent groups and
interests to build a
broad electoral coalition
to maximize the chances of
winning

PUBLIC POLICY

Ordinarily, incremental
change

Sharp policy change only
under exceptional circumstances—
"mandate" election, executive-
legislative coherent ideological
majority, restive public about
perceived foreign or domestic
crisis

party.[22] The public dimension of the party is on display when larger questions of public policy are brought before the legislature. As often occurs on these questions, party lines fail to hold, factions ease away from the party, and biparty coalitions are born, empowered for the moment as the majority. The party's public appearance, in the judgment of many critics, leaves much to be desired. The fundamental flaw is that the party nominally in control of government, but rent by factionalism and fragmentation, cannot be held responsible by the public for its decisions. The problem is not that party unity collapses on all issues but that it collapses with sufficient frequency to make it less than a dependable agent for carrying out commitments presumably made to the electorate.

In sharp contrast is the private personality of the party. Though it is an exaggeration to argue that the party is engaged in steady introspection, it is surely true, as Schattschneider has observed, that "the party knows its private mind better than it knows its public mind." [23] It has a sharp sense of where the best opportunities lie for partisan advantage and an equally keen sense of the perils and pitfalls that can threaten or damage party interests. Numerous occasions arise for transmitting benefits to the party organization and its members. Patronage can be extracted from government at all levels. In some jurisdictions literally hundreds and thousands of jobs are available for distribution to party stalwarts. At the national level, the custom of "senatorial courtesy" guarantees that senators will have the dominant voice in the selection of candidates to fill various positions, such as district court judges and U.S. marshals. This custom calls on the president, before nominating a person for a position in a state, to consult with the senators of that state (if they belong to the same party as he does) to learn their preference for the position. If he should nominate someone objectionable to the senators of that state, the prospects are strong that the full Senate will reject the nominee, irrespective of his qualifications. On questions of this sort—those that touch the careers and political fortune of members—party unity is both high and predictable.

Legislators have never won reputations for queuing up behind proposals that might limit maneuvering in the interest of their careers or their party's welfare. With only a few exceptions, for example, they have opposed plans to extend the merit system, to take judges out of politics, and to empower independent boards or commissions to assume responsibility for reapportionment and redistricting. There is a private side to such public questions—to extend the merit system is to cut back party patronage, to remove judges from the election process is to cut off a career avenue for legislators with their sights on the court, and to give a nonlegislative commission control over redistricting is to run the risk of a major rearrangement of legislative districts and a resultant loss of offices. Legislators and the parties they represent take seriously their role as guardians of the welfare of the organization and the personal interests of its members. As a collectivity, the American party is most resourceful and cohesive when it is monitoring party business. And party business is about as likely to intrude on the great public questions as it is on those of narrow or parochial concern. Opportunities to advance the party cause—through debate, legislation, or investigations—are limited only by a failure of imagination.

The Ambiguity of Party Membership

For those people who set great store by neat and orderly arrangements, the American major party is vastly disappointing. There are numerous examples of the party in disarray. A particularly good one, in the judgment of some students of American politics, involves the concept of party "membership."

Who is a party member in the United States? The answer is not clear, though a stab at the question can be made by considering the legal aspects of party membership. Closed primary states have tests of membership. Legal party membership in these states is determined by self-classification at the stage of registration. The significance of establishing membership is that each party's primary is open only to members registered in that party.[24] About one-half of the states have authentic closed primary systems. By contrast, open primary states have no test of party affiliation. Gaining membership consists merely of the voter's request for the ballot of the party in whose primary he wishes to participate. In certain open primary states the voter is automatically given the ballots of all the parties, with instructions to mark one and discard the rest.

Apart from primary voting in closed primary states, membership in a major party is of slight moment. In effect, anyone who considers himself a Democrat is a Democrat; anyone who considers himself a Republican is a Republican. A citizen may register one way and vote another or not vote at all. No obligations intrude on the party member. He can be a member without applying for admission, a beneficiary without paying dues or contributing to campaigns, a critic without attending meetings, an interpreter without knowing party vocabulary, an apostate without fearing discipline. To the citizen who takes politics casually, it may be the best of all worlds. The typical American is insensitive to the claims, problems, and doctrine of his party. His principal participation in party life is through the act of voting— sometimes for his party and sometimes not.

The Indomitable Party?

The party in America is at the center of the political process. Nonetheless, its grip on political power is far from secure. To be sure, the people who are recruited for party and public offices, the issues that they bring before the electorate, the campaigns in which they participate, and the government that they help to organize and direct—all are influenced by party. The basic problem remains, however, that the party is unable to control all the routes to political power. In some jurisdictions, nonpartisan election systems have been developed to try to remove parties from politics, and to a degree they have succeeded. Moreover, so thoroughly are some states and localities dominated by one party that party itself has come to have little relevance for the kinds of men and women recruited for office or for the voters in need of cues for casting their votes. Devices such as the direct primary have also cut into the power of the party organization, serving in particular to discourage national party agencies from attempting to influence nominations, including those for national office, and to open up the nominating process to all kinds of candidates. In addition, divided party control of government has become a chronic problem of both state and national governments. Typically one party winds up controlling the executive branch and the other party one or both houses of the legislative branch. Determining which party in fact is the majority party has become increasingly difficult.

The party-in-the-electorate—voters who regard themselves as party members—probably has never been weaker than it is right now. Nearly one-third of all voters profess to be independents. Strong partisans are less numerous than in the past. More than half of all voters regularly cast split ballots in presidential elections. Most voters do not view parties in a favorable light or believe that party control over government is desirable. On the whole, the nation's political culture is a hostile environment for parties. The absence of citizen interest in elections also takes a toll on party vitality. It is a spectacular fact that more than 100 million citizens who might have voted in the 1986 congressional elections chose to "stay home," and voter turnout (37.3 percent of the voting-age population) was the third-lowest in the nation's history.[25] In the midst of the signs of party deterioration, it is not surprising that the influence of the mass media, public relations experts, campaign management firms, and political action committees has grown markedly in virtually all phases of campaigns and elections.[26]

Perhaps the wonder of American politics is that the party system functions as well as it does. From the perspective of party leaders, the Constitution is a vast wasteland, scarcely capable of supporting vigorous parties; federalism, separation of powers, checks and balances, and staggered elections all have proved inimical to the organization of strong parties. National and state constitutions apparently were drafted by those who were suspicious of the concentration of power in any hands; their designs have served to fracture or immobilize party power. The party itself is an uneasy coalition of individuals and groups brought together for limited purposes. Within government, power is about as likely to be lodged in nooks and crannies as it is in central party agencies. Conflict within the parties is sometimes as intense as it is between the parties. As for the individual party member, he has a great many rights but virtually no responsibilities for the well-being of the party.

Public disillusionment over the parties places a further strain on their capacities. Many voters believe that the parties have not posed imaginative solutions for such nagging issues as racial injustice, urban decay, inflation, unemployment, and poverty. Similarly, citizens are concerned about the "old" politics that seems to dominate the parties, manifested in a preoccupation with patronage, perquisites, and the welfare of the organization instead of public policy. The parties are also subject to harsh criticism for their apparent willingness to yield to the blandishments of pressure groups and local interests, while too frequently ignoring broad national interests and problems. For many citizens, parties appear as starkly conservative institutions, fearful of innovation and unable to shape intelligent responses to contemporary dilemmas. At no time in the last century have the American major parties occupied such troubled ground as they do today. The party reforms of the modern period have done more to weaken the parties than to strengthen them. The spread of presidential primaries, the opening up of caucuses, the ideology of popular participation, and the federal campaign finance law (and Supreme Court rulings concerning it) have diminished the role of parties and party leaders in presidential elections. All too often, parties are nothing more than spectators to the campaign clashes of candidate organizations. As for the members of Congress, they have become even more independent of party. In the current state of free-floating politics, interest groups have gained increasing influence over election outcomes and public policies. Their role in financing congressional campaigns is one of the main reasons that campaign expenditures are out of control, increasing at a rate that far outstrips inflation. In sum, the politics of today looks much different from that of the 1960s.

For those citizens who believe that democratic politics depends on the presence of viable parties, conditions must surely appear grim. Even so, it is by no means clear that the major parties are in the process of withering away, to be replaced by government without parties or government by multiple-party coalitions. Survival in this weakened state seems much more likely. And finally, it is useful to remember that, whatever else may be said of American parties, they have never been particularly strong.

Notes

1. On the decentralization of American parties, see Robert Harmel and Kenneth Janda, *Parties and Their Environment* (New York: Longmans, 1982), especially Chapter 5.
2. *Cousins v. Wigoda*, 419 U.S. 477 (1975). This case involved the seating of the Illinois delegation to the 1972 Democratic national convention. The Court upheld the right of the Democratic convention to refuse to seat the Illinois delegation, which, according to findings of the credentials committee, had violated national party rules concerning the selection process for delegates and whose makeup inadequately represented youth, women, and minorities. The right of the national party to establish rules concerning delegate selection was further strengthened by the Court in a case involving Wisconsin's open presidential primary: *Democractic Party of the U.S. v. LaFollette*, 101 S. Ct. 1010 (1981). (See the discussion in Chapter 3.)
3. The centralizing reforms in the delegate selection process of the Democratic party have not altered the basic decentralization of the party. See William J. Crotty, "The Philosophies of Party Reform," in *Party Renewal in America: Theory and Practice*, ed. Gerald M. Pomper (New York: Praeger Special Studies, 1980), especially 45-48.
4. See Paul S. Herrnson's analysis of the growing role of national party committees in providing services, such as fund raising and advertising, for House candidates. The Republican party has been significantly more active in this respect. "Do Parties Make a Difference?: The Role of Party Organizations in Congressional Elections," *Journal of Politics* 48 (August 1986): 589-615. Also see Elizabeth Drew, "Politics and Money," *New Yorker*, December 6, 1982, 64.
5. Austin Ranney and Willmoore Kendall, *Democracy and the American Party System* (New York: Harcourt, 1956), 497.
6. See the discussion of political action committees in Chapter 3.
7. James M. Burns, *The Deadlock of Democracy: Four Party Politics in America* (Englewood Cliffs, N.J.: Prentice-Hall, 1963), 236-237. For an instructive

study of state party organizations and leaders, see Robert J. Huckshorn, *Party Leadership in the States* (Amherst: University of Massachusetts Press, 1976).

8. This section on law and the parties is based primarily on the findings of David E. Price, *Bringing Back the Parties* (Washington, D.C.: CQ Press, 1984), especially Chapter 5. Contrast the heavily regulated parties of today with those of half a century ago described by E. E. Schattschneider in *Party Government* (New York: Holt, Rinehart and Winston, 1942), 11: "The extralegal character of political parties is one of their most notable qualities."

9. The competitiveness of presidential elections also can be examined from the perspective of the electoral college. Of the forty-six presidential elections held between 1876 and 1968, twenty-one can be classified as "hairbreadth elections"—those in which a slight shift in popular votes in a few states would have changed the outcome in the electoral college. See Lawrence D. Longley and Alan G. Braun, *The Politics of Electoral College Reform* (New Haven, Conn.: Yale University Press, 1972), especially 37-41.

10. On this point, see especially Richard F. Fenno, Jr., *Home Style: House Members in Their Districts* (Boston: Little, Brown, 1978), 10-18; and Thomas E. Mann, *Unsafe at Any Margin: Interpreting Congressional Elections* (Washington, D.C.: American Enterprise Institute for Public Policy Research, 1978).

11. The literature on legislative-constituency relations, which includes examination of the incumbency factor in elections, is impressive. Anyone who takes the time to read the following studies on the subject will know vastly more than any normal person should know: David R. Mayhew, "Congressional Elections: The Case of the Vanishing Marginals," *Polity* 6 (Spring 1974): 295-317; Gary C. Jacobson, "The Effects of Campaign Spending in Congressional Elections," *American Political Science Review* 72 (June 1978): 469-491; Jon R. Bond, Gary Covington, and Richard Fleisher, "Explaining Challenger Quality in Congressional Elections," *Journal of Politics* 47 (May 1985): 510-529; Donald A. Gross and James C. Garrand, "The Vanishing Marginals, 1824-1980," *Journal of Politics* 46 (February 1984): 224-237; Robert S. Erikson and Gerald C. Wright, "Voters, Candidates, and Issues in Congressional Elections," in *Congress Reconsidered*, 3d ed., ed. Lawrence C. Dodd and Bruce I. Oppenheimer (Washington, D.C.: CQ Press, 1985), 87-108; John C. McAdams and John R. Johannes, "Constituency Attentiveness in the House: 1977-1982," *Journal of Politics* 47 (November 1985): 1108-1139; Glenn R. Parker and Suzanne L. Parker, "Correlates and Effects of Attention to District by U.S. House Members," *Legislative Studies Quarterly* 10 (May 1985): 223-242; Melissa P. Collie, "Incumbency, Electoral Safety, and Turnover in the House of Representatives, 1952-1976," *American Political Science Review* 75 (March 1981): 119-131; John R. Alford and John R. Hibbing, "Increased Incumbency Advantage in the House," *Journal of Politics* 43 (November 1981): 1042-1061; James E. Campbell, "The Return of the Incumbents: The Nature of the Incumbency Advantage," *Western Political Quarterly* 36 (September 1983): 434-444; Diana Evans Yiannakis, "The Grateful Electorate: Casework and Congressional Elections," *American Journal of Political Science* 25 (August 1981): 568-580; Richard Born, "Generational Replacement and the Growth of Incumbent Reelection Margins in the U.S. House," *American Political Science Review* 73 (September 1979): 811-817; Candice J. Nelson, "The Effect of Incumbency on Voting in Congressional Elections, 1964-1974," *Political Science Quarterly* 93 (Winter 1978-1979): 665-678; John R. Johannes and John C. McAdams, "The Congressional Incumbency Effect: Is it Casework, Policy Compatibility, or Something Else?," *American Journal of Political Science* 25 (August 1981): 512-542; Warren Lee Kostroski, "Party and Constituency in

Postwar Senate Elections," *American Political Science Review* 67 (December 1973): 1213-1234; and Lyn Ragsdale, "Incumbent Popularity, Challenger Invisibility, and Congressional Voters," *Legislative Studies Quarterly* 6 (May 1981): 201-218. And see these books: David R. Mayhew, *Congress: The Electoral Connection* (New Haven, Conn.: Yale University Press, 1974); Fenno, *Home Style: House Members in Their Districts;* Gary C. Jacobson and Samuel Kernell, *Strategy and Choice in Congressional Elections* (New Haven, Conn.: Yale University Press, 1981); and Gary C. Jacobson, *The Politics of Congressional Elections* (Boston: Little, Brown, 1987), especially Chapter 3.

12. See Austin Ranney, "Parties in State Politics," in *Politics in the American States,* ed. Herbert Jacob and Kenneth Vines (Boston: Little, Brown, 1976), 63-65; and John F. Bibby, Cornelius P. Cotter, James L. Gibson, and Robert J. Huckshorn, "Parties in State Politics," in *Politics in the American States,* ed. Herbert Jacob and Virginia Gray (Boston: Little, Brown, 1983), 59-96.

13. It is worth noting here that the elements that influence voting decisions also vary by office. One study suggests that the importance of parties (as cue givers), experience and incumbency, personal qualifications, and issues in shaping voter decisions depends on the nature and level of the office—for example, presidential-subpresidential, executive-legislative, incumbent-nonincumbent. The personal qualifications of candidates appear to have the greatest impact on the vote. Issues usually loom more important in presidential and gubernatorial voting, parties more important in gubernatorial and senatorial voting, and candidate experience most important in senatorial voting. Typically, voters have much less political information about senatorial candidates than they do about presidential and gubernatorial candidates. See Barbara Hinckley, Richard Hofstetter, and John Kessel, "Information and the Vote: A Comparative Election Study," *American Politics Quarterly* 2 (April 1974): 131-158.

14. For analysis of the dualism theme, see V. O. Key, Jr., *Politics, Parties, and Pressure Groups* (New York: Crowell, 1964), 207-208.

15. Major party nominees are automatically given access to the general election ballot. Minor, new party, and independent candidates have to qualify for the ballot by establishing a certain level of support, which is set by state law. For an analysis of ballot access laws, see Bruce W. Robeck and James A. Dyer, "Ballot Access Requirements in Congressional Elections," *American Politics Quarterly* 10 (January 1982): 31-45.

16. Maurice Duverger, *Political Parties* (New York: Wiley, 1965), 17.

17. *Congressional Quarterly Weekly Report,* November 15, 1986, 2907-2912.

18. For a study of the decline of party unity in both parties in the lower house of Congress, see Barbara Deckard Sinclair and John Stanley, "Party Decomposition and Region: The House of Representatives, 1945-1970," *Western Political Quarterly* 27 (June 1974): 249-264. A major explanation for the decline has been the growth of regional and ideological cleavages within the parties. Most notable for their declining party unity scores from 1945 to 1970 were eastern Republicans (more liberal than their party colleagues) and southern Democrats (more conservative than their party colleagues). For the most part, regional cleavages within the parties are due to ideological differences.

19. The differences between Democratic and Republican members of Congress are examined at greater length in Chapter 5.

20. See an analysis by Jeff Fishel of the ideological differences between Democratic and Republican candidates who challenge incumbent members of Congress. A majority of Democratic challengers in his study see themselves as liberal, and a majority of the Republican challengers see themselves as conservative. About one-third of the candidates in each party see themselves as middle-of-the-road.

Only a handful of candidates label themselves as conservative Democrats or liberal Republicans. *Party and Opposition: Congressional Challengers in American Politics* (New York: McKay, 1973), 64-94.

21. Key, *Politics, Parties, and Pressure Groups,* 221.
22. From *Party Government,* by E. E. Schattschneider. Copyright 1942 by E. E. Schattschneider. Reprinted by permission of Holt, Rinehart and Winston, 133-137.
23. From Schattschneider, *Party Government,* 134.
24. In 1973 the United States Supreme Court upheld, in a 5-4 decision, a New York state law that requires a voter to register his party affiliation thirty days in advance of a general election to be eligible to vote in that party's next primary election. Had the Court not upheld this "closed" provision, nothing would prevent voters from switching parties as often as they like, permitting Democrats to vote in Republican primaries and Republicans to vote in Democratic primaries. *Rosario v. Rockefeller,* 410 U.S. 752 (1973).
25. The turnout estimate is taken from the *New York Times,* November 8, 1986.
26. The impact of the mass media and professional campaign management firms on the electorate and the party system is considered in Chapter 6.

c h a p t e r   t h r e e

Political Parties and
the Electoral Process

IT IS PROBABLE that no nation has ever experimented as fully or as fitfully with mechanisms for making nominations as has the United States. The principal sponsor of this experimentation is the federal system itself. Under it, responsibility for the development of election law lies with the states. Their ingenuity, given free rein, has often been remarkable. A wide variety of caucuses, conventions, and primaries—the three principal methods of making nominations—have been tried out in the states. The devices that have lasted owe their survival not so much to a widespread agreement on their merits as to the inability of opponents to settle on alternative arrangements and to the general indifference of the public at large to major institutional change.

Nominating Methods

Caucus

The oldest device for making nominations in the United States is the caucus. In use prior to the adoption of the Constitution, the caucus is an informal meeting of political leaders held to decide questions concerning candidates, strategies, and policies. The essence of the caucus idea, when applied to nominations, is that by sifting, sorting, and weeding out candidates before the election, leaders can assemble substantial support behind a single candidate, thus decreasing the prospect that the votes of like-minded citizens will be split among several candidates. Historically, the most important form of caucus was the *legislative caucus,* which, until 1824, was used successfully for the nomination of candidates for state and national offices, including the presidency. The major drawback to the legislative caucus was that membership was limited to the party members in the legislature, thereby exposing the caucus to the charge that it was unrepresentative and undemocratic. A modest reform in the legislative caucus occurred when provisions were made for seating delegates from districts held by the opposition party. Nevertheless, when the (Jeffersonian) Republican caucus failed to nominate Andrew Jackson for the presidency in 1824, it came under severe criticism from many quarters and shortly thereafter was abandoned for the selection of presidential nominees. (But another form of caucus survives in the presidential nominating process. See the subsequent analysis of the caucus-convention system for choosing delegates to the parties' national nominating conventions.)

Party Conventions

Advocates of reform in the nominating process turned to the party convention, already in use in some localities, as a substitute for the legislative caucus. The great merit of the convention system, it was argued, was that it could provide for representation, on a geographical basis, of all elements within the party. The secrecy of the caucus was displaced in favor of a more public arena, with nominations made by conventions composed of delegates drawn from various levels of the party organizations. As the convention method gained in prominence, so did the party organizations; state and local party leaders came to play a dominant role in the selection of candidates.

The convention system, however, failed to consolidate its early promise. Although it has been used for the nomination of presidential candidates from the 1830s to the present, it has given way to the direct primary for most other offices. Critics found that it suffered from essentially the same disabling properties as the caucus. In their view, it was sheer pretense to contend that the conventions were representative of the parties as a whole; instead, they were run by party bosses without regard either for the views of the delegates or for the rules of fair play. An endless array of charges involving corruption in voting practices and procedures were made, and doubtless there was much truth in them. Growing regulation of conventions by the legislatures failed to assuage the doubts of the public. The direct primary came into favor as reformers came to understand its potential as a device for dismantling the structure of boss and machine influence and for introducing popular control over nominations.

The Direct Primary

Popular control of the political process has always been an important issue in the dogma of reformers. The direct primary, with its emphasis on voters instead of on party organization, was hard to resist. Once Wisconsin adopted it for nomination of candidates for state elective offices in 1903, its use spread steadily throughout the country. Connecticut became the last state to adopt it, in 1955, but only after much tampering with the idea. The Connecticut model (the "challenge" primary) combines convention and primary under an arrangement in which the party convention continues to make nominations, but with this proviso: if the party nominee at the convention is challenged by another candidate who receives as much as 20 percent of the convention votes, a primary must be held later. Otherwise, no primary is required, and the name of the convention nominee is automatically certified for the general election.

Part of the attractiveness of the primary is its apparent simplicity. From one perspective, it is a device for transferring control of nominations from the party leadership to the rank-and-file voters; from another, it shifts this control from the party organization to the state. The primary rests on state law: it is an official election held at public expense, on a date set by the legislature, and supervised by public officials. It has often been interpreted as an attempt to institutionalize intraparty democracy.

It is not surprising that the direct primary has always had a better reception in reformist circles than anywhere else. For the party organization, it poses problems, not opportunities. If the organization becomes involved in a contested primary for a major office, it probably will have to raise large sums of money for the campaign of its candidate. If it remains neutral, it may wind up with a candidate who either is hostile to the organization or is unsympathetic toward its programs and policies. Even if it abandons neutrality, there is no guarantee that its candidate will win; indeed, a good many political careers have been launched in primaries in which the nonendorsed candidate has convinced the voters that a vote for him is a vote to crush the machine. Finally, the primary often works at cross purposes with the basic party objective of harmonizing its diverse elements by creating a "balanced" ticket for the general election. The voters are much less likely to nominate a "representative" slate of candidates, one that recognizes all major groups within the party, than is the party leadership. Moreover, if the primary battle turns out to be bitter, the winner may enter the general election campaign with a sharply divided party behind him.[1] It is no wonder that some political leaders have viewed the primary as a systematically conceived effort to bring down the party itself.

Types of Primaries

Four basic types of state primaries are in use: *closed, open, blanket,* and *nonpartisan.* Two special forms of primaries are also used: *runoff* and *presidential* (the latter is analyzed in the section on the presidential nominating process).

Closed Primary

Twenty-six states use a closed primary to make nominations.[2] The key feature of this primary is that the voter can participate in the nomination of candidates only in the party to which he belongs—and this is established through *registration* as a party member.[3] State laws vary substantially in the ease with which voters can switch back and forth between the parties. Voters in the closed primary states of Iowa, Ohio, and Wyoming, for example, can change their party registration on election day—a provision that makes their systems palpably "open." Other closed primary states establish a deadline for changing parties sometime prior to primary election day. South Dakota sets this deadline at a mere fifteen days and Oregon at twenty days, while New York and Kentucky set it at about eleven months. The mean requirement is roughly two months. Some closed primary states prohibit voters from switching parties once the candidates have filed declarations of candidacies, while other less restrictive states encourage "voter floating" by permitting changes in party registration after candidates have declared themselves. Sharp differences exist among closed primary states in how they foster or protect party efficacy and integrity.[4]

Other differences in closed primary systems likely will follow in the wake of the 1986 Supreme Court ruling in *Tashjian v. Republican Party of Connecticut.*[5] The case arose from the efforts of the Connecticut state Republican party to attract independents by permitting them to vote in its primary elections. Unable to change the state's closed primary law in the legislature, the party successfully challenged it in court. By a 5-4 vote, the Supreme Court ruled that states may not require political parties to hold closed primaries that permit only voters previously enrolled in a party to vote. This ruling leaves the choice of primary system to the parties instead of to state legislatures. Hence, a state party may choose to open its primary to unaffiliated (or independent) voters or it may choose to bar their participation. The *Tashjian* decision does not outlaw closed primaries, and presumably many state parties will continue to permit only registered party members to vote in their primaries.

Open Primary

From the point of view of the party organization, the open primary is less desirable than the closed primary. Twenty-one states (not counting states that use blanket or nonpartisan primaries) have some form of open primary—defined as one in which the voter is not required to register as a party member to vote in a party primary. Provisions for open primaries differ from state to state. In nine states the voter is given the ballots of all parties, with instructions to vote for the candidates of only one party and to discard the other ballots.[6] Nothing can prevent Democrats from voting to nominate Republican candidates or Republicans from voting to nominate Democratic candidates. The strongest appeal of this form of open primary is that it preserves the secrecy of the voter's affiliation or preference.

In the other twelve open primary states voters are required to declare a party preference at the polls to obtain a ballot. In some states the declaration is recorded by election officials and in other states it is not. Here and there a voter's right to participate in a particular primary may be challenged. Interestingly, switching parties from one primary to the next in certain open primary states, such as Rhode Island, is more difficult than switching in certain closed primary states, such as Iowa.

Party leaders suffer from a special anxiety in open primary states: the possibility that voters of the competing party will "raid" their primary, hoping to nominate a weak candidate who would be easy to defeat in the general election. Whether raiding occurs with any frequency is difficult to say, but in some states large numbers of voters do cross over to vote in the other party's primary when an exciting contest is present. One of the central arguments used by the state of Connecticut in the *Tashjian* case was the party's need to protect itself from raiding by members of the other party. The Supreme Court found this defense of the closed primary "insubstantial."

The use of open (crossover) primaries in the presidential nominating process has been a continuing source of aggravation for some party leaders, since these primaries permit nonparty members to influence the choice of a party's nominee. In Wisconsin, one study has shown, roughly

8 to 11 percent of all voters in presidential primaries are "partisan crossovers"—that is, Democrats voting in the Republican primary or Republicans voting in the Democratic primary. And a surprising one-third of each party's primary participants are self-styled independents. In a close race, the presence of these "outsiders" can make a difference in the outcome.[7]

To combat crossover voting, the charter of the Democratic party, adopted in 1974, specified that delegates to the party's national convention be chosen through procedures that limit participation to Democratic voters. Despite this provision, Wisconsin continued to permit voters to participate in the state's Democratic presidential primary without regard to party affiliation. When delegates were later chosen in the Democratic caucus sytem, they were obligated to vote in accordance with the voters' presidential preferences as revealed in the open primary. In a decision clearly designed to protect party processes, the Supreme Court ruled in 1981 that states could continue to hold open presidential primaries, but that the results did not have to be recognized in selecting state party delegates to the convention.[8] The effect of this decision was to require Wisconsin in 1984 to select its delegates in closed caucuses—that is, caucuses limited to Democrats only. This restriction did not last long. In the belief that the "Democrats only" provision had produced considerable ill will and had narrowed the party's base, the Democratic National Committee voted in 1986 to permit Wisconsin Democrats to return to their traditional open primary, in which independents and Republicans can participate. This new rule thus accepts the open-primary heritage of states such as Wisconsin and Montana, but it does not permit other states to change their systems by opening their delegate selection processes to members of other parties. (See Rules 2A, 2C in Table 3-1.)

Blanket Primary

The states of Alaska and Washington complete the circle of open primary systems with what is known as a blanket primary. No primary is quite so open. Nor does any other provide voters with a greater range of choice. Under its provisions the voter is given a ballot listing all candidates of all parties under each office. Voters may vote for a Democrat for one office and for a Republican for another office. Or they may vote for the candidate of a third party. They cannot, of course, vote for more than one candidate per office. The blanket primary is an invitation to ticket splitting.

Nonpartisan Primary

In a number of states, judges, school board members, and other local government officials are selected in nonpartisan primaries. State legislators in Nebraska are also selected on this basis. The scheme itself is simple: the two candidates receiving the greatest number of votes are nominated; in turn, they oppose each other in the general election. No party labels appear on the ballot in either election. The nonpartisan primary is defended on the grounds that partisanship should not be permitted to intrude on the selection of certain officials, such as judges. By eliminating the party label, runs the assumption, the issues and divisiveness that dominate national and state party politics can be kept out of local elections and local offices. Although nonpartisan primaries muffle the sounds of party, they do not, however, eliminate them. It is not uncommon for the party organizations to slip quietly into the political process and to recruit and support candidates in these primaries; in such cases, about all that is missing is the party label on the ballot.

Since 1975 Louisiana has had an "open elections" law that renders its primaries nonpartisan. Under this system, all candidates for an office are grouped together in a primary election. A candidate who receives a majority of the primary vote is elected, thus eliminating the need for a general election. If no candidate obtains a majority of the votes cast, the top two, irrespective of party affiliation, face each other in a runoff general election. Among the apparent effects of the open elections law have been a pronounced advantage for incumbents, new difficulties for the Republican party, a growing number of candidates who have no party affiliation, costlier campaigns, and, perhaps most important, the development of "institutionalized multifactionalism"—marked by intensified campaigning at the primary stage with numerous candidates competing for the same office. (Fourteen candidates for the U.S. Senate, for example, were on the Louisiana primary ballot in 1986.) Party obviously counts for little in the Louisiana setting. Even the ballot has been modified, changing from party column to office block as a means of inhibiting straight party voting.[9]

Runoff Primary

The runoff or second primary is a by-product of a one-party political environment. As used in southern states, this primary provides that if no candidate obtains a majority of the votes cast for an office, a runoff is held between the two leading candidates. The runoff primary is an attempt to come to terms with a chronic problem of a one-party system— essentially all competition is jammed into the primary of the dominant party. With numerous candidates seeking the nomination for the same office, the vote is likely to be sharply split, with no candidate receiving a majority. A runoff between the top two candidates in the first primary provides a guarantee, if only statistical, that one candidate will emerge as the choice of a majority of voters. This is no small consideration in those southern states where the Democratic primary has long been the "real" election and where factionalism within the party has been so intense that no candidate would stand much of a chance of consolidating his party position without two primaries—the first to weed out the losers, and the second to endow the winner with the legitimacy a majority can offer.

An Overview of the Primary

The great virtue of the direct primary, in the perspectives of its early Progressive sponsors, was its democratic component, its promise for changing the accent and scope of popular participation in the political system. Its immediate effect, it was hoped, would be to diminish the influence of political organization on political life. What is the evidence that the primary has accomplished its mission? What impact has it had on political party organization?

An important outcome of having the primary system is that party leaders have been sensitized to the interests and feelings of the most active rank-and-file members. Fewer nominations are cut and dried. Even though candidates who secure the organization's endorsement win more frequently than they lose, their prospects often are uncertain.[10] The possibility of a revolt against the organization, carried out in the primary, forces party leaders to take account of the elements that make up the party and to pay attention to the claims of potential candidates. There is always a chance—in some jurisdictions, a strong possibility— that an aspirant overlooked by the leadership will decide to challenge the party's choice in the primary. The primary thus induces caution among party leaders. A hands-off policy—one in which the party makes no endorsement—is sometimes the party's only response. If it has no candidate, it cannot very well lose; some party leaders have been able to stay in business by avoiding the embarrassment that comes from primary defeats. In some jurisdictions, party intervention in the primary is never even considered, so accustomed is the electorate to party-free contests.

For the public at large, the main contribution of the primary is that it opens up the political process.

The primary has not immobilized party organizations, but it has caused a number of problems for them. Party leaders' lack of enthusiasm for primaries is not hard to understand knowing that, among other things, the primary (1) greatly increases party campaign costs (if the party backs a candidate in a contested primary); (2) diminishes the capacity of the organization to reward its supporters through nominations; (3) makes it difficult for the party to influence nominees who establish their own power bases in the primary electorate; (4) creates opportunities for people hostile to party leadership and party policies to capture nominations; (5) permits anyone to wear the party label and opens the possibility that the party will have to repudiate a candidate who has been thrust upon it; and (6) increases intraparty strife and factionalism.[11] It seems no institution is better designed than the primary to stultify party organization and party processes.

On the whole, the primary has not fulfilled the expectations of its sponsors. Several things have gone awry. To begin, competitiveness has been absent in primaries. The suprising number of nominations won by default may be because of any of several reasons. For one, uncontested primaries may be evidence of party strength—that is, potential candidates stop short of entering the primary because their prospects appear slim for defeating the organization's choice. Second, the "deserted" primary simply may demonstrate the pragmatism of politicians: they do not struggle to win nominations that are unlikely to lead anywhere. As V. O. Key and others have shown, primaries are most likely to be contested when the chances are strong that the winner will be elected to office in the general election and will be least likely to be contested when the nomination appears to have little value.[12] Thus, the tendency is for electoral battles to occur in competitive districts or in the primary of the dominant party. Third, the presence of an incumbent reduces competition for a nomination. In House elections between 1956 and 1974, Harvey L. Schantz has shown, 55 percent of all Democratic primaries were contested when no incumbent was running, and only 37 percent when an incumbent was in the race; for Republican primaries, the percentages were 44 and 20, respectively. Overall, the prospects for primary contests are greatest in districts in which a party has no incumbent but has a reasonable chance to win in November.[13]

Experience with the primary has also shown that it is one thing to shape an institution so as to induce popular participation and quite another to realize it. No fact about primaries is more familiar than that large numbers of voters assiduously ignore them. A majority of voters usually stay away from the polls on primary day, even when major statewide races are to be settled. A turnout of 25 to 30 percent of the eligible electorate is the norm in many jurisdictions. The promise of the primary is thus only partially fulfilled. The reality is that the public is not keenly interested in the nominating process.

The National Convention

The American national convention is surely one of the most remarkable institutions in the world for making nominations. In use since the Jacksonian Era, it is the official agency for the selection of each party's candidates for president and vice president and for the ratification of each party's platform. At the same time, it is the party's supreme policy-making authority, empowered to make the rules that govern party affairs.

The national convention historically has served another function of prime importance to the parties. It has been a meeting ground for the party itself, one where leaders could tap rank-and-file sentiments and where the divergent interests that make up each party could, at least in some fashion, be accommodated. In its classic role, the national convention presents an opportunity for the national party—the fifty state parties assembled—to come to terms with itself, permitting leading politicians to strike the necessary balances and to settle temporarily the continuing questions of leadership and policy. Under the press of other changes in the presidential nominating process, however, the party role in conventions has recently been diminished.

Until the 1970s, national convention decisions could best be explained by examining the central role of national, state, and local party leaders and the behavior of state delegations. These were the "power points" in the classic model of convention politics, aptly described by the authors of *Explorations in Convention Decision Making:*

> Historically, state delegations have been thought to be the key units for bargaining in conventions; operating under the unit rule, they bargain with each other and with candidate organizations. The rank-and-file delegates are manipulated by hierarchical leaders holding important positions in national, state, and local party organizations. In order to enhance their bargaining position, these leaders often try to stay uncommitted to any candidate until the moment that their endorsement is crucial to victory for the ultimate nominee. After the

presidential balloting is over, the vice presidential nomination is awarded to a person whose selection will mollify those elements of the party who did not support the presidential choice. At the end of the convention, all groups rally around the ticket and the party receives a boost in starting the fall campaign.[14]

The classic model of convention decision making bears only modest resemblance to the patterns of influence at play in the most recent party conventions. In broad terms, decentralization of power is now the chief characteristic of the struggle for the presidential nomination. State delegations have given way to candidate blocs in importance, and party leaders have been displaced by the leaders of candidate organizations. Party leaders have few resources with which to bargain in those state delegations that are split among candidates. The governor who heads a state delegation may be nothing more than a figurehead; meetings of many state delegations are concerned more with announcements (for example, bus departures for the convention site) and ceremonies than with strategy. In contrast, the action is found in the candidate caucuses, where the strategy sessions on candidates, rules, and platform planks occur. Uncommitted delegates have become less numerous than in the past. (But see the subsequent discussion of a change that increases the number of uncommitted delegates at the Democratic convention.) Today's party conventions are dominated by candidates and their organizations. Accordingly, the influence that party and elected officials wield in conventions is largely a product of their affiliation with one of the candidate organizations.

The decline of the party presence in national conventions results from a confluence of forces: the new delegate selection rules that both opened up the parties to amateur activists and contributed to the spread of presidential primaries, to the capacity of candidates to dominate campaign fund raising (using government subsidies under a matching system since 1976), and to the general weakness of state and local party organizations.[15] The reliance of candidates on party leaders in the preconvention period has never been less—in most states, party leaders cannot do much either to help or to hurt a candidate's chances to win delegates. What matters to the candidate is winning the immediate primary or placing well (as judged by the mass media) to attract new funds and to build momentum for the next contest. In the modern scheme of campaigning, expert consultants, an active personal organization spread out around the state, and the mass media loom much more important to the candidates than the party structures and party leaders.

Selection of Delegates

National convention delegates are chosen by two methods: presidential primaries and caucus-conventions. Each state chooses its own system, and it is not unusual for a state to switch from one method to another between elections in response to criticisms by the press, by the public, and by politicians unhappy about recent outcomes.

Loosely managed by the parties, the caucus-convention system provides for the election of delegates by rank-and-file members (mixed with "candidate enthusiasts") from one level of the party to the next—ordinarily from precinct caucuses to county conventions to the state convention and from there to the national convention. The first-tier caucuses (mass meetings at the precinct level) are crucial, since they establish the delegate strength of each candidate in the subsequent conventions, including the national. Hence it is extremely important for candidates and their organizations to turn out their supporters for these initial party meetings; a loss at this stage cannot be reversed.

At one time the chief criticism of the caucus-convention system was that it was essentially closed, dominated by a few party leaders who selected themselves, key public officials, "fat cats" (major financial contributors), and lesser party officials as delegates. The "democratizing" reforms of the 1970s changed all this, opening up the caucuses to participation by average party members and short-term activists willing to spend an afternoon or evening in discussion and voting. Today, the delegate-selection caucuses are dominated by competing candidate organizations and their enthusiasts, and prominent party officials may or may not be found in their ranks. Preoccupied with the struggle for delegates, the media pay scant attention to the caucus as a party event.

In 1984 twenty-seven states, mainly small and medium-sized ones, used the caucus-convention system to select delegates. Although party leaders no longer dominate caucus decisions and vastly more people now participate in the caucus process, caucus turnout is still not high in comparison with primary states. Less than one million voters took part in the states' first-round Democratic caucuses in 1984. On the Republican side, where President Reagan had no major opposition, participation in the caucuses was extremely light. Overall, in none of the caucus-convention states did turnout for the first-round meetings surpass 4 percent of the eligible electorate.[16]

The other system for selecting delegates is the presidential primary. This method was introduced in the early twentieth century. Like the direct primary used to nominate national, state, and local officials, the presidential primary was designed to wrest control of nominations from the "bosses" (the party professionals) and to place it in the hands of the people by permitting them to choose the delegates to the nominating conventions in a public election. In 1904 Florida became the first state to adopt a presidential primary law. In little more than a decade, about half of the states had adopted some version of it. Its use since then has fluctuated. Only sixteen states and the District of Columbia held presidential primaries in 1968. The popularity of this device grew in the 1970s, and thirty-five states, plus Puerto Rico and the District of Columbia, held primaries in 1980. The number fell again in 1984, when the Democratic party held primaries in twenty-eight states, the District of Columbia, and Puerto Rico, and the Republican party held them in twenty-four states. In four of the states where Democratic primaries were held (Idaho, North Dakota, Vermont, and Wisconsin), the results were nonbinding, with delegates chosen later in party caucuses. In addition, none of the Democratic candidates even bothered to file in the 1984 Montana primary; the state's delegates were chosen through the caucus process. Nearly two out of three states scheduled primaries for the 1988 election, including virtually all of the populous states.

The broad thrust of presidential primaries is to encourage popular participation in the presidential nominating process.[17] In 1984 nearly eighteen million people voted in Democratic primaries and some six million voted in Republican primaries. Even so, this level of participation is far from impressive. In the thirty Democratic and twenty-four Republican primaries the median turnout was only 13 percent of the voting-age population on the Democratic side and 10 percent on the Republican side.[18]

The nominating electorate—the voters who take part in caucuses and primaries—is a modest share of the total electorate. In 1984 about one out of seven eligible voters attended a first-tier caucus or voted in a primary. Perhaps twenty-six million voters took part in the presidential nominating process,[19] as contrasted with some ninety-two million people who voted in the general election.

Prior to the 1970s, the manner in which national convention delegates were selected was left to the states. Today, the Democratic party in particular tightly regulates the methods of delegate selection. The dimensions of national party control can best be appreciated by examining Table 3-1, which includes certain major rules in effect for the 1988 Democratic National Convention. In the selection of delegates, the rules make clear, not much is left to chance or to the discretion of individual state parties.

TABLE 3-1   Major Delegate Selection Rules for the 1988 Democratic National Convention

Rule	1A:	State parties shall adopt affirmative action and delegate selection plans which contain explicit rules and procedures governing all aspects of the delegate selection process....
	1C:	State delegate selection and affirmative action plans shall be submitted to the Compliance Assistance Commission [CAC] for approval....
	2A:	Participation in the delegate selection process is open to all voters who wish to participate as Democrats.
	2C:	Nothing in this rule shall be interpreted to encourage or permit states with party registration and enrollment, or states that limit participation to Democrats only, to amend their systems to open participation to members of other parties.
	3A:	All official party meetings and events related to the national convention delegate selection process ... shall be scheduled for dates, times, and public places which would be most likely to encourage the participation of all Democrats.
	5C:	With respect to groups such as ethnics, youth, persons over sixty-five years of age, lesbians and gay men, persons with a high school education or less, the physically handicapped, persons of low and moderate income, and other groups significantly underrepresented in our party affairs, each state party shall develop ... outreach programs ... in order to achieve full participation by such groups in the delegate selection process and at all levels of party affairs.
	6A:	In order to encourage full participation by all Democrats in the delegate selection process and in all party affairs, the national and state Democratic parties shall adopt and implement affirmative action programs with specific goals and timetables for blacks, Hispanics, native Americans, Asian/Pacific Americans, and women.
	6C:	State delegation plans shall provide for equal division between delegate men and delegate women and alternate men and alternate women in the convention delegation.
	7C:	Seventy-five percent (75%) of each state's base delegation shall be elected at the congressional district level or lower. Twenty-five percent (25%) of each state's base delegation shall be elected at large.
	7D:	In those states with more than one congressional district, after the election of district-level delegates and prior to the selection of at-large delegates, each state Democratic chair shall: (1) certify as unpledged party delegates each member of the Democratic National Committee [DNC] from that state; (2) certify each Democratic governor, if any, as an unpledged delegate; (3) certify as unpledged delegates those members of the U.S. Congress from that state who have been selected by the House Democratic Caucus and the Senate Democratic Conference ... ; (4) certify pledged party leader and elected official delegates equal to 15 percent of the state's base delegation....
	8A:	... the Democratic Caucus of the U.S. House of Representatives and the Democratic Conference of the U.S. Senate shall meet and select four-fifths of their respective memberships to serve as national convention delegates....
	9A:	The election of at-large delegates shall be used, if necessary, to achieve the equal division of positions between men and women and the representation goals established in the state party's affirmative action plan.

10A: No meetings, caucuses, conventions, or primaries which constitute the first determining stage in the presidential nominating process ... may be held prior to the second Tuesday in March or after the second Tuesday in June in the calendar year of the national convention. Provided, however, that the Iowa precinct caucuses may be held no earlier than twenty-two days before the second Tuesday in March; that the New Hampshire primary may be held no earlier than fourteen days before the second Tuesday in March; that the Maine first tier caucuses may be held no earlier than nine days before the second Tuesday in March; and that the Wyoming first tier caucuses may be held no earlier than four days before the second Tuesday in March.

11A: All candidates for delegate in caucuses, conventions, committees and on primary ballots shall be identified as to presidential preference, uncommitted or unpledged status at all levels of a process which determines presidential preference.

11H: Delegates elected to the national convention pledged to a presidential candidate shall in all good conscience reflect the sentiments of those who elected them.

12A: Delegates shall be allocated in a fashion that fairly reflects the expressed presidential preference or uncommitted status of the primary voters or, if there is no binding primary, the convention and caucus participants. States shall choose one of the following plans for allocating delegates to presidential candidates at the district level: (1) *Proportional representation.* District level delegates shall be allocated in proportion to the percentage of the primary or caucus vote won in that district by each preference, except that preferences falling below a 15 percent threshold shall not be awarded any delegates. (2) *Bonus delegate plan.* One delegate position per district shall initially be awarded to the primary or caucus-convention winner in that district. The remainder of the delegate positions in the district shall be allocated in proportion to the percentage of the primary or caucus-convention vote won in that district by each preference, except that preferences falling below the 15 percent threshold shall not be awarded any delegates. (3) *Direct-election primaries.* Individual candidates for delegate and alternate may be voted for directly on the primary ballot....

16A: The unit rule, or any rule or practice whereby all members of a party unit or delegation may be required to cast their votes in accordance with the will of a majority of the body, shall not be used at any stage of the delegate selection process.

18A: A Compliance Assistance Commission ... shall be appointed ... to assist in the administration and enforce affirmative action and delegate selection requirements for the national and state Democratic parties.

20A: Wherever any part of any section contained in these rules conflicts with existing state laws, the state party shall take provable positive steps to achieve legislative changes to bring the state law into compliance with the provisions of these rules.

20C: A state party may be required by a vote of the DNC Executive Committee upon a recommendation of the CAC to adopt and implement an alternative party-run delegate selection system which does not conflict with these rules, regardless of any provable positive steps the state may have taken.

SOURCE: *Delegate Selection Rules for the 1988 Democratic National Convention* (Washington, D.C.: Democratic National Committee, 1986).

An amalgam of recommendations by five party study commissions, stretching from 1969 to 1985, the rules were designed to serve several major objectives: (1) to stimulate the participation of rank-and-file Democratic voters in the presidential nominating process; (2) to increase the representation of certain demographic groups (particularly women, blacks, and young people) in the convention through the use of guide-lines on delegate selection; (3) to eliminate procedures held to be undem-ocratic (such as the unit rule, under which a majority of a state delegation could cast the state's total vote for a single candidate); (4) to enhance the local character of delegate elections (by requiring 75 percent of the delegates in each state to be elected at the congressional district level or lower); and (5) to provide through proportional representation that elected delegates fairly reflect the presidential candidate preferences of Democratic voters in primary states and Democratic participants in caucus-convention states. (The proportional representation rule was relaxed in the 1980s.)

For many members of the first commission, the McGovern-Fraser Commission, the underlying objective was to diminish the power of party professionals in the convention, while at the same time increasing that of party members and activists at the local level. They succeeded in extraor-dinary degree. A new type of participant, to whom candidates and issues were central, came to predominate in the Democratic convention. Party professionals were thoroughly overshadowed in the 1972 and 1976 conventions.[20] Party leaders and public officials gradually have been "readmitted" since then. Following a recommendation of the Winograd Commission, the Democratic National Committee adopted a provision to expand each 1980 state delegation by 10 percent to include prominent party and elected officials. That provision set the stage for further change. In 1982 the Democratic party again revised its rules to augment the influence of professional politicians in the convention. Adopting a recommendation of the Hunt Commission, the DNC added a bloc of 568 uncommitted party and elected officials as delegates to the 1984 conven-tion. Members of this group—sometimes referred to as "superdele-gates"—were chosen by virtue of the public or party office that they held; nearly two hundred Democratic members of Congress, for exam-ple, were selected by House and Senate party caucuses. Continuing to grope for the proper balance in the 1988 convention, the Fairness Commission (the fifth such reform commission in a decade and a half) recommended an increase in the number of superdelegates to about 650. With DNC approval of this recommendation in 1986, an even larger proportion of delegate positions has been reserved for the party's governors, members of Congress (roughly 80 percent), DNC members, and assorted state and local officials. (See Rule 7D, Table 3-1.)

The rules governing the selection and allocation of convention delegates vary from state to state and from party to party. The national delegate selection rules of the Democratic party have been changed in one respect or another for each presidential election since 1968, undoubtedly contributing to confusion about the objectives of the party. (Losing an election is a special incentive to go back to the drawing board.) But whatever the rules in force, complexity has been their leading characteristic. A close look at them is warranted.

Currently, national Democratic rules permit state parties to choose from among three broad plans. (See Rule 12A, Table 3-1.) First, states may select the *proportional representation* method, under which any Democratic candidate who reaches the threshold of the primary or caucus vote (15 percent in 1988, lowered from the 20 percent level used in most states in 1984) is entitled to a proportionate share of the delegates; candidates who fail to reach the threshold do not qualify for any delegates. Second, states may adopt what amounts to a *winner-take-all* system. In this direct-election form, voters cast ballots for individual delegates who may be pledged to candidates or uncommitted. The candidate who comes in first in a district can win all or most of the delegates instead of sharing them with the trailing candidates.[21] Third, states may choose a *winner-take-more* plan. Here, the winning candidate in each district gains a bonus delegate before the rest are divided proportionally.

Either nonproportional scheme is an attractive option for a populous state, since by permitting a candidate to claim a disproportionate number of delegates a state magnifies the importance of its primary or caucus. An impressive victory in California or Pennsylvania, large winner-take-all primary states, is likely to yield more delegates and garner more media attention than modest victories in half a dozen or more smaller states where delegates are allocated proportionally and hence scattered among several candidates.

Proportional representation has had two controversial side effects. First, it permits the candidate who builds an early lead, the front-runner, to continue to pile up numerous delegates even in those states won by another candidate. It still takes a long time to nail down the nomination, however, since some other contenders will always reach the threshold and thus share in the distribution of delegates. Second, proportional representation prevents a trailing candidate from winning big—capturing a large share of the delegates in a populous state, as could occur under a winner-take-all arrangement.

Democratic Party's Delegate Selection Rules . . .

In the Democratic party, national rules prescribe in detail how delegates to the national nominating convention are to be chosen. State party organizations must comply with these rules. Developed by various reform commissions, they have fluctuated sharply over the past two decades. Initially, the reformers focused on means to make the party more open, the delegate selection process more democratic, and the delegates themselves more representative of major demographic groups. The recent commissions, by contrast, have sought chiefly to restore the influence of professional politicians in the convention and to give state parties somewhat wider latitude to formulate methods for selecting delegates.

For party officials, rule making is no day at the beach. Hard choices are involved. Candidates, interests, party blocs, and state politicians must be accommodated or mollified. New rules, moreover, produce unanticipated consequences as well as winners and losers.

The one constant in Democratic presidential selection politics is change.

Intraparty Democracy

McGovern-Fraser Commission (1969-1972)

Developed rules to permit all Democratic voters a "full, meaningful, and timely" opportunity to take part in the presidential nominating process.

Required each state party to include in its delegation blacks, women, and young people in numbers roughly proportionate to their presence in the state population.

Required at least 75 percent of each state delegation to be selected at a level no higher than the congressional district.

Eliminated practices held to be undemocratic, such as the unit rule.

Mikulski Commission (1972-1973)

Reaffirmed many McGovern-Fraser guidelines.

Dropped "quotas" but required states to establish affirmative action plans to encourage full participation by all Democrats, with special efforts required to include minority groups, native Americans, women, and youth.

Required a fair reflection of voters' presidential preferences (thus proportional representation) at all levels of the delegate selection process, with a few exceptions.

Created a national party compliance review commission to monitor implementation of state affirmative action and delegate selection programs.

...*Key Provisions of Reform Commissions*

Intraparty Democracy and Party Renewal

Winograd Commission (1975-1978)

Specifically identified women, blacks, Hispanics, and native Americans as the objects of "remedial action to overcome the effects of past discrimination."

Shortened the period for delegate selection from six to three months.

Eliminated last vestiges of winner-take-all systems.

Outlawed "crossover" primaries under which Republicans and independents could vote in Democratic primaries.

Increased the size of state delegations by 10 percent to augment representation of top party leaders and elected officials.

Required delegates to vote for the presidential candidate they were elected to support for at least first ballot.

Voted not to require each state to have an equal number of men and women in its delegation, but the Democratic National Committee later adopted equal-division rule.

Party Renewal

Hunt Commission (1981-1982)

Retreated from proportional representation by permitting state parties to adopt winner-take-all or winner-take-more systems.

Provided that 14 percent of the delegates to the 1984 convention be chosen on the basis of their public office or party status ("superdelegates").

Tightened the primary-caucus "window" by reducing the period between the Iowa caucuses and the New Hampshire primary from thirty-six days to eight.

Eliminated binding first ballot for delegates.

Fairness Commission (1984-1985)

Increased number of superdelegates from 568 to about 650 for the 1988 convention.

Lowered threshold from 20 to 15 percent, thus making it easier for trailing candidates to share in the distribution of delegates.

Permitted Wisconsin and Montana to conduct open (or crossover) primaries, banned earlier by the Winograd Commission.

For these and other reasons the Democratic National Committee has eased its commitment to proportional representation by permitting state parties to choose winner-take-all or winner-take-more systems. Party leaders make no bones about their preference for a convention that merely ratifies the voters' choice. They do not want a brokered convention, marked by "backroom politicking," impasse, and television's merciless eye on frustrated delegates casting ballot after ballot. Preference for a system that winnows out candidates well in advance of the convention has also prompted the party to retain the controversial threshold rule. The overall purpose of the current rules is to build consensus behind a single candidate prior to the convention.[22] There is no assurance, however, that this will happen every time.

The Republican party was considerably less active than the Democratic party in the 1970s and 1980s in restructuring its delegate selection rules, but it did make a few changes. Its current rules require open meetings for delegate selection, ban automatic (ex officio) delegates, and provide for the election, not the selection, of congressional district and at-large delegates (unless otherwise provided by state law). State Republican parties are urged to develop action plans for increasing the participation of women, young people, minorities, and other groups in the presidential nominating process, but they are not required to do so. The push to nationalize party rules, pronounced among Democratic reformers for the past two decades, finds only limited support among Republicans. Rather, Republicans continue to stress the federal character of their party; the basic authority to reshape delegate selection rules rests accordingly with state parties.[23]

Republican delegate selection practices differ in several major respects from those of the Democrats. In the first place, Republicans have resisted the allure of proportionality in delegate allocation, placing much more emphasis on some version of winner-take-all. As observed by the chief counsel of the Republican National Committee, "the allocation of delegates to our convention has always been based in part on the electoral college, which is winner-take-all. People who don't like that should argue with James Madison or Thomas Jefferson." [24] Second, the Republican party has no provision for the automatic selection of party or party officials—superdelegates in Democratic nomenclature. Third, the party has no requirement that state delegations be evenly divided between men and women, a rule imposed on state Democratic parties beginning in 1980. (Women delegates are nonetheless numerous in Republican conventions.) And finally, each state Republican party is free to schedule its presidential primary or caucus as it sees fit. The

Michigan Republican party, for example, begins its delegate selection process almost two years in advance of the party's national convention.[25] On the Democratic side, the primary-caucus calendar is tightly governed by national party rules.[26] Party differences in delegate selection reflect basic party differences in philosophy and organization that can be summed up in the appellations "federal" Republicans and "national" Democrats.

Evaluating Presidential Primary and Caucus-Convention Systems

Sometimes it appears as though the only persons who are satisfied with the presidential nominating process are the winners—the nominees and their supporters. Everyone else, it seems, can find reasons to be unhappy or frustrated about the process.

To the initiated and uninitiated voter alike, the primaries and caucuses are a mass of oppositions and paradoxes. Unpredictability reigns. Victory in a single state can be the key to the nomination. And victories in the early primaries and caucuses are usually crucial. Consider recent outcomes. In the judgment of many observers, on the day that John F. Kennedy defeated Hubert H. Humphrey in the West Virginia primary in 1960—a Catholic winning in an overwhelmingly Protestant state—he sewed up the nomination. In 1964 the critical Republican primary took place in California, where Barry Goldwater narrowly defeated Nelson Rockefeller. In 1972 George McGovern's nomination seemed to be guaranteed by his win in California. Jimmy Carter's string of early primary victories in 1976, beginning with his narrow win in New Hampshire, gave him a commanding lead. His weakness in late primaries, marked by several losses to California governor Jerry Brown, had no effect on the nomination. Challenged by Edward M. Kennedy and Jerry Brown in 1980, Carter again won the New Hampshire primary and five of the next six primaries, forcing Brown out of the race. Kennedy won ten of thirty-four primaries, but half of those victories came on the last day of the primary season, too late to matter. Although the Democratic struggle in 1984 was much different, a case can be made that Walter Mondale's successes in Alabama and Georgia on "Super Tuesday," the second Tuesday in March, were indispensable, serving to keep him from elimination after a series of media and real victories by Gary Hart.

Where the key state victories occur makes a difference. When

Presidential Nominating Politics . . .

Which presidential primaries or caucus-conventions were most important in 1984? On the Democratic side, scene of all the action, consider these states:

Iowa (February 20): The first caucus-convention state. Walter F. Mondale won almost 50 percent of the vote of caucus participants. But the real winner may have been Gary Hart, who won about 15 percent of the vote while placing second—a boost for his New Hampshire campaign.

New Hampshire (February 28): First primary state, known for its unpredictability. Hart, 37 percent; Mondale, 27 percent. Permitted to vote in the Democratic primary, independents strongly supported Hart. Benefited by media hype, his outsider campaign accelerated.

"Super Tuesday" (March 13): Mondale won the Alabama and Georgia primaries. Hart won the Florida, Massachusetts, and Rhode Island primaries and caucuses in three western states. Jesse Jackson ran well in the South.

Michigan and Illinois (March 17, 20): Key victories for Mondale, arresting the Hart surge.

New York (April 3): Major victory for Mondale in a "Democrats only" primary. Hart narrowly edged Jackson.

Pennsylvania (April 10): "Democrats only" primary and winner-take-all within districts. Impressive victory for Mondale. Mondale's margin in delegates was now almost two-to-one over Hart. (Can the front-

---

California emerges as the focus in the preconvention struggle, no one thinks much about it. California is the nation's most populous state, and its primary comes late. When bucolic Iowa and contrary New Hampshire vault a dark horse into prominence, however, it is a different matter. Both George McGovern in 1972 and Jimmy Carter in 1976 owed their nominations to their strong showings in these states. And Gary Hart, another outsider, almost parlayed a better-than-anticipated vote in the Iowa caucuses in 1984 (15 percent to Mondale's 45 percent) and a victory in New Hampshire into the nomination. The most important result of an early victory (or good showing) is the extraordinary "free" media time it produces for winners, strong finishers, and underdogs.

At bottom, the issue is the representativeness of Iowa and New Hampshire of the entire Democratic electorate. Neither state has a major

... *Mondale and Hart in 1984 Campaign*

runner be overtaken when many of the remaining states use a proportional representation scheme for allocating delegates? Answer: unlikely.)

Indiana and Ohio (May 8): How to stop the bleeding: narrow victories for Hart. Independents allowed to vote in both primaries. But Mondale won the Maryland and North Carolina primaries as well as the Texas caucuses the same week.

California and New Jersey (June 5): The season ends. California won by Hart, New Jersey by Mondale. Counting "pledges" from uncommitted delegates, Mondale claimed he had won the nomination and, as it turned out, he was right.

For Hart, the most important primaries or caucus-conventions probably were Iowa and New Hampshire, in which he gained media victories, celebrity status, momentum, campaign funds, and a few delegates. The western primaries and caucuses, where Hart was strong, came too late to change the result. In addition, many of Hart's victories came in proportional representation states, where he gained only a few more delegates than Mondale.

For Mondale, probably the Alabama and Georgia primaries on Super Tuesday (since they kept his candidacy alive) and those in the large states of Illinois, New York, and Pennsylvania were most important. Each of the latter three states used a winner-take-all or winner-take-more system for awarding delegates.

metropolitan area, a large urban (unionized) workforce, or a sizable minority population. The voters in these states are patently not a cross section of the majorities that elect Democratic presidents. In fact, these states are much more likely to vote Republican than Democratic in November. Thus their prominence in eliminating contenders, in turning long shots into viable candidates, and in controlling the route to the nomination leaves Democrats in the other forty-eight states and the District of Columbia baffled, if not wholly incredulous.

Regional variation in candidate strength also can be decisive. If, in 1976, the western primaries and caucuses had been held at the beginning of the nominating season instead of near the end, both Jimmy Carter and Ronald Reagan might have fared differently.[27] In 1980 both Carter and Reagan gained critical momentum—the bandwagon effect—by winning a string of early southern primaries. And in 1984 Mondale's virtual sweep of the industrial Northeast gave him a lead that Hart's later victories in western states could not overcome. Sequence makes a difference.

The electoral results in the early caucus-convention and primary states are the peculiar dynamic of the presidential nominating process. And overemphasis of the results by the media is the norm. Often speaking with greater finality than the voters themselves, the media create winners and losers, front-runners and also-rans, candidates who should "bail out" and candidates who have earned "another shot." Voters learn who did better than expected and who did worse than expected. Winning or placing well is translated into a major political resource, with the psychological impact greater than the body count of delegates won. The rewards for capturing the media's attention are heightened visibility, an expanded and more attentive journalistic corps, television news time, interest group cynosure, endorsements, campaign funds, and a leg up on the next contest.

In the nominating process the media have become the new parties:

> The television news organizations in this country are an enormously dominant force in primary elections. They're every Tuesday night, not only counting the votes, but, in some cases, setting the tone. . . . (A member of the Jimmy Carter organization)

> . . . [if] you're short of delegates, the real determining factor's going to be the psychological momentum the press creates. Is he a winner? Can he get the nomination? (A member of the Fred Harris organization)

> You go into a place like New Hampshire and you've got two things in mind. Primarily is winning New Hampshire. Secondly is getting out the stories about your candidate and where he stands and all that to the rest of the country. . . . (A member of the Ronald Reagan organization)

> Everywhere we go, we're on a media trip; I mean we're attempting to generate as much free television and print, as much free radio, as we can get. Any angle can play. . . . (A member of the Morris Udall organization)[28]

> If you're not first or second in New Hampshire, you might as well pack your bags. (John Sears, Republican political consultant)[29]

What really matters is the interpretation of election results by the print and broadcast media. Christopher Arterton writes:

> Those who manage presidential campaigns uniformly believe that interpretations placed upon campaign events are frequently more

important than the events themselves. In other words, the political contest is shaped primarily by the perceptual environment within which campaigns compete. *Particularly in the early nomination stages, perceptions outweigh reality in terms of their political impact.* Since journalists communicate these perceptions to voters and party activists and since part of the reporter's job is creating these interpretations, campaigners believe that journalists can and do affect whether their campaign is viewed as succeeding or failing, and that this perception in turn will determine their ability to mobilize political resources in the future: endorsements, volunteers, money, and hence, votes.[30]

The opening weeks of the nominating process are likely to be even more important in the future, since a number of states have shifted the dates of their primaries or caucuses to the early part of the season—"front loading," in the argot of analysts and political junkies. For 1988 nearly every southern and border state switched its delegate-selection event to early March in a concerted move to enhance southern influence in the nominating process and, on the Democratic side at least, to improve the prospects of moderate or conservative candidates. Whether this de facto regional primary will reduce or increase the significance of the Iowa and New Hampshire outcomes remains to be seen. The salient point is that candidates who fail to get out of the blocks fast may find themselves out of the race before most of the nation's voters have had a chance to express their preferences. Inconclusive results in the early caucuses and primaries mean that the struggle for the nomination may continue to the end of the season (second Tuesday in June) and perhaps beyond to the convention itself. Trying to predict how the calendar will affect individual candidacies, state or regional influence, or voting patterns is impossible. Too many imponderables, including the peculiar mix of candidacies, are present. And what serves certain interests in one election, moreover, may not in the next.

The Democratic party has sought, more or less unsuccessfully, to diminish the significance of the early phase of the presidential nominating process. In 1982 the Democratic National Committee adopted a rule proposed by the Hunt Commission to restrict the nominating season (the caucus-primary "window") to the period of early March to early June, with a few exceptions. Under its terms Iowa will continue to open the nominating season in February, about three weeks in advance of the window, followed by New Hampshire eight days later. Maine and Wyoming tip-toe in slightly in advance of the window. (See Rule 10A, Table 3-1.) Despite these exceptions, the overall schedule is more compact. In 1976 the Iowa caucuses were held in January, more than five weeks before the New Hampshire primary. This long interval permitted "unknown" Jimmy Carter to capitalize on his strong Iowa showing, giving him increased media attention, new supporters, and additional campaign funds that were vital for the New Hampshire primary and elsewhere. The rule narrowing the window may be an advantage for well-known candidates with campaign organizations in place and significant national followings. But not too much should be made of that. The major development is front loading. By day's end on Super Tuesday, more than 40 percent of the states will have held their primary or first-round caucuses. For most candidates, doing poorly and running out of funds, this day marks the end of the race, even though three months of the nominating calendar remain. If a clear-cut front-runner has emerged, the last twelve weeks of the season may be nothing more than the "mop-up" stage.[31] But if two or more strong candidates survive after Super Tuesday, the race has just begun (and the front-loading states have miscalculated).

A realistic campaign for the presidential nomination is expensive. Money is the sine qua non. It separates the serious candidate from the dilettante or the rank outsider. Of course there is never enough of it, and the law does not make it easy to raise. Under the Federal Election Campaign Act, no individual can contribute more than $1,000 to any campaign. Moreover, candidates can qualify for matching federal funds only after they have raised $100,000 in small sums ($250 or less, $5,000 per state) in twenty states. Political action committees may contribute up to $5,000 to a candidate, but their gifts are not eligible for matching public money.[32] The long and short of it is that candidates are compelled to develop a large network of small contributors, spread around the country—making fund raising a chore for all candidates and a major obstacle for some. Plans and activities to raise money must be launched long in advance of the election year. It is thus easy to mark the opening of a new campaign. It begins with the creation of fund-raising committees and the scramble for money. The money hassle is aptly described by the press secretary to Fred Harris, who sought the Democratic nomination in 1976:

> You're caught in a kind of vicious circle. In order to raise money, especially money from more than twenty states, then you have to have national media attention, not just good local media that Fred has been able to generate. . . . But in order to raise that kind of money dispersed among twenty states then you need national media exposure. You need it because people do judge by national media exposure as to

whether the campaign is serious or not and, believe me, they hesitate before they give money.... They're going to wait until they see Fred's smiling face on national television.[33]

The system of caucus-conventions and presidential primaries is a crazy quilt of activity. Candidates fly from one end of the country to the other, then back again, emphasizing certain states, deemphasizing others, and doing their best to impose their interpretation on the most recent results. Candidates are never wholly confident about how or where they should spend their time or money; voters are not quite sure what is going on. Yet there is more to the system than its awkwardness, complexity, and unpredictability.

Popular participation in the presidential nominating process generally was not of much consequence prior to the reforms of the 1970s. Candidates, following their instincts and the advice of assorted national and state politicians, chose to enter primaries, to avoid them, or to participate in certain ones while skipping others. As recently as 1968, only sixteen states even held primaries. And Hubert Humphrey captured the Democratic nomination that year even though he did not contest any primaries (which were dominated by Eugene McCarthy and Robert F. Kennedy). In states using the caucus-convention system, the chief method of nomination, one or a few leaders typically controlled the selection of delegates and thus the outcome. To win the nomination, candidates spent much of their time cultivating key state party leaders. Only a few candidates at any time, moreover, were even thought to be "available" for the office—that is, possessed of attributes that would prompt party leaders around the country and the media to take them seriously. Presidential nominees were chosen in a relatively closed system from among a very select group.

That ambiance and the rules and practices that fostered it have disappeared. Today the system is remarkably open. The impact of party leaders and organizations is minimal in the process. No leader can "deliver" a state. Candidates rarely "write off" a primary or caucus, and surely not one scheduled early. And most important, the rank-and-file voters now play a central role in the presidential nominating process. In 1976 nearly twenty-nine million voters cast ballots in both parties' primaries. The number rose to about thirty-two million in 1980 and, with fewer primaries and no contest on the Republican side, declined to about twenty-four million in 1984. Overall, roughly one-fourth of the eligible electorate now votes in presidential primary states. Perhaps one million voters turn out for the first-tier caucuses in the caucus-convention states.[34] The presidential nominating process is much more responsive to popular preferences than ever in the past. It is a new participatory system. Nothing looks quite the same. Even an incumbent president may have reason to fear a challenge to renomination (for example, Carter versus Kennedy in 1980) in the free-for-all of primaries and caucuses. Whether the new system produces better candidates (or better presidents) than those previously chosen in "smoke-filled rooms" is another matter.

Presidential primaries, because they tap voters' preferences in a more direct fashion than caucuses, and at the same time involve a much larger sector of the electorate, present a particularly good opportunity for testing candidates, policies, and issues in a variety of states.[35] Consider evidence of the past two decades. The Vietnam War was the pivotal issue in both the 1968 and 1972 Democratic primaries. It contributed to President Johnson's decision not to seek reelection in 1968 and, four years later, was central to George McGovern's nomination. When an outsider, Jimmy Carter, won a large majority of the Democratic primaries in 1976, the intensity of voters' resentment toward the "Washington establishment" was revealed. Voter attitudes toward conservatism were brought to light in 1980. Ronald Reagan easily won the first primary in New Hampshire (following a narrow loss to George Bush in Iowa, the first caucus-convention state), lost narrowly to Bush in Massachusetts, and then won six primaries in a row—all by large margins. Most of the other contenders for the Republican nomination, faring poorly in the early primaries, soon withdrew. Reagan lost only four of the thirty-two primaries he entered. Finally, on the Democratic side in 1984, an intense struggle culminated in a close victory for Walter Mondale—one that he gained without either a majority of the national primary (or caucus) vote and one that revealed both the party's contradictions and its bleak prospects in the November election. Primaries make and break politicians' careers, while illuminating the problems of the party, in particular factional conflict and an absence of consensus on program and policy.

What has been the overall impact of the preconvention struggle on the choice of nominees? The primary and convention-caucus process has become decisive, sharply constricting the significance of the national conventions in the selection of presidential nominees. John F. Kennedy owed his nomination in 1960 to, more than anything else, his successes in primary states. Numerous state and local Democratic candidates would have preferred a "safer" candidate, but they found it impossible to withstand the surge of public support behind Kennedy. Democratic party professionals were again confounded in 1972 and 1976 when party outsiders, George McGovern and Jimmy Carter, respectively, won numerous primary victories and, coupled with their successes in nonprimary states, the nominations. On the Republican side, despite the advantage of the presidency, Gerald R. Ford barely escaped with the nomination in 1976 after an extraordinary preconvention challenge by Ronald Reagan, who won ten primaries. President Ford won seventeen. After the first wave of primaries in 1980, there was not much doubt concerning the eventual winners. Carter won nine of the first thirteen Democratic primaries, and Reagan won ten of the first thirteen Republican primaries. In 1984, benefiting from delegate selection and delegate distribution rules that diminished the chances of outsiders and winning where it counted, Mondale had captured the nomination by the end of the primary and caucus season. And Reagan, of course, had virtually no opposition.

The preconvention struggle, however, may not always settle the choice of the nominee. If it does not, the selection will turn on convention bargaining. A "brokered" convention, characterized by sparring between leading candidates (perhaps including some who avoided the primaries and caucuses) and by a more important role for party leaders and public officials, is thus still a possibility. Sooner or later, doubtlessly, there will be one.

The Convention Delegates

The ramifications of political reforms are often much larger than anticipated. The new emphasis on popular participation in the delegate selection process, coupled with the requirements for affirmative action plans to promote the representation of disadvantaged groups, has sharply changed the composition of Democratic national conventions. Prior to the 1970s, Democratic delegates were preponderantly male, middle-aged, and white. And they were usually party regulars—officials of the party, important contributors, and reliable rank-and-file members. Public officeholders were prominent in all state delegations. The selection process itself was dominated by state and local party leaders.

The reforms produced a new breed of delegate. As a result of the guidelines adopted by the McGovern-Fraser Commission, the representation of women, blacks, and young persons in the national convention increased dramatically. For example, the proportion of women delegates grew from 13 percent in 1968 to 40 percent in 1972, and of blacks from 5.5 to 15 percent. Under current rules, each Democratic state party is required to develop "outreach programs" to increase the number of

The Characteristics of National Convention Delegates, 1944-1984

	1944		1968		1976		1984 [a]	
	D	R	D	R	D	R	D	R
By sex:								
Men	89%	91%	87%	83%	67%	69%	49%	54%
Women	11	9	13	17	33	31	51	46
By education:								
High school or less	24	23	b	b	b	b	11	12
Some college	18	18	b	b	b	b	18	25
College grad	12	16	19	—	21	27	20	28
More than college degree	46	41	44	34	43	38	51	35
Average age (in years)	52	54	49	49	43	48	44	51
By occupation:								
Lawyer	38	37	28	22	16	15	17	14
Union leader	2	—	4	—	6	—	6	—
Executive	9	10	27	40	17	30	14	26
Other profession/ teacher	24	35	8	2	26	12	36	27
Public official	11	6	13	13	12	9	9	6
Housewife	6	5	c	c	7	15	4	13
Never attended convention before	63	63	67	66	80	78	74	69
By ideology:								
Liberal	c	c	c	c	40	3	50	1
Moderate	c	c	c	c	47	45	42	35
Conservative	c	c	c	c	8	48	5	60

SOURCE: Barbara G. Farah, "Delegate Polls: 1944 to 1984," *Public Opinion* 7 (August/September 1984): 44.

NOTE: D = Democrat; R = Republican.

[a] 1984 figures are a combination of the CBS News poll, the *New York Times* poll, and the *Los Angeles Times* poll; the 1968 and 1976 figures come from the CBS News poll. The occupation categories are not the same in the 1944 study and the later polls, which explains the discrepancy between "Executive" in the early year and the later ones.
[b] Not available.
[c] Questions not asked.

delegates from groups that have been significantly underrepresented in the past, such as persons over sixty-five years old, the physically handicapped, and persons of low and moderate income. Another affirmative action rule specifies that in the selection of at-large delegations, preference shall be given to blacks, Hispanics, native Americans, Asian/Pacific Americans, and women. Moreover, all state delegation selection plans must provide for an equal division of delegates between men and women. These mandated changes have had a profound impact on the composition of state delegations.

The chief losers in the reordering of the 1970s were Democratic party professionals and public officeholders, as "issue" and "candidate enthusiast" delegates ("amateurs," in broad terms) replaced them in state after state. Recent changes in party rules, such as adding superdelegates in 1984 and 1988, have increased the number of professional politicians. A survey of Democratic delegates in 1984 found that 42 percent held some party office and 29 percent held an elective (or public) office. Nearly 70 percent of the delegates reported that they were engaged in party activities on a year-round basis. Twenty-eight percent of the delegates, by contrast, said that they engage in party work only when the issues or candidates are important to them.[36] The broad point is that professional politicians have reemerged in the Democratic conventions of the 1980s after being sidelined in the 1970s by various party reform commissions. Whether their presence will make much difference remains to be seen. Recent conventions have been cut and dried, the presidential nominees having been chosen earlier by primary voters and caucus participants.

Changes in the composition of Republican convention delegations have come more gradually. Even so, a larger proportion of women, blacks, and young people are being elected as Republican delegates than ever before. Amateur activists are also more numerous in Republican conventions now, but clearly not on the scale found on the Democratic side. Party leaders, longtime party members, and public officials have steadily played key roles in Republican conventions.

Convention delegates do not reflect a cross section of the population or a cross section of the party membership. Two demographic characteristics in particular differentiate delegates from the wider public and rank-and-file party members: high income and substantial education. In 1984 71 percent of the Democratic delegates and 63 percent of the Republican delegates had completed four years of college; a surprising 51 percent of the Democrats and 35 percent of the Republicans had undertaken graduate work. Among Democratic delegates, 42 percent had annual incomes in excess of $50,000; among Republicans, 57 percent. In addition, Protestants were more numerous in the Republican convention (71 percent) while Catholics and Jews were more fully represented in the Democratic convention (32 percent and 9 percent, respectively). Blacks made up 18 percent of the Democratic membership but only 4 percent of the Republican membership, while the percentages for Hispanics were 7 and 4, respectively.

Liberals are overrepresented in the Democratic convention, conservatives in the Republican convention. Fifty percent of the Democratic delegates in 1984 described themselves as liberals, a proportion considerably larger than for the Democratic party membership as a whole (25 percent). And while 40 percent of rank-and-file Republicans saw themselves as conservatives, 60 percent of the Republican delegates described themselves in that fashion. Only 1 percent of the Republican delegates viewed themselves as liberals and only 5 percent of the Democrats emerged as conservatives. Ideological distinctiveness clearly is more characteristic of delegates than of average party members.[37]

The Politics of the Convention

Three practical aims dominate the proceedings of the national convention: to nominate presidential and vice-presidential candidates, to draft the party platform, and to lay the groundwork for party unity in the campaign. The way in which the party addresses itself to the tasks of nominating the candidates and drafting the platform is likely to determine how well it achieves its third objective, that of healing party rifts and forging a cohesive party. To put together a presidential ticket and a platform that satisfies the principal elements of the party is exceedingly difficult. The task of reconciling divergent interests within the party occupies the convention from its earliest moments until the final gavel— at least in most conventions. By and large, convention leaders have been successful in shaping the compromises necessary to keep the national party, such as it is, from flying apart.

The Convention Committees

The initial business of the convention is handled mainly by four committees. The *committee on credentials* is given the responsibility for determining the permanent roll (official membership) of the convention. Its specific function is to ascertain the members' legal right to seats in the convention. In the absence of challenges to the right of certain delegates to be seated or of contests between two delegations from the same state, each trying to be seated, the review is handled routinely and with dispatch. Most state delegations are seated without difficulty. When disputes arise, the committee holds hearings and takes testimony; its recommendations for seating delegates are then reported to the convention, which ordinarily (but not invariably) sustains them. The *committee on permanent organization* is charged with selecting the permanent officers of the convention, including the permanent chairman, the clerks, and the sergeant at arms. The *committee on rules* devises the rules under which the convention will operate and establishes the order of business.

Ordinarily the most important convention committee is the *committee on resolutions,* which is in charge of the drafting of the party platform. The actual work of this committee begins many weeks in advance of the convention, so that usually a draft of the document exists by the time the convention opens and the formal committee hearings begin. When a president seeks reelection, the platform is likely to be prepared under his direction and accepted by the committees (and later by the floor) without major changes.

A fight over the nomination may influence the drafting of the platform, since the leading candidates have an interest in securing planks that are compatible with their views. Indeed, the outcomes of clashes over planks may provide a good indication of which candidate will capture the nomination. In the 1968 Democratic convention, for example, it was all but certain that Hubert Humphrey would win the nomination when the convention, after a lengthy and emotional floor debate, adopted by a comfortable margin a plank that reflected the Johnson administration's position on the Vietnam War. Humphrey's two principal opponents, senators Eugene McCarthy and George McGovern, were the most prominent supporters of the losing minority plank, which called for an unconditional halt to the bombing of North Vietnam. In the 1976 Republican convention, intense struggles occurred in the platform committee between the forces of President Ford and those of Ronald Reagan. Almost all the planks adopted represented victories for the supporters of Ford, thus auguring well for his nomination.

The 1980 Republican and Democratic platforms were fashioned in sharply different ways. Harmony prevailed at the Republican convention, and the members quickly approved a platform with planks that meshed comfortably with the views of its nominee, Ronald Reagan. The document of the platform committee was adopted without change. Debate over the Democratic platform, by contrast, was acrimonious and protracted. Numerous minority reports were adopted on the floor. In the end, the delegates adopted a platform that in major respects (particularly in its economic and human needs planks) was more in line with the liberal views of Senator Kennedy and his partisans than with those of President Carter. The high level of conflict over the platform was surprising given that an incumbent president, the certain nominee, was seeking reelection. No one expects the president's forces to lose on key convention votes. In 1984 scarcely a discordant note was struck at the Republican convention as it renominated President Reagan and approved the platform without debate. On the Democratic side, compromises on the platform among the Walter Mondale, Jesse Jackson, and Gary Hart forces were sufficient to avert divisive floor fights, and the party, stressing family and eschewing tradition, chose Geraldine A. Ferraro as its vice-presidential nominee.[38]

Selecting the Presidential Ticket

To some party leaders, the best convention is the one that opens with significant uncertainties and imponderables—a good, though not sure-fire, prescription for generating public interest in the convention, the party, and its nominees. In the usual convention, however, uncertainties are far from numerous. Doubts are much more likely to surround the choice of the vice-presidential nominee than the presidential nominee. So many presidential candidates are screened out during the primary-caucus season that by the time the convention opens the range of choice has become sharply narrowed, perhaps nonexistent.

The early stages of the nominating process are especially important for the selection of presidential candidates (see Table 3-2). Typically, the candidate leading the public opinion polls at the start of the year (before the first delegate has even been chosen) winds up with the nomination. New opportunities for challenging leading candidates in primaries and caucuses may alter this pattern. In 1972 and 1976 the Democratic nomination was won by an outsider whose poll standings were unimpressive at the start of the year. And in 1980 Ronald Reagan won the Republican nomination, although he trailed in the early polls. Walter Mondale had a wide lead in the initial polls in 1984 and, after an early scare, nailed down the nomination before the Democratic convention opened.

The experience of recent conventions is instructive. In the 1960, 1968, and 1972 Republican conventions, Richard Nixon's nomination

TABLE 3-2 Continuity and Change in Presidential Nominating Politics, 1936-1984

Year	Leading candidate at beginning of election year	Nominee
Party in power		
1936 (D)	Roosevelt	Roosevelt
1940 (D)	Roosevelt	Roosevelt
1944 (D)	Roosevelt	Roosevelt
1948 (D)	Truman	Truman
1952 (D)	Truman	Stevenson
1956 (R)	Eisenhower	Eisenhower
1960 (R)	Nixon	Nixon
1964 (D)	Johnson	Johnson
1968 (D)	Johnson	Humphrey
1972 (R)	Nixon	Nixon
1976 (R)	Ford	Ford
1980 (D)	Carter	Carter
1984 (R)	Reagan	Reagan
Party out of power		
1936 (R)	Landon	Landon
1940 (R)	?	Willkie
1944 (R)	Dewey	Dewey
1948 (R)	Dewey-Taft	Dewey
1952 (R)	Eisenhower-Taft	Eisenhower
1956 (D)	Stevenson	Stevenson
1960 (D)	Kennedy	Kennedy
1964 (R)	?	Goldwater
1968 (R)	Nixon	Nixon
1972 (D)	Muskie	McGovern
1976 (D)	Kennedy-Humphrey	Carter
1980 (R)	Ford	Reagan
1984 (D)	Mondale	Mondale

SOURCE: Donald R. Matthews, "Presidential Nominations: Process and Outcome," in *Choosing the President,* ed. James David Barber (Englewood Cliffs, N.J.: Prentice-Hall, 1974), 54 (as updated).

NOTE: D = Democrat; R = Republican.

occurred on the first ballot, without significant opposition. In 1964, in the judgment of most party professionals, Barry Goldwater's nomination was assured by his victory over Nelson Rockefeller in the California primary. The great bulk of the Goldwater delegates had been captured earlier in state conventions. The Democratic experience is about the same. Lyndon Johnson's nomination in 1964 was a foregone conclusion, following the custom (at that time) that incumbent presidents were entitled to another term if they chose to run. In 1968, with the forces opposed to the Johnson administration in disarray following the assassination of Robert F. Kennedy, there was scarcely any doubt but that Vice President Hubert Humphrey would become the party standardbearer. In 1972 George McGovern arrived at the Democratic convention with over twice as many delegate votes as any other candidate, and his nomination on the first ballot, though it could not have been predicted a few months earlier, was anything but a surprise at the convention. In 1976 Jimmy Carter came to the Democratic convention in Madison Square Garden with the nomination locked up. Some months earlier, that feat could not have been predicted either. First-ballot nominations occurred at both conventions in 1980 and 1984.

The stark fact is that in only a few conventions in the last three decades has there been substantial doubt about the ultimate winner: both conventions in 1952 (Dwight D. Eisenhower versus Robert A. Taft in the Republican convention and a wide-open contest in the Democratic convention), the Democratic convention in 1960 (John F. Kennedy, who won the presidential primaries, versus the field), and the 1976 Republican convention (Gerald R. Ford versus Ronald Reagan). It is unusual for a front-runner—the candidate holding the most delegate votes prior to the convention—to lose out at the convention. Often the front-runner is nominated on the first ballot.

The final major item of convention business is the selection of the party's vice-presidential nominee. Here the task of the party is to come up with the right political formula—the candidate who can add the most to the ticket and detract the least. The presidential nominee most often makes the choice, following rounds of consultation with various party and candidate organization leaders.[39] Although a great deal of suspense is usually created over the vice-presidential nomination, convention ratification comes easily once the presidential nominee has decided and cleared the selection with key leaders. Unless the presidential nominee is inclined to take a major risk to serve the interest of his own faction or ideology (as Barry Goldwater did in choosing Republican national chairman William E. Miller in 1964), he selects a candidate who can help to balance the ticket and unify the party.[40] Jimmy Carter's choice of Sen. Walter F. Mondale in 1976 fits neatly into this category, as does Ronald Reagan's choice of George Bush in 1980. Walter Mondale's selection of Geraldine Ferraro in 1984 broke with major party tradition in more ways than one: Representative Ferraro was the first woman to be nominated for the vice presidency, the first Italian-American to be nominated for national office, and the first nominee to be "anointed" prior to the opening of the convention. The presidential nominee ordinarily has a great deal of leeway in choosing a running mate, although the need to reward or placate a particular party element can drastically reduce the list of possible candidates.

A National Primary? Regional Primaries?

Dissatisfaction with the current system has led some politicians and analysts to prefer a single, one-day national primary. Under a typical proposal, to win the nomination a candidate would be required to obtain a majority of the popular vote cast in his party primary; if no candidate received a majority, a runoff election would be held between the top two finishers. A separate vote would be held for vice-presidential candidates. The national convention would be retained for writing the platform and fashioning party rules.

Another plan calls for regional primaries—all those states holding primaries within a region would be required to hold them on the same day.[41] A total of perhaps five regional primaries would be conducted, one each month from March through July in the presidential year, their order to be determined by lot. The national convention would continue, at least formally, to select the presidential candidate. When the primaries failed to produce a clear-cut winner, the actual choice would be made by the convention.

Still another proposal would require all states using primaries to choose one of four dates (in March, April, May, or June) on which to hold them—thus bringing a measure of order to the system and diminishing the significance of a single state's early primary. Left to the decision of each state, a caucus-convention system could be used in place of a primary. The national convention would continue in its present form.

The adoption of a national primary law would represent the sharpest departure from the current system. It would favor well-known, well-financed candidates and would hurt outsiders—those lesser-known candidates who gain visibility and momentum through a win or an impressive showing in an early primary or caucus state. Inevitably, a national primary would have a destructive impact on the political parties, eliminating them from any role in the selection of presidential candidates. Austin Ranney writes:

> [The] clear gainers in influence from the dismantling of the party organizations would be the national news media—the national television and radio networks, the major newspapers, and the wire serv-

ices. . . . [Their] interpretations of the state primaries and caucuses, especially the early ones, already have a powerful influence on who wins or who loses. . . . In a national primary . . . the only preelection facts relevant to who was winning would be public opinion polls and estimates of the sizes of crowds at candidate meetings. The former are scientifically more respectable than the latter, but neither constitutes hard data in the sense that election returns do. And hard data of that sort would be available only after national primary day. Thus, a one-day national direct primary would give the news media even more power than they now have to influence the outcomes of contests for nominations by shaping most people's perceptions of how these contests were proceeding.[42]

Political Campaigns

Political campaigns are difficult to describe for one very good reason: they come in an extraordinary variety of shapes and sizes. Whether there is such a thing as a typical campaign is open to serious doubt. Campaigns will differ depending upon the office sought (whether executive, legislative, or judicial), the level of government (national, state, or local), the legal and political environments (partisan or nonpartisan election, competitive or noncompetitive constituency), and the initial advantages or disadvantages of the candidates (incumbent or nonincumbent, well known or little known), among other things.

The standards by which to measure and evaluate the effectiveness of campaigns are not easy to discover because of the vast number of variables that intrude both on campaign decisions and on voter choice. Does the party that wins an election owe its victory to a superior campaign or would it have won in any case? Data needed to answer the question are elusive. What is evident is that strategies that are appropriate to one campaign may be less appropriate or even inappropriate to another. Tactics that work at one time or in one place may not work under other circumstances. Organizational arrangements that satisfy one party may not satisfy the other. Campaigns are loaded with imponderables. Neither the party organizations nor the candidates have any control over numerous factors in a campaign. Moreover, there is no way for parties and candidates to develop an immunity against campaign mistakes. Even so, in most cases it is not immediately clear when a miscalculation has been made, how serious it may have been, or how best to restore the damage.

Despite the variability and uncertainty that characterize political campaigns, a few general requirements are imposed on all candidates and parties. The candidate making a serious bid for votes must acquire certain resources and meet certain problems. Whatever his perspective of the campaign, the candidate will have to deal with matters of organization, strategy, and finances.

Campaign Organization

Very likely the single most important fact to know about campaign organization is that the regular party organizations are ill equipped to organize and conduct campaigns by themselves. Of necessity, they look to outsiders for assistance in all kinds of party work and for the development and staffing of auxiliary campaign organizations. A multiplicity of organizational units is created in every major election for the promotion of particular candidacies. Some businessmen will organize to support the Republican nominee and other businessmen will organize to support the Democratic candidate. And the same will be true for educators, lawyers, physicians, advertising executives, and even independents, to mention but a few. At times these groups work in impressive harmony with the regular party organizations (perhaps to the point of being wholly dominated by them), and at other times they function as virtually independent units, seemingly oblivious to the requirements for communication or for coordination of their activities with those of other party or auxiliary units.

The regular party organizations share control of campaigns not only with citizen groups but also with political action committees that operate under the sponsorship of interest groups. Among the best known are the AFL-CIO Committee on Political Education (COPE), the American Medical Association Political Action Committee, and the National Committee for an Effective Congress. Like other campaign groups, these committees raise campaign funds, endorse candidates, and otherwise support those candidates in sympathy with their positions and programs.

At the top of the heterogeneous cluster of party and auxiliary campaign committees are the campaign organizations created by the individual candidates. Virtually all candidates for important, competitive offices feel they must develop personal campaign organizations to counsel them on strategy and issues, to assist with travel arrangements and speeches, to raise money, to defend their interests in party circles, and to try to coordinate their activities with those of other candidates and campaign units. The size of a candidate's personal organization is likely to vary according to the significance of the office and the competitiveness of the constituency. The member from a safe district, for example, habituated to easy elections, has less need of an elaborate campaign organization than a candidate from a closely competitive district. Some congressional districts are so safe (at least for the candidate, if not the party) that were it not for having to attend certain district party and civic rites, the incumbent could easily skip campaigning and remain in Washington.

In some campaigns the regular party organization is reduced to being just another spectator. It is not unusual for candidates to employ professional management firms to direct their campaigns instead of relying on the party organizations.[43] All facets of American politics today come under the influence of public relations specialists and advertising firms. Possessing resources that the party organizations cannot match, they raise funds, recruit campaign workers, develop issues, gain endorsements, write speeches, arrange campaign schedules, direct the candidate's television appearances, and prepare campaign literature, films, and advertising. Indeed, they sometimes create the overall campaign strategy and dominate day-to-day decision making. Their principal task is to build images of candidates by controlling the way they appear to the general public. A campaign adviser to Richard Nixon's 1968 presidential election campaign made the point in this observation:

> [Nixon] has to come across as a person larger than life, the stuff of legend. People are stirred by legend, including the living legend, not by the man himself. It's the aura that surrounds the charismatic figure more than it is the figure itself that draws the followers. Our task is to build that aura. . . .[44]

Campaign Strategy

The paramount goal of all major party campaigns is to form a coalition of sufficient size to bring victory to the candidate or party. Ordinarily, the early days of the campaign are devoted to the development and testing of a broad campaign strategy designed to produce a winning coalition. In the most general sense, strategy should be seen as "an overall plan for acquiring and using the resources needed for a campaign." [45] In developing a broad strategy, candidates, their advisers, and party leaders must take into consideration a number of factors. These include (1) the principal themes to be developed during the campaign; (2) the issues to be emphasized and exploited; (3) the candidate's personal qualities to be emphasized; (4) the specific groups and geographical areas to which appeals will be directed; (5) the acquisition of financial support and endorsements; (6) the timing of campaign activities; (7) the relationship of the candidate to the party organization and to factions within it; and (8) the uses to be made of the communications media, particularly television.

To the casual observer, there appear to be no limits to the number of major and minor strategies open to a resourceful candidate. However, important constraints serve to shape and define the candidate's options. For example, campaign strategy will be affected by the political, social, and economic environments that are present. Among the factors that intrude on campaign strategy are the competitiveness of the district, the nature of the electorate, the quality and representativeness of the party ticket, the unity of the party, the presence of an incumbent, the election timetable (for example, presidential or off-year election), and the predispositions and commitments of political interest groups. Although difficult to weigh its significance, the temper of the times will also affect the candidate's overall plan of action. "In eras of general complacency and economic well-being," V. O. Key has written, "assaults against the interests and crusades against abuses by the privileged classes seem to pay small dividends. Periods of hardship and unrest move campaigners to contrive strategies to exploit the anxieties of people—or to insulate themselves from public wrath." [46] Whatever the impact of these constraints on campaign strategy, most of them are beyond the control of the candidate; they are, purely and simply, conditions to which the candidate must adjust and adapt. The overall strategy that the candidate fashions or selects must be consonant with the givens of the campaign environment.

Opportunities and constraints vary from campaign to campaign and from candidate to candidate. Although this results in great diversity, it is nevertheless possible to depict the three overarching strategies that serious candidates usually follow. The most important is for the candidate to get his *supporters out to vote.* A great many elections are won or lost depending on the turnout of the party faithful. Minority party candidates probably would win most elections if they could increase the rate of turnout of their own supporters (assuming turnout for the major party candidates remained the same). The second general strategy is to *activate latent support.* Successful campaigns often turn on the ability of the candidate to activate potential voters among the groups that ordinarily support his party. For the Democratic candidate, this means that special effort must be directed to involving such segments of the population as Catholics, Jews, blacks, blue-collar workers, union members, and urban residents; for the Republican candidate, this rule prescribes a similar effort to activate Protestants, whites, suburban and rural residents, and professional, business, and managerial elements. The third general strategy is to *change the opposition.*[47] In recent years this strategy has been spectacularly successful. A large number of Democrats, for example, voted for Dwight D. Eisenhower in the elections of 1952 and 1956, and a large number of Republicans bolted their party to vote for Lyndon B. Johnson in 1964. Similarly, in 1972 Democrats in great numbers abandoned their party's candidate, George McGovern, to vote for Richard Nixon (though it is probable that they were not so much attracted to Nixon as repelled by McGovern). In 1980 about one-fourth of all Democrats voted for Ronald Reagan and in 1984, about one-fifth. These switchers played a crucial role in both Republican victories.

Myths and facts are mixed in about equal proportion in the lore of campaign strategy. Strategies are not easily devised, sorted out, or tested. Indeed, it is scarcely ever apparent in advance which strategies are likely to be most productive and which least productive or even counterproductive. However disciplined and well managed campaigns may appear to those who stand on the outskirts, they rarely are in reality. As Stimson Bullitt has observed:

> A politician, unlike a general or an athlete, never can be invincible, except within a constituency which constitutes a sinecure. Furthermore, a candidate cannot even be sure that his campaigning will change the election result. . . . [A] politician must act on his hypotheses, which are tested only by looking backward on his acts. A candidate cannot even experiment. Because no one knows what works in a campaign, money is spent beyond the point of diminishing returns. To meet similar efforts of the opposition all advertising and propaganda devices are used—billboards, radio, TV, sound trucks, newspaper ads, letter writing or telephone committee programs, handbills, bus cards. No one dares to omit any approach. Every cartridge must be fired because among the multitude of blanks one may be a bullet. . . .
>
> A common mistake of post-mortems is to assert that a certain event or a stand or mannerism of a candidate caused him to win or lose. Often no one knows whether the election result was because of this factor or despite it. Spectacular events, whether a dramatic proposal, an attack, or something in the news outside the campaign, are like a revolving door. They win some votes and lose others. . . .[48]

The evidence of many studies suggests that campaign decisions are about as likely to be shaped by chance and by the ability of the candidate to seize on events as they are by the careful formulation of a broad and

The Democratic Party's Dilemma

The Democratic party is the nation's majority party. It maintains a continuing advantage in voters' party identification and regularly controls Congress, a majority of state legislatures and governorships, and virtually all major cities. Presidential elections are another matter. The party's ability to win this office is often frustrated by its failure to hold its own partisans. The record shows that Democratic voters play a decisive role in the election of Republican presidents.

Party identification	Voting behavior							
	1968		1972		1980		1984	
	D	R	D	R	D	R	D	R
Democrat	74%	12%	67%	33%	69%	26%	79%	21%
Republican	9	86	5	95	8	86	4	96
	Nixon wins, 43.4% to 43.0%, over Humphrey		Nixon wins, 62% to 38%, over McGovern		Reagan wins, 51% to 41%, over Carter		Reagan wins, 59% to 41%, over Mondale	

SOURCE: Developed from data in *Gallup Report*, November 1984, 8-9.

NOTE: D = Democrat; R = Republican. In 1968 George C. Wallace received 14% of the vote of Democratic identifiers and 5% of the vote of Republican identifiers. In 1980 John B. Anderson received 4% of the vote of Democratic identifiers and 5% of the vote of Republican identifiers. Even when Jimmy Carter won in 1976, 18% of all Democratic identifiers voted for the Republican nominee, Gerald R. Ford.

coherent plan of attack. Consider the decision of John F. Kennedy in the 1960 presidential campaign to telephone Coretta Scott King to express his concern over the welfare of her husband, the Rev. Dr. Martin Luther King, Jr., who had been jailed in Atlanta following a sit-in in a department store. There is no evidence that Kennedy's decision—perhaps as critical as any of the campaign—was based on a comprehensive assessment of alternatives or possible consequences. Instead, according to Theodore H. White, the decision came about in this way:

> The crisis was instantly recognized by all concerned with the Kennedy campaign. . . . [The] suggestion for meeting it [was made by] Harris Wofford. Wofford's idea was as simple as it was human—that the

candidate telephone directly to Mrs. King in Georgia to express his concern. Desperately Wofford tried to reach his own chief, Sargent Shriver, head of the Civil Rights Section of the Kennedy campaign, so that Shriver might break through to the candidate barnstorming somewhere in the Middle West. Early [the next] morning, Wofford was able to locate Shriver . . . and Shriver enthusiastically agreed. Moving fast, Shriver reached the candidate [as he] was preparing to leave for a day of barnstorming in Michigan. The candidate's reaction to Wofford's suggestion of participation was impulsive, direct, and immediate. From his room at the Inn, without consulting anyone, he placed a long-distance telephone call to Mrs. Martin Luther King, assured her of his interest and concern in her suffering and, if necessary, his intervention. . . . The entire episode received only casual notice from the generality of American citizens in the heat of the last three weeks of the Presidential campaign. But in the Negro community the Kennedy intervention rang like a carillon.[49]

The development of critical issues is not invariably of great importance in designing campaign strategy. Although some voters are highly sensitive to the specific issues generated in a campaign, many others are preoccupied with the candidate's image, personality, and style. Candidates often are judged less by what they say than by how they say it, less by their achievements than by their personality. Voters' perceptions of a candidate's character are highly important—perhaps especially in presidential contests. Scandals in government, such as the Watergate affair, typically have a major impact on the strategies of subsequent campaigns, serving to heighten the significance of the candidate's alleged personal virtues—especially those of honesty and sincerity—and to diminish the significance of issues. "I don't think issues mean a great deal about whether you win or lose," observed a newly elected senator. "I think issues give you a chance to [demonstrate] your intellectual capacity. Issues are a vehicle by which voters determine your honesty and candor. I don't think a right or wrong answer on an issue makes up anyone's mind but the ideologues. . . ."[50]

Yet, in some elections, issues lie at the center of campaign manipulations. And vogue appears in issues as in other things. The passage of Proposition 13 (a California referendum that reduced property taxes) had a dramatic impact on campaigns in 1978 as candidates at all levels sought to outstrip one another in their opposition to taxes, higher spending, and big government. Politicians know a good issue when they see it. Attacks against Washington, such as those made by Jimmy Carter two years earlier, found their way into congressional campaigns throughout the country.

Increasingly, gimmickry is a key element in creative campaign strategy. Statewide walking tours have become commonplace since Lawton Chiles of Florida used this technique to win a seat in the Senate in 1970. Lately candidates have engaged in different forms of blue-collar work, dutifully filmed by the media for news stories and by the candidate's public relations team for television advertising. A relatively unknown state senator who won the Democratic nomination for governor in Florida in 1978 (and later the election) worked at one hundred different jobs in a period of more than a year prior to the primary. His laboring experiences included work as a shrimp fisherman, a citrus fruit picket, a stable boy, a bellboy, a Tallahassee policeman, an airline attendant, and an orderly in a nursing home. Not surprisingly, wealthy candidates seem to find blue-collar work stunts an attractive campaign technique, undoubtedly because it permits them to develop their image as an "average, hard-working citizen."[51] Stunts are a matter of image making. However ingenious and beguiling, they beg the question: can a public officeholder understand the problems of the shrimp industry without having labored as a shrimp fisherman, or the problems of nursing homes without the learning that comes from dumping bedpans? The answer is yes.

Campaign Money

Of all the requirements for successful campaigns, none may be more important than a strong infusion of money. Campaign costs have risen steadily over the years. In 1952 expenditures for the nomination and election of public officials at all levels of government came to about $140 million. By 1968 this figure had climbed to $300 million. Candidates and parties spent approximately $425 million in 1972, $540 million in 1976, $1.2 billion in 1980, and $1.8 billion in 1984.[52]

Most of the cost of American elections is borne by private individuals and groups. In presidential elections, however, public financing is available. Under amendments adopted to the Federal Election Campaign Act in 1974, candidates for the presidential nomination can qualify for matching public funds. Once the nominations have been settled, the candidates can elect to receive full federal funding in the general election campaign. Even so, private money dominates the financing of political campaigns at all levels of government.

The spiraling costs of running for office result from a number of factors. The steady increase in the general price level is one reason: inflation affects campaign costs as well as everything else. Additional

The Public's Role in Financing Political Campaigns

During the past year did you give any money to an individual candidate, a political party organization, people supporting a ballot proposition, or to a particular issue or interest group?

Yes	12.5%
No	87.5

Did you give any money to a political party organization during the election year?

Yes	4.4%
No	95.6

Did you give any money to an individual candidate running for public office?

Yes	3.9%
No	96.1

Did you use the one-dollar checkoff option on your federal income tax return to make a political contribution?

Yes	31.2%
No	63.0
Don't know	5.8

SOURCE: These questions are drawn from the 1984 presidential election survey, National Election Study, Center for Political Studies, University of Michigan.

costs stem from the utilization of new techniques in campaigning (particularly television and computerized mailings), the growth in population, and the enlargement of the electorate. The substitution of presidential primaries for caucus-convention systems appears to have increased campaign expenditures. Considerable sums are spent by candidates in hiring political consultants to direct their campaigns. Finally, the availability of private money in large quantities, particularly from the political action committees of interest groups,[53] encourages candidates to add to their campaign treasuries. Many congressional incumbents believe, for example, that the best way to discourage challengers is to amass a large campaign fund well in advance of the next election. Thus it is common for members of Congress to solicit and accept PAC funds even when they have no serious electoral opposition. Some members use surplus funds to make contributions to the campaigns of colleagues.

Because of the restrictions placed on contributions to presidential campaigns, perhaps the best way to begin the analysis of money in national political campaigns is to examine the sources from which congressional candidates secure funds. Several features of the money hustle of the 1984 election (covering the two-year election cycle and including primary, runoff, and general elections) stand out (see Table 3-3). First, the contributions of individuals represent the major source of campaign money for congressional candidates. And because FECA limits individual contributions to $1,000 per election, these gifts arrive in relatively small sums. In 1984 private contributions made up nearly 50 percent of the funds raised by House candidates and more than 60 percent of the funds raised by Senate candidates (for Senate incumbents, 65 percent). Second, PACs are also a key source of congressional campaign funds. Indeed, they have become critical in the campaigns of House incumbents, making up 42 percent of their total receipts in 1984. Although not as dependent on interest groups, Senate incumbents nevertheless raised 23 percent of their funds from PACs. Third, congressional campaign fund raising is an incumbent-dominated system. Challengers do not fare nearly as well in the PAC sweepstakes (see Table 3-3). Seventy-three percent of all PAC funds in 1984 were given to incumbents, 16 percent to challengers, and 11 percent to candidates for open seats. The average House incumbent received $142,000 from PACs, while challengers averaged only $31,000.[54] Thirty-seven House incumbents each accepted more than $250,000 from PACs; one member reported receiving $662,861 and another $419,438. Among senators, Phil Gramm (R-Texas) easily led the way with PAC gifts exceeding $1.3 million; twenty-eight Senate candidates each accepted more than half a million dollars from political action committees.[55]

The rate of growth of PAC contributions has been tremendous (see Table 3-4). PACs contributed three times as much money to House and Senate candidates in 1984 as in 1978. The numbers themselves are instructive: a total of $34.1 million was contributed in the 1978 election cycle and $104.9 million in the 1984 election cycle.

Political action committees target their contributions carefully, taking into consideration incumbency, party, and legislative position. In 1984 labor PACs contributed $23.9 million to congressional candidates, with 95 percent given to Democrats. Corporate PACs gave $34.6 million to congressional candidates, of which 62 percent went to Republicans.[56]

TABLE 3-3   The Sources of Funding for 1984 Congressional Candidates

	Individual contributions	PAC contributions	Party contributions	Party expenditures	Candidate contributions	Candidate loans	Other receipts
House							
Incumbents	46%	42%	1%	2%	0%	1%	7%
Challengers	46	21	5	9	1	13	4
Candidates for open seats	46	26	3	7	1	14	4
Senate							
Incumbents	65	23	1	5	0	1	6
Challengers	64	16	1	11	0	3	4
Candidates for open seats	48	9	0	8	4	28	3

SOURCE: *Federal Election Commission Record* (Washington, D.C.: Federal Election Commission, July 1985), 9.

NOTE: PAC = political action committee. This analysis includes primary, runoff, and general election funds of all candidates running in the November 1984 general election. A PAC is a political committee that is neither a candidate committee nor a party committee. Party expenditures are limited expenditures made by party committees on behalf of federal candidates in the general election. Other receipts include loans, rebates, refunds, contributions from unregistered entities and other campaign committees, interest, and dividends.

Committee chairmen and party leaders are major beneficiaries of interest group largesse. Committee membership is also taken into consideration. Members of the tax and commerce committees, for example, invariably receive more PAC money than members of the judiciary or foreign policy committees. The pattern of contributions is illustrated by these observations:

The main goal is to support our friends who have been with us most of the time. (An official of the UAW)

The prevailing attitude is that PAC money should be used to facilitate access to incumbents. (The director of governmental and political participation for the Chamber of Commerce of the United States)

We're inclined to support incumbents because we tend to go with those who support our industry. We are not out looking to find challengers. Our aim is not to change the tone of Congress. (A spokesperson for the Lockheed Good Government Program)

We're looking especially for members who serve on key committees, and people who help us on the floor. (A spokesperson for the Automobile and Truck Dealers Election Action Committee)[57]

TABLE 3-4   The Contributions of Political Action Committees (PACs) to
Congressional Campaigns, 1978-1984

	1978	1980	1982	1984
Total PAC contributions	$34.1	$55.2	$83.6	$104.9
House campaigns	24.4	37.9	61.1	75.6
Senate campaigns	9.7	17.3	22.5	29.3
PAC percentage of all funds raised by:				
House candidates	21%	26%	29%	34%
Senate candidates	11	16.5	16	17

SOURCE: Data from press release, Federal Election Commission, May 16, 1985.

NOTE: Dollar figures are in millions.

Political action committees are many-sided. Parties as well as candidates now depend on them. In 1984 the two major parties collected assorted PAC gifts totaling $10.4 million, up from $6 million in 1982.[58] Putting those numbers in perspective, for every one dollar that PACs gave to the party organizations they gave ten dollars to candidate organizations.

In addition to making direct contributions to candidates, PACs are permitted to make *independent* expenditures, spending for or against candidates. No limits are placed on the amounts they may spend, but they are prohibited from consulting candidates concerning these expenditures. In 1984 independent PAC expenditures totaled $22.2 million, most of which was spent on the presidential race. The biggest PACs now hire media consultants and polling experts to make their independent aid as effective as possible. In 1986 the American Medical Association (AMA) budgeted $300,000 to support the opponent of Rep. Andrew Jacobs, Jr., (D-Ind.) who had incurred the AMA's wrath for urging House colleagues, in a debate on Medicaid, to "vote for the canes, not for the stethoscopes." [59] Despite AMA opposition, Jacobs was reelected by a comfortable margin. Under the Federal Election Campaign Act, direct PAC contributions to any candidate in any election are limited to $5,000. Independent spending is thus a way of circumventing this restriction.

So popular is the PAC idea that many members of Congress have created their own political action committees to raise and disburse campaign funds. The thrust of some member PACs is simply to help to reelect partisan or ideological allies. But for most member PACs the dominant purpose appears to be self-promotion. The most active congressional PACs are those created by members with aspirations for the presidency, the speakership, and a range of other positions, such as floor leader, whip, or committee chairman. These "leadership PACs" distribute campaign funds to members (and occasionally to challengers) as a way of building good will and creating support. For presidential hopefuls in particular, having one's own PAC is invaluable in meeting the expenses of political travel necessary to capture public attention or to campaign for other congressional candidates. Probably the best known member PAC is North Carolina Republican senator Jesse Helms's National Congressional Club. Among the other influential member PACs are Campaign America (Sen. Robert Dole, R-Kan.), Campaign for Prosperity (Rep. Jack F. Kemp, R-N.Y.), Fund for a Democratic Majority (Sen. Edward M. Kennedy, D-Mass.), Majority Congress Committee (Rep. Jim Wright, D-Texas), and America's Leaders Fund (Rep. Dan Rostenkowski, D-Ill.). Of no particular surprise, most of the money contributed to member PACs come from other PACs.[60]

The availability of PAC money makes life easier for incumbents. They and their aides understand the PAC network, know how to curry favor with PACs (or at least how to avoid their enmity), know how to solicit funds from them, and know how to respond to their initiatives. Members are largely comfortable in this world of organization money even though they resent the amount of time required to raise funds and worry over possible obligations to their benefactors. Nonetheless, access to PAC money is not the most important advantage of incumbents. Their main advantage is simply the opportunities and resources that are attached to holding congressional office: the franking privilege, a public record, name recognition, generous travel allowance, opportunities to make news, opportunities to take credit for "pork" brought into the constituency, and, perhaps most important of all, a large staff (many of whom are assigned to the district or state). "The Hill office," writes David Mayhew, "is a vitally important political unit, part campaign management firm and part political machine." [61] The office is a political unit financed by the Treasury, and the contributions to incumbents are substantial. Michael Malbin estimates that House incumbents enjoy perquisites of office, supporting constituent contact, worth at least $1 million over the period of a two-year term ($400,000 for constituent-service staff; $400,000 for district office expenses, travel, phones, computers, and the like; and $250,000 for unsolicited mailings to constituents).[62] Hence the heavy support of political action committees is simply icing on the cake—double-rich.

The third most important source of campaign funds for congressional candidates is the political party. The party's role is limited, however, by the Federal Election Campaign Act, both in terms of how much money it can contribute directly to candidates and how much it can spend on their behalf. In making direct contributions to House candidates, national party committees (national committee and congressional campaign committee) face the same limitation as PACs—each is limited to a contribution of $5,000 per candidate per campaign. Candidates for the Senate can receive up to $17,500 in direct contributions from the national committee and the senatorial campaign committee, combined, in a calendar year. State and local committees can also make limited contributions to congressional campaigns. Much more important are national party expenditures made on behalf of congressional candidates—so-called *coordinated* expenditures. Permitted only in the general election, coordinated expenditures are made by the party committees alone, though they may consult with the candidates' organizations to decide how the money is to be spent. Based on state voting-age populations, the amounts permitted are sizable for Senate campaigns in populous states. In California, for example, each party in 1986 could spend $851,000 on behalf of its senatorial candidate, in New York $581,000, in Texas $504,000, in Pennsylvania $391,000, and in some dozen relatively small states $43,000. For House candidates in 1986, coordinated expenditures were limited to $21,810.[63]

In addition, fortified by a Supreme Court ruling,[64] a state party committee can transfer its spending authority to the national committee, which has the effect of doubling the expenditures the national party can make on behalf of its candidates. These "agency agreements" have been a boon to the spending plans of the Republican party in particular.

Party support for congressional candidates has been growing (see Figure 3-1). In 1984 coordinated expenditures totaled about $20 million for the Republican party and almost $10 million for the Democratic party. These are significant sums, but they do not make the national parties the major source of campaign funds. Gary Jacobson estimates that national party committees can supply perhaps one-fourth of the money necessary for a serious House campaign and, in some states, perhaps up to half of the funds necessary for a full-scale Senate campaign.[65] In their assistance to candidates, parties in fact do not stack up especially well in comparison with PACs. Not counting independent expenditures, PACs contributed more than three and one-half times as much money to House and Senate candidates in 1984 as the two national parties. What is more, if analysis is confined simply to House incumbents, PAC contributions in 1984 were fourteen times as great as party contributions and expenditures (see Table 3-4). National party commit-

FIGURE 3-1   Major Party Support Provided to Congressional Candidates,
1977-1984

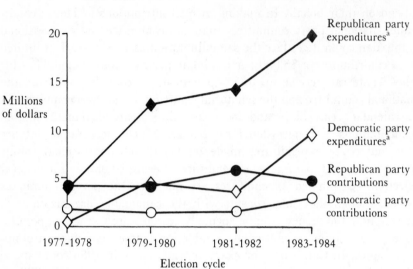

SOURCE: *Federal Election Commission Record* (Washington, D.C.: Federal Election Commission, July 1985), 10.

[a] Party expenditures are limited expenditures made by party committees on behalf of federal candidates in the general election.

tees are a more important source of funds for challengers and for candidates for open seats. If the behavior of officeholders is influenced by campaign money, as Herbert E. Alexander has observed, the parties do not have an unusually strong claim for preference, particularly in view of the contributions to legislators by individuals and political action committees.[66]

Spending campaign money intelligently is problematical at the least. Candidates spend as heavily as they do because neither they nor their advisers know which expenditures are likely to produce the greatest return in votes. Lacking systematic information, they jump at every opportunity to contact and persuade voters—and every opportunity costs money.

Political money is not a subject that lends itself to easy analysis. Tracing exactly how it is raised and how it is spent is far from simple. In a federal and fragmented system campaign money is collected and spent by a multiplicity of competing political actors and institutions. If there is fashion at all, it is helter-skelter. In addition, the effects of money on elections, political behavior, and public policy are not fully understood.

One point about which there is substantial agreement, however, is that campaign spending has grown dramatically in recent years.

Congressional campaigns provide a good example. They are expensive. In 1976 House and Senate candidates collectively spent about $100 million.[67] In 1984 they spent about $374 million, almost four times as much (see Figure 3-2).[68] The consumer price index rose rapidly from 1976 to 1984, but "only" about 80 percent. Inflation thus does not account for the lion's share of the increase.

Spending by winners and losers in 1984 House elections suggests several conclusions (see Table 3-5). First of all, the most expensive races involve incumbents who think or know they are in trouble with the voters. Half-million dollar campaigns are common for apprehensive House incumbents. At the same time, incumbents who expect to win and do win easily spend less than anyone except "hopeless" challengers. But even safe incumbents (some of whom faced no opposition) had average expenditures of $228,000 in 1984. Second, with relatively few exceptions, incumbents outspend their challengers, many of whom are severely underfinanced. For about two-thirds of all House challengers in 1984, the average campaign expenditure was only $71,000. Third, spending in campaigns for open seats (no incumbent) is nearly always high, averaging more than $450,000 for winners in 1984. Fourth, the costs of some House campaigns border on the scandalous. One New York Democrat spent nearly $2 million in 1984, losing to his Republican opponent who spent in excess of $1 million. Twenty-six House candidates spent more than $700,000 on their campaigns. In several Senate races in 1984,

FIGURE 3-2   Total Spending by Congressional Candidates, 1975-1984

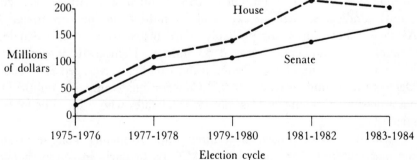

SOURCE: *Federal Election Commission Record* (Washington, D.C.: Federal Election Commission, July 1985), 8.

NOTE: This figure covers all campaign spending (primary, runoff, and general) of major party candidates running in congressional elections.

TABLE 3-5   The Expenditures of Winners and Losers in U.S. House Elections, Shown in Relation to Electoral Margins, 1984

	Winning with 60 percent or more of vote	Winning with 55-59.9 percent of vote	Winning with less than 55 percent of vote
Average expenditures of winning:			
Incumbents	(315) $228,135	(48) $391,986	(31) $500,011
Challengers	(2) 372,369	(2) 527,876	(17) 441,981
Candidates for			
open seats	(7) 401,213	(6) 427,408	(11) 508,907

	Losing with 45 percent or more of vote	Losing with 40-44.9 percent of vote	Losing with less than 40 percent of vote
Average expenditures of losing:			
Incumbents	(15) $425,992	(2) $553,259	—
Challengers	(29) 339,695	(48) 250,776	(187) $ 71,238
Candidates for			
open seats	(9) 381,448	(7) 377,473	(10) 126,280

SOURCE: Data from press release, Federal Election Commission, May 16, 1985.

NOTE: Number of House candidates in each category shown in parentheses.

spending was spectacular. In the most expensive campaign in Senate history, Jesse Helms spent $16.4 million to win reelection, while his opponent, James Hunt, spent $9.4 million. John D. Rockefeller IV (D-W.Va.) captured an open seat with expenditures of $9.4 million. Phil Gramm also spent $9.4 million to win an open seat. Altogether, ten Senate candidates spent in excess of $4 million on their campaigns. Average expenditures are probably more instructive: for the Senate, Republican incumbents averaged $3 million, Democratic incumbents $1.7 million; for the House, Republican incumbents averaged $279,000, Democratic incumbents $275,000.[69] Congressional campaign politics is not a poor man's game, at least not for candidates who want to be taken seriously.

Of all the issues raised concerning campaign finance, none seems to stir more interest than the role of PACs, particularly in congressional campaigns. The national press frequently focuses on their contributions. Common Cause has prepared dozens of studies over the years, and their findings point to the dangers of the PAC movement.[70] Even Congress itself occasionally becomes exercised over the "PAC problem"—the growing reliance of members on interest group money and the suspicion that these gifts undermine the independence of members. Are members' votes influenced by the PAC gifts they receive? It is hard to demonstrate in any overall pattern. On certain narrow economic issues, such as dairy price supports and cargo preference, a relationship between contributions and voting behavior has been found.[71] Nonetheless, influence is hard to establish: Does money follow votes or votes follow money? Not surprisingly, members evaluate PACs in sharply different ways, as the following observations show:

> It is fundamentally corrupting. At best, people say they are sympathetic to the people they are getting money from before they get it; at worst, they are selling votes. But you cannot prove cause and effect. I take the money from labor, and I have to think twice in voting against their interests. I shouldn't have to do that. (Rep. Richard L. Ottinger, D-N.Y.)

> There's a danger that we're putting ourselves on the auction block every election. It's now tough to hear the voices of the citizens in your district. Sometimes the only things you hear are the loud voices in the three-piece suits carrying a PAC check. (Rep. Leon E. Panetta, D-Calif.)

> PAC money is destroying the electoral process. (Sen. Barry Goldwater, R-Ariz.)

> I don't worry about being bought, because I'm not for sale. The truth is I am proud of the PACs and the people who support me. (Sen. Phil Gramm, R-Texas)

> If you're not able to fund your campaign and keep your responsibility to the people who send you here, you don't belong in office. (Rep. John D. Dingell, D-Mich.)

> PACs facilitate the political participation of hundreds of thousands of individuals who might not otherwise become involved in the election of an individual. (Sen. John W. Warner, R-Va.)[72]

Bills to curtail PAC influence in campaigns have been introduced frequently in Congress over the last decade. Currently, the proposal with the best chance of winning acceptance is sponsored by Sen. David L. Boren (D-Okla.). Under the Boren bill, limits would be placed on the total amount of PAC funds that congressional candidates could accept. For House candidates, the limit would be $100,000 for the two-year election cycle (or $125,000 for the member with both a primary and general election challenge), and for Senate candidates, $175,000 to

$750,000, depending on state size. Adoption of this provision, it is argued, would reduce PAC spending by about one-half. Second, the bill would reduce PAC contributions to candidates from $5,000 to $3,000 per election (or from $10,000 to $6,000 for a primary and general election). At the same time, the contribution limit for individuals would be raised from $1,000 to $1,500 per election. Other provisions would tighten the definition of independent spending by PACs and close a loophole in the law that permits PACs to receive individual contributions, bundle them together, and pass them along to candidates in the PAC's name but without falling under the limitations on spending.[73] The Boren measure was adopted by the Senate in 1986 as an amendment to an unrelated bill; it was lost when the bill failed in the closing days of the Ninety-ninth Congress.

The availability of PAC funds represents a major advantage incumbents have over their challengers, and whether members will be willing to give it up remains to be seen. Yet if PAC contributions continue unabated, the intensity of this "special interest" issue will also grow. Merits aside, PAC power is an issue made in heaven for "good government" groups, reformers, certain insiders, and the press. At some point, probably sooner than later, members may find themselves forced to impose restrictions on PAC contributions. If and when that happens, the initial limitations are likely to be modest. For advocates of all kinds, the reasoning goes, something is better than nothing.

The Regulation of Campaign Finance

Public restiveness over the role of money in American politics has long been present. Dissatisfaction focuses around three main complaints. The first is simply that campaign costs have risen to such an extent that candidates with limited resources are seriously disadvantaged in the electoral process. The doubt persists that some talented people never seek public office because they lack financial support or are unwilling to solicit funds from others because of the risk of incurring political indebtedness and of compromising their independence.[74] Moreover, the high cost of elections may mean that the public hears only one side of the campaign, that of the candidate with access to large sums of money.

The second complaint is that the individuals, families, and groups that contribute lavishly to parties and candidates are suspected of buying influence and gaining preferments of some kind in return for the money they channel into campaigns. Whether this is true may not be as important as the fact that the public believes it to be true. In some measure, public suspicion about campaign financing contributes to public suspicion of government.

And finally, as a result of the Watergate exposé, there has been a heightened awareness of the potential for corruption and abuse when huge sums of money are collected and spent for political purposes.

To deal with a variety of maladies associated with the financing of federal political campaigns, Congress passed the Federal Election Campaign Act of 1971. This act, the first serious attempt since 1925 to reform campaign financing, is of unusual importance. Adopted prior to the Watergate incident, the act anticipated public financing of federal election campaigns by providing that taxpayers could earmark one dollar on their personal income tax returns for use in the 1976 presidential election. Of at least equal importance, the act provided for rigorous disclosure requirements concerning campaign contributions, expenditures, and debts. Finally, a provision to stimulate private contributions to political campaigns was placed in the act. Under a tax-incentive system, taxpayers were permitted to deduct small campaign contributions from their tax obligations. In retrospect, the extraordinary dimensions of the 1972 presidential election scandal certainly would not have been uncovered without the disclosure requirements for political contributions and expenditures contained in the law.

Crisis is often a spur to legislative action. Largely in response to Watergate, Congress in 1974 passed comprehensive amendments to the Federal Election Campaign Act. Designed to curtail the influence and abuse of money in campaign politics, these amendments placed tight restrictions on contributions, expenditures, disclosure, and reporting. Most important, the 1974 legislation provided for at least partial public financing of presidential primaries, elections, and nominating conventions. The constitutionality of the provisions relating to the presidential electoral process was promptly tested in the courts. In *Buckley v. Valeo*,[75] decided in 1976, the Supreme Court held that the act's limitations on individual expenditures (either those of the candidate[76] or those of individuals spending independently on behalf of a candidate) were unconstitutional, since they interfered with the right of free speech under the First Amendment. Political money, in a sense, is political speech. The Court upheld the limitations on contributions to campaigns, the disclosure requirements, and the public-funding provisions for presidential primaries and elections. The main features of the nation's campaign finance law are included in Table 3-6.

The leading characteristic of the campaign finance law is its focus on the presidency. No provision is made for the public financing of

TABLE 3-6   Major Provisions for the Regulation of Campaign Financing in
              Federal Elections

I. Contribution Limits

   A. No individual may contribute more than $1,000 to any candidate or
       candidate committee per election. (Primary, runoff, and general elections
       are considered to be separate elections.)

   B. Individual contributions to a national party committee are limited to
       $20,000 per calendar year and to any other political committee to $5,000
       per calendar year. (The total contributions by an individual to all federal
       candidates in one year cannot exceed $25,000.)

   C. A multicandidate committee (one with more than fifty contributors that
       makes contributions to five or more federal candidates) may contribute no
       more than $5,000 to any candidate or candidate committee per election, no
       more than $15,000 to the national committee of a political party, and no
       more than $5,000 to any other political committee per calendar year.

   D. The national committee and the congressional campaign committee may
       each contribute up to $5,000 to each House candidate, per election; the
       national committee together with the senatorial campaign committee may
       contribute up to a combined total of $17,500 to each Senate candidate for
       the entire campaign period (including a primary election).

   E. Political action committees formed by businesses, trade associations, or
       unions are limited to contributions of no more than $5,000 to any
       candidate in any election. No limits apply to their aggregate contributions.

   F. Banks, corporations, and labor unions are prohibited from making con-
       tributions from their treasuries to federal election campaigns. Government
       contractors and foreign nationals are similarly restricted. Contributions
       may not be supplied by one person but made in the name of another
       person. Contributions in cash are limited to $100.

II. Expenditure Limits

   A. Candidates are limited to an expenditure of $10 million each plus COLA
       (cost-of-living adjustment) in all presidential primaries.

   B. Major party presidential candidates may spend no more than $20 million
       plus COLA in the general election (a total of $40.4 million each in 1984).

   C. Presidential and vice-presidential candidates who accept public funding
       may spend no more than $50,000 of personal funds in their campaigns.

   D. Each national party may spend up to two cents per voter on behalf of its
       presidential candidate.

   E. In addition to making contributions to candidates, the national committee,
       together with congressional and senatorial campaign committees, may
       make expenditures on behalf of House and Senate candidates. For each
       House member—in states with more than one district—the sum is
       $10,000 plus COLA. For each Senate candidate the sum is $20,000 plus
       COLA or two cents for each person in the state's voting-age population,
       whichever is greater. (Under the second formula, party committees could

spend $851,000 on behalf of a California Senate candidate in 1986.) State party committees may make expenditures on behalf of House and Senate candidates up to the same limits.

F. As a result of the *Buckley v. Valeo* decision, there are no limits on how much House and Senate candidates may collect and spend in their campaigns (or on how much they may spend of their own or their family's money).

G. Also in the wake of *Buckley v. Valeo,* there are no limits on the amount that individuals and groups may spend on behalf of any presidential or congressional candidate so long as the expenditures are independent—that is, not arranged or controlled by the candidate.

III. Public Financing

A. Major party candidates for the presidency qualify for full funding ($20 million plus COLA) prior to the campaign, the money to be drawn from the federal income-tax dollar checkoff. Candidates may decline to participate in the public funding program and finance their campaigns through private contributions. Candidates who accept public funding may not accept private contributions.

B. Minor party and independent candidates qualify for lesser sums, provided their candidates received at least 5 percent of the vote in the previous presidential election. New parties or parties that received less than 5 percent of the vote four years earlier qualify for public financing after the election, provided they drew 5 percent of the vote.

C. Matching public funds up to $5 million (plus COLA) are available for presidential primary candidates, provided that they first raise $100,000 in private funds ($5,000 in contributions of no more than $250 in each of twenty states). Once that threshold is reached, the candidate receives matching funds up to $250 per contribution. No candidate is eligible for more than 25 percent of the total available funds.

D. Presidential candidates who receive less than 10 percent of the vote in two consecutive presidential primaries become ineligible for additional campaign subsidies.

E. Optional public funding of presidential nominating conventions is available for the major parties, with lesser amounts for minor parties.

IV. Disclosure and Reporting

A. Each federal candidate is required to establish a single, overarching campaign committee to report on all contributions and expenditures on behalf of the candidate.

B. Frequent reports on contributions and expenditures are to be filed with the Federal Election Commission.

V. Enforcement

A. Administration of the law is the responsibility of a six-member, bipartisan Federal Election Commission. The Commission is empowered to make rules and regulations, to receive campaign reports, to render advisory opinions, to conduct audits and investigations, to subpoena witnesses and information, and to seek civil injunctions through court action.

campaigns for Congress. For those who believe that what is good for the goose is good for the gander, the observations of Sen. Edward M. Kennedy (D-Mass.) are especially appropriate:

> Abuses of campaign spending and private campaign financing do not stop at the other end of Pennsylvania Avenue. They dominate congressional elections as well. If the abuses are the same for the presidency and Congress, the reforms should also be the same. If public financing is good enough for presidential elections, it should also be good enough for Senate and House elections.[77]

Attempts since 1974 to extend public financing to congressional elections have been unsuccessful. The chief opponents have been Republicans and southern Democrats, joined by some northern big-city Democrats. In general, Republicans see proposals for public financing of congressional elections as designed to protect incumbents—which translates into the safeguarding of heavy Democratic majorities, especially in the House. Prospects for the Republican party, they may reason, are better under the present system of private financing. In contrast, some Democrats who oppose public financing legislation worry that the public funds made available would heighten competitiveness in their states and districts and thus threaten their reelection. (Doubtlessly some Republicans share their anxieties.) As a Democratic representative from New York observed, "the more of a challenger's bill public financing gets to be, the harder it is to pass it." [78] Consider these aspects of the matter:

First, whatever the motives that underlie members' attitudes toward public financing, it is plain that this issue bears peculiarly on congressional careers. The temptation will be strong for members to evaluate public financing in personal and political terms, favoring or opposing proposed legislation in light of its probable impact on their electoral security and on the welfare of their party. At the same time, the pressure for some form of public financing of congressional campaigns, linked to tighter restrictions on total expenditures, is likely to become more intense given the runaway campaign costs of recent years and the heavy involvement of PACs in political spending.

Second, the absence of a provision for public financing of congressional campaigns represents a triumph for incumbent members of Congress. Past experience has shown that it is scarcely ever easy to defeat a member of Congress,[79] and the new law does nothing to make it easier. Incumbents invariably are much more successful than challengers in securing campaign contributions, particularly from the political action committees of interest groups. In 1984, for example, PACs contributed four and one-half times as much money to congressional incumbents as to their challengers.

Third, the law places third or minor parties, especially those newly created, at a disadvantage. Minor parties can qualify for some public funding only if their candidates received 5 percent of the vote in the previous presidential election. New parties or parties that failed to receive at least 5 percent of the vote in the previous election cannot qualify for public funds until after the election has been held and then only if they reach the 5 percent threshold. On the other hand, a third party that qualifies for funding in one election will automatically qualify for funding in the next, contributing perhaps to the institutionalization of a multiple party or, more accurately, to a multiple candidate system of presidential elections—an anomaly worth pondering by those concerned about the fragmentation of American politics.

Although it is altogether unlikely that Congress has written its last word on campaign finance, it is useful to take stock of what has happened since the adoption of the Federal Election Campaign Act and its subsequent amendments. A decade and a half of experience with campaign finance legislation provides support for a number of observations concerning its impact on citizens, parties, candidates, and the political system:[80]

1. *The campaign finance law and its amendments have encouraged citizen contributions to the parties and candidates.* Until recently, only about 10 percent of the electorate had contributed money to political parties or individual candidates in election campaigns. As a result of the adoption of income tax checkoff provisions at the federal and state levels, financial participation has increased significantly. Nearly one-third of the electorate now takes advantage of the checkoff option available to them. This type of contribution is a relatively low-cost activity, since it does not increase the individual's tax liability; its cumulative impact is nevertheless enormous in financing presidential preconvention and general election campaigns. Altogether, about $115 million in federal funds were distributed to presidential candidates in these election phases in 1984. Direct contributions by citizens are also made. In 1982 7 percent of the electorate made contributions to various candidate organizations, 9 percent contributed to political action committees, and 4 percent contributed to political parties—about the same pattern as in 1980. In 1984 4 percent of the electorate contributed to candidate organizations and 4 percent to political parties (with no data available on contributions to PACs). Overall, in these three recent campaigns, contributors were more likely to make gifts to a PAC or to a candidate organization than to a

party. Political parties face more competitors than in the past, and they no longer are able to dominate the organization and funding of campaigns.[81]

2. *The campaign finance law has aided the parties in some respects and weakened them in others.* Among the provisions of the Federal Election Campaign Act that benefit the parties are these: (a) individual contributors can give more money to the parties ($20,000) than they can to candidates ($1,000); (b) each national party can spend money on behalf of its presidential and congressional candidates (coordinated expenditures); (c) both national and state party committees can make direct contributions to House and Senate candidates; (d) public funds are available to defray the costs of presidential nominating conventions; (e) under a 1979 amendment, state and local parties can spend unlimited sums on campaign materials, voter registration, and get-out-the-vote drives in presidential elections—so-called "party-building activities."

Other features of the law, however, do not serve the party interest. The parties' impact on presidential elections has been diminished. The public funds made available in the nominating and election phases go directly to the candidates instead of to the parties; each major party candidate received $40.4 million in 1984. In this major feature, the law is plainly candidate-centered. Moreover, the parties are limited in the amounts they can contribute to their candidates and in the amounts they can spend on behalf of them. Many observers believe that the limits are too stringent, and some believe they should be abolished altogether. PACs and individuals can spend unlimited amounts on federal campaigns (opposing as well as supporting candidates) as long as these expenditures are made independently—that is, made without consulting the candidate or the candidate's organization. And, as noted, direct contributions by PACs to candidates for Congress have increased substantially in recent years. On the whole, the campaign finance law has increased the influence of nonparty groups in American politics. No one apparently planned for that to happen.

3. *Spending in congressional and senatorial primaries and elections has increased dramatically.* The 1976 ruling of the Supreme Court in *Buckley v. Valeo* that restrictions on the personal and total expenditures of candidates for Congress were unconstitutional led to an explosion of spending. Winning candidates for the Senate in 1976 spent a total of $20.1 million; in 1984 they spent $97.5 million, almost five times as much. Winning candidates for the House in 1976 spent a total of $38 million; in 1984 they spent $126.5 million, nearly three and one-half times as much. In 1984 thirty-seven Senate candidates spent more than

$1 million on their campaigns. Four House candidates spent more than $1 million and forty-one spent more than $600,000.[82] And as a result of the *Buckley* decision, it is not unusual today for a candidate to spend half a million dollars or more of personal funds in a campaign. A few spend much more than that. The sky is the limit. Whatever can be raised can be spent. The overall spending record belongs to North Carolina, where the two Senate candidates in 1984 spent in excess of $25 million. The most expensive campaign in 1986 took place in California, where the two Senate candidates spent about $18 million.

4. *Interest group involvement in campaign funding is greater than in the past.* The impact of interest groups is especially pronounced at the congressional level. In 1974 political action committees made campaign contributions of about $12.5 million to congressional candidates. In 1984 their contributions totaled $104.9 million—an increase of more than 700 percent in a decade. Currently there are about four thousand political action committees, about seven times as many as in 1974.

5. *Although the Federal Election Campaign Act places certain restrictions on the parties in raising and spending funds, their role in campaigns is nevertheless growing—dramatically in the case of the Republican party.* According to Federal Election Commission studies, Republican party committees at national, state, and local levels raised about $300 million in 1984, while corresponding Democratic committees raised $96.7 million. Six years earlier, for the 1977-1978 election cycle, Republican committees had raised $84.5 million and Democratic committees $26.4 million. In 1984, for every one dollar raised and spent by the Democratic party, the Republican party raised and spent three dollars.[83] The amount of money now spent by the parties on behalf of congressional candidates and through "agency agreements" is impressive—particularly on the Republican side.

6. *The direct influence of fat cats (wealthy contributors) on electoral politics has declined, at least at the national level.* The contributions of an individual to federal candidates are limited to $1,000 for each election and to a total of $25,000 in a calendar year. This, however, is not a stringent limitation. Wealthy individuals, like PACs, can spend an unlimited amount of money to help elect a candidate if the money is spent independently. In 1984 $15.8 million was spent independently in support of the Reagan campaign, while $803,000 was spent on behalf of Mondale.[84] Independent funds are also used in campaigns to defeat candidates, but not on such a large scale. In addition, wealthy candidates can give $5,000 to state parties (all fifty if they like), knowing that this money will help the overall ticket. Thus it is a myth that private money

is excluded from the presidential campaign and that strict limitations govern contributions to federal campaigns. Only direct contributions to federal candidates are effectively limited.

7. *The importance of raising large amounts of money in small sums has become apparent to all candidates, and particularly to those seeking the presidential nomination.* As provided by the Federal Election Campaign Act, matching federal funds become available for presidential primary and caucus candidates who first raise $100,000 in small sums— obtaining $5,000 in contributions of $250 or less in each of twenty states. Once a candidate has reached the $100,000 threshold, the government matches the first $250 of any gift. In the preconvention campaign of 1984, eleven candidates (ten Democrats and one Republican) raised about $105 million, with 60 percent of it received from individuals and most of the remainder from federal matching funds.[85] One result of the new emphasis on small gifts is that firms that engage in direct mail solicitations, working with computerized mailing lists, have assumed even greater importance in the fund-raising efforts of candidates. In fund raising, as in certain other respects, the party organizations now face major competition from other quarters.

8. *Opportunities for persons to engage in corrupt practices in the use of money in federal elections have been constricted.* The risks of detection are greater as a result of timely and comprehensive disclosure provisions, requirements for centralized accounting of contributions and expenditures, curbs on cash contributions, and the existence of a full-time agency, the Federal Election Commission, to administer the law and to investigate alleged infractions of it. Every major presidential candidate organization has numerous accountants and lawyers to analyze and monitor the candidate's financial activities. Bookkeeping has thus become a major feature and expense of campaigns for federal office, congressional as well as presidential.

9. *While paying lip service to the finance law, both parties have nevertheless searched imaginatively for ways around its restrictions—and clearly they have been successful.* As noted earlier, the finance law limits the amount of money that national party committees can give directly to candidates and the amount that party committees can spend on behalf of candidates—coordinated expenditures. Actually, these restrictions are not taken seriously. Under regulations of the Federal Election Commission, a party is permitted to collect checks from donors that are earmarked for specific candidates, bundle them together, and pass them on to designated candidates. These sums do not count against FECA party limits. Awash in funds and adept at "bundling," the National Republi-

can Senatorial Committee funneled more than $6 million into Senate campaigns in 1986, greatly exceeding the amounts permitted in direct contributions and coordinated expenditures.[86] And bundling is only part of the problem. Other controversies have arisen concerning party solicitation of contributions from corporations to pay for a national television address by the president on the eve of the election, the apparent use of "soft money" (limited to party-building activities such as paying for campaign headquarters or get-out-the-vote drives) for the promotion of candidates,[87] and the explosion of PAC independent spending, effectively bypassing the limits on direct contributions to candidates. At a minimum, the parties and PACs are now skirting, if not violating, the law. New techniques for raising and allocating funds, combined with unprecedented spending, seem likely to place new pressures on Congress to revise the basic law.

10. *Adoption of the Federal Election Campaign Act (and its 1974, 1976, and 1979 amendments) has not by any means solved all the problems of financing American elections.* Inequities, confusion, and uncertainties persist. Have campaigns become too costly? Some close observers argue that they are underfinanced.[88] Should congressional as well as presidential campaigns be publicly financed? Thus far, Congress has said no. And if public financing of these campaigns is adopted, should spending limits also be established? And what of interest groups, now spending with a vengeance and undoubtedly gaining improved access to policy makers or securing questionable preferments? Should new limits on PAC direct and independent expenditures be imposed? On one or both, and how much regulation will the Supreme Court permit? And if tighter limits on PAC contributions are adopted, will PACs be encouraged to make even heavier independent expenditures? Is it realistic to think of passing new campaign finance legislation that makes elections more competitive by diminishing the advantages of incumbents over their challengers? As it stands, the massive advantages of office for incumbents, who are benefited additionally by one-sided PAC campaign support, ordinarily leave challengers with no more than an outside chance of winning, particularly in House elections. And in some years Senate challengers find their prospects equally bleak. Both law and practice have combined to build a comprehensive incumbent-protection system. Can campaign finance legislation be designed to strengthen the parties, and should this be a public policy goal? Should party committees be permitted to contribute larger sums to House and Senate candidates and to spend more on their behalf or on behalf of presidential candidates? These are some of the questions that will inform debate on

campaign finance and its reform. Answers to them are not easy to fashion. The consequences of change, moreover, are not easy to anticipate. Protecting the status quo is the best single safeguard against the unanticipated consequences that invariably accompany change.[89]

The manner in which political campaigns are financed has long been a source of controversy. Devising acceptable public policy on the subject has proved to be difficult, as it usually is on complex questions. But the objectives of regulation have been clear: to increase public confidence in the political process by curbing the abusive uses of political money, to enhance the opportunities for citizens to participate in politics by running for public office, and to reduce the vulnerability of candidates and public officials to the importunings and pressures of major benefactors. The campaign finance law has contributed in varying measure to the achievement of these objectives. It has also created new problems, accentuated certain old ones, fostered uncertainties, conferred advantages on some politicians and disadvantages on others and, arguably, done more to weaken the parties than to strengthen them.

Notes

1. Does a hard fought, divisive primary hurt the party's chances in the general election? Politicians and political observers tend to believe that it does—that supporters of the candidate or candidates who lost in the primary will switch their allegiance or decline to vote in the general election. Although the question is not settled, the preponderance of evidence suggests that conflictual (or competitive) primaries do have an adverse impact on the parties' chances for victory in the general election. The candidate who survives a primary battle is not as likely to win in November as a candidate who had little or no primary opposition. Support for this interpretation appears in Patrick J. Kenney and Tom W. Rice, "The Effect of Primary Divisiveness in Gubernatorial and Senatorial Elections," *Journal of Politics* 46 (August 1984): 904-915, and Robert A. Bernstein, "Divisive Primaries Do Hurt: U.S. Senate Races, 1956-1972," *American Political Science Review* 71 (June 1977): 540-545. But for a study that finds the relationship weak, see Richard Born, "The Influence of House Primary Divisiveness on General Election Margins 1962-76," *Journal of Politics* 43 (August 1981): 640-661. The "carryover effect" has also been studied in presidential elections by Walter J. Stone. He finds a strong carryover effect among partisan and committed activists; that is, activists who supported candidates who lost the nomination were less active in the general election. See his article, "The Carryover Effect in Presidential Elections," *American Political Science Review* 80 (March 1986): 271-279.

2. This discussion of closed and open primaries rests largely on an analysis by Craig L. Carr and Gary L. Scott, "The Logic of State Primary Classification Schemes," *American Politics Quarterly* 12 (October 1984): 465-476. Also see Malcolm E. Jewell and David M. Olson, *American State Political Parties and Elections* (Homewood, Ill.: Dorsey Press, 1978), 127-131, and David E. Price,

Bringing Back the Parties (Washington, D.C.: CQ Press, 1984), 127-131.

3. The closed primary states, listed from least to most restrictive in terms of the length of time necessary to change party affiliation, are: Iowa, Ohio, Wyoming, South Dakota, Oregon, Kansas, North Carolina, Delaware, Massachusetts, West Virginia, Pennsylvania, Florida, Colorado, Arizona, New Jersey, Nevada, Oklahoma, Maine, Nebraska, New Hampshire, New Mexico, Maryland, Connecticut, Kentucky, New York, and California.

4. Do members of the U.S. House of Representatives from closed primary states have higher party support scores than members elected from states with less restrictive, or more open, systems? The answer is that closed primary states do tend to produce more partisan officeholders; their partisanship, however, appears to be a function of party strength and other attitudes toward parties present in the state rather than the result of a closed primary nominating system. See Steven H. Haeberle, "Closed Primaries and Party Support in Congress," *American Politics Quarterly* 13 (July 1985): 341-352.

5. *Tashjian v. Republican Party of Connecticut*, 107 S. Ct. 544 (1986).

6. The states with the "purest" form of open primary are Hawaii, Idaho, Michigan, Minnesota, Montana, North Dakota, Utah, Vermont, and Wisconsin.

7. The "crossover" voting data are drawn from Ronald D. Hedlund and Meredith W. Watts, "The Wisconsin Open Primary, 1968 to 1984," *American Politics Quarterly* 14 (January-April 1986): 55-73. Also see Ronald D. Hedlund, Meredith W. Watts, and David M. Hedge, "Voting in an Open Primary," *American Politics Quarterly* 10 (April 1982): 197-218; David Adamany, "Communication: Cross-over Voting and the Democratic Party's Reform Rules," *American Political Science Review* 70 (June 1976): 536-541; and James I. Lengle and Byron E. Shafer, "Primary Rules, Political Power, and Social Change," *American Political Science Review* 70 (March 1976): 25-40.

8. *Democratic Party of the U.S. v. LaFollette*, 101 S. Ct. 1010 (1981).

9. The observations made in this paragraph are based mainly on an analysis by Charles D. Hadley, "The Impact of the Louisiana Open Elections System Reform," *State Government* 58, no. 4 (1986): 152-157. Also consult Thomas A. Kazee, "The Impact of Electoral Reform: 'Open Elections' and the Louisiana Party System," *Publius* 13 (Winter 1983): 132-139 and, for a general analysis of factionalism, see Earl Black, "A Theory of Southern Factionalism," *Journal of Politics* 45 (August 1983): 594-614.

10. Laws in a few states make provisions for the parties to hold *preprimary conventions* for the purpose of choosing the "organization slate." The candidates selected by these conventions will usually appear on the ballot bearing the party endorsement. In the great majority of states, however, slating is an informal party process; the party depends on its organizational network and the communications media to inform the voters which candidates carry party support.

11. These themes appear in Frank J. Sorauf, *Party Politics in America* (Boston: Little, Brown, 1980), 220-224.

12. V. O. Key, Jr., *American State Politics: An Introduction* (New York: Knopf, 1956); William H. Standing and James A. Robinson, "Inter-Party Competition and Primary Contesting: The Case of Indiana," *American Political Science Review* 52 (December 1958): 1066-1077; and Malcolm E. Jewell, "Party and Primary Competition in Kentucky State Legislative Races," *Kentucky Law Journal* 48 (Summer 1960): 517-535.

13. See Harvey L. Schantz, "Contested and Uncontested Primaries for the U.S. House," *Legislative Studies Quarterly* 5 (November 1980): 545-562.

14. Denis G. Sullivan, Jeffrey L. Pressman, and F. Christopher Arterton, *Explora-*

tions in Convention Decision Making (San Francisco: Freeman, 1976), 17. Reprinted by permission.

15. Sullivan, Pressman, and Arterton, *Explorations in Convention Decision Making*, 20-21.
16. *Congressional Quarterly Weekly Report,* June 2, 1984, 1316.
17. Turnout in presidential primaries tends to be highest in those states distinguished by high levels of education, facilitative legal provisions on voting, and competitive two-party elections. Interestingly, high turnout is not associated with high levels of campaign spending. See Patrick J. Kenney and Tom W. Rice, "Voter Turnout in Presidential Primaries: A Cross-Sectional Examination," *Political Behavior* 7, no. 1 (1985): 101-112. In terms of participation in presidential primaries, there is little or no difference between Democrats and Republicans. See Jack Moran and Mark Fenster, "Voting Turnout in Presidential Primaries," *American Politics Quarterly* 10 (October 1982): 453-476. Candidate strategy does influence turnout. See a study of how the number of candidates in the opposition party and the intensity of campaigning in the presidential party influence aggregate turnout levels: Barbara Norrander and Gregg W. Smith, "Type of Contest, Candidate Strategy, and Turnout in Presidential Primaries," *American Politics Quarterly* 13 (January 1985): 28-50. Turnout for first-tier caucuses is heightened by the presence of significant ideological choice among candidates, although no relationship exists between ideological range and turnout in primary states. See Steven E. Schier, "Turnout Choice in Presidential Nominations," *American Politics Quarterly* 10 (April 1982): 231-245.
18. *Congressional Quarterly Weekly Report,* July 7, 1984, 1619-1620.
19. *Congressional Quarterly Weekly Report,* July 7, 1984, 1619-1620.
20. See an analysis of the decline of success-minded professionals in party conventions and the growing "principle mindedness" of national convention delegates by John R. Petrocik and Dwaine Marvick, "Explaining Party Elite Transformation: Institutional Changes and Insurgent Politics," *Western Political Quarterly* 36 (September 1983): 345-363.
21. Winner-take-all has a dramatic impact on the allocation of delegates. Consider these results in 1984: Walter Mondale received 45 percent of the vote in New Jersey but more than 80 percent of the delegates. The situation was reversed in California where Gary Hart received 41 percent of the vote and 63 percent of the delegates.
22. See an interesting account of party leaders' views on a brokered convention in *Congressional Quarterly Weekly Report,* March 15, 1986, 627.
23. William J. Crotty, *Political Reform and the American Experiment* (New York: Crowell, 1977), 255-260.
24. *Congressional Quarterly Weekly Report,* August 25, 1984, 2092.
25. Operating under its primary-caucus hybrid system, Michigan Republicans in August 1986 elected about ten thousand precinct delegates to attend first-round caucuses in early 1988.
26. See *Congressional Quarterly Weekly Report,* March 1, 1986, 509-510.
27. William R. Keech and Donald R. Matthews, "Patterns in the Presidential Nominating Process, 1936-1976," in *Parties and Elections in an Anti-Party Age,* ed. Jeff Fishel (Bloomington: Indiana University Press, 1978), 216.
28. This observation and the previous three are drawn from F. Christopher Arterton, "Campaign Organizations Confront the Media-Political Environment," in *Race for the Presidency: The Media and the Nominating Process,* ed. James David Barber, 5. © 1978 The American Assembly, Columbia University. Reprinted by permission of Prentice-Hall Inc., Englewood Cliffs, N.J.

29. *Congressional Quarterly Weekly Report,* August 23, 1986, 1999.
30. F. Christopher Arterton, "Campaign Organizations Confront the Media-Political Environment," 10 (emphasis added).
31. *Congressional Quarterly Weekly Report,* August 23, 1986, 1997-2002.
32. In 1984 fourteen presidential candidates spent $107 million in the prenomination campaign. Of this sum, 60 percent was contributed by individuals, 34 percent came in matching funds, and 1.2 percent was contributed by PACs; the remainder was made up of loans. On the Democratic side, Walter Mondale raised $37 million and Gary Hart $23 million; Mondale received nearly $9 million in federal matching funds while Hart received about $5 million. Ronald Reagan raised nearly $29 million in the prenomination campaign, of which $10.1 million (the maximum permissable) was in federal matching funds. Press release, Federal Election Commission, June 4, 1986.
33. F. Christopher Arterton, "Campaign Organizations Confront the Media-Political Environment," 9.
34. These figures on participation are derived from several sources: Austin Ranney, *Participation in American Presidential Nominations, 1976* (Washington, D.C.: American Enterprise Institute for Public Policy Research, 1977), 15-20; *Congressional Quarterly Weekly Report,* July 5, 1980, 1869; *Congressional Quarterly Weekly Report,* June 2, 1984, 1315-1317; and *Congressional Quarterly Weekly Report,* July 7, 1984, 1618-1620.
35. But see a study of the 1980 presidential primaries by Barbara Norrander that finds that voters made little use of candidates' issue positions in deciding how to vote. The most frequent correlates of vote choice are the qualities of the candidates. "Correlates of Vote Choice in the 1980 Presidential Primaries," *Journal of Politics* 48 (February 1986): 156-166.
36. *New York Times,* July 15, 1984.
37. Data for this paragraph and the preceding one are drawn from various CBS and *New York Times* polls, as reported in the *New York Times,* August 24, 1984.
38. Few contributions of the major parties are more likely to be criticized or ridiculed than the party platforms. Commentators have found them meaningless, irrelevant, and all but useless in charting the direction of the government by the winning candidate and party. The truth is something else. Platform pledges tend to be adopted by the parties once they take control of government. Recently, about two-thirds of all platform promises have been fulfilled in some measure. See Gerald M. Pomper and Susan S. Lederman, *Elections in America* (New York: Longman, 1980), especially 161-167, and Alan D. Monroe, "American Party Platforms and Public Opinion," *American Journal of Political Science* 27 (February 1983): 27-42.
39. An exception to this rule occurred in 1956 when Adlai Stevenson, the Democratic presidential nominee, created a stir by declining to express a preference for his vice-presidential running mate. Left to its own devices, the convention quickly settled on a choice between senators Estes Kefauver and John F. Kennedy. Kefauver, who had been an active candidate for the presidency, won a narrow victory. Kennedy came off even better—he launched his candidacy for the presidential nomination in 1960.
40. The preference of party professionals for a balanced ticket grows out of their instinct for the conservation of the party and their understanding of the electorate. In the view of party professionals, the ticket should be broadly appealing instead of narrowly ideological or sectional. The factors that ordinarily come under review in the consideration of balance are geography, political philosophy, religion, and factional recognition.

41. A variation of this regional plan would require all states to hold a presidential primary.

42. Austin Ranney, *The Federalization of Presidential Primaries* (Washington, D.C.: American Enterprise Institute for Public Policy Research, 1978), 36-37. This monograph provides a comprehensive analysis of the proposals discussed in this section.

43. For an analysis of the new style of campaigning, particularly in terms of the role of campaign management firms, see Robert Agranoff, *The New Style in Election Campaigns* (Boston: Holbrook Press, 1972).

44. Quoted by Joe McGinniss, *The Selling of the President, 1968.* © 1969 by Joemac Inc. Reprinted by permission of Trident Press/Division of Simon and Schuster Inc.

45. David A. Leuthold, *Electioneering in a Democracy* (New York: Wiley, 1968), 3. Leuthold's study of congressional campaigns shows that "the problems of acquisition are more significant than the problems of using the resources. As a result, the decision on making an appeal for the labor vote, for example, will depend not only on the proportion of the constituency which is labor-oriented, but also on the success that the candidate has had in acquiring such resources as the support of labor leaders, the money and workers needed to send a mailing to labor union members, and information about issues important to labor people."

46. V. O. Key, Jr., *Politics, Parties, and Pressure Groups* (New York: Crowell, 1964), 464.

47. Lewis A. Froman, Jr., "A Realistic Approach to Campaign Strategies and Tactics," in *The Electoral Process,* ed. M. Kent Jennings and L. Harmon Zeigler (Englewood Cliffs, N.J.: Prentice-Hall, 1966), 7-8.

48. Stimson Bullitt, *To Be a Politician* (Garden City, N.Y.: Doubleday, 1961), 72-73.

49. From *The Making of the President, 1960,* by Theodore H. White. Copyright © 1961 by Atheneum House Inc. Reprinted by permission of the author and Atheneum Publishers, 322-323. For analysis of the major models of campaign decision making, see Karl A. Lamb and Paul A. Smith, *Campaign Decision-Making: The Presidential Election of 1964* (Belmont, Calif.: Wadsworth, 1968).

50. "Campaign Consultants: Pushing Sincerity in 1974," *Congressional Quarterly Weekly Report,* May 4, 1974, 1105.

51. *Congressional Quarterly Weekly Report,* October 21, 1978, 3060-3061.

52. See Herbert E. Alexander, *Financing the 1980 Election* (Washington, D.C.: CQ Press, 1983), and William J. Crotty and Gary C. Jacobson, *American Parties in Decline* (Boston: Little, Brown, 1980), 816-823. The estimate for total expenditures in 1984 was made by Herbert Alexander.

53. The development of political action committees represents a major change in American electoral politics. See an article by Frank J. Sorauf that examines the organizational lives of PACs, the role of donors to PACs, and PAC accountability: "Who's in Charge? Accountability in Political Action Committees," *Political Science Quarterly* 99 (Winter 1984-1985): 591-614. Also see the studies of PAC goals, organization, and decision making by Theodore J. Eismeier and Philip H. Pollock III, "An Organizational Analysis of Political Action Committees," *Political Behavior* 7, no. 2 (1985): 192-216, and "Strategy and Choice in Congressional Elections: The Role of Political Action Committees," *American Journal of Political Science* 30 (February 1986): 197-213. The authors distinguish three PAC roles: *accommodationist* (seek access in Congress through gifts to incumbents); *partisan* (basically financial auxiliaries of the major parties); and *adversary* (seek to defeat members whom they regard as hostile to their

interests).
54. *Congressional Quarterly Weekly Report,* April 13, 1985, 701.
55. Press release, Federal Election Commission, May 16, 1985.
56. Press release, Federal Election Commission, May 16, 1985.
57. *Congressional Quarterly Weekly Report,* April 8, 1978, 850-851, and November 11, 1978, 3260-3262.
58. Press release, Federal Election Commission, May 19, 1985.
59. *Wall Street Journal,* September 9, 1986.
60. *Congressional Quarterly Weekly Report,* August 2, 1986, 1751-1754.
61. David R. Mayhew, *Congress: The Electoral Connection* (New Haven, Conn.: Yale University Press, 1974), 84.
62. *Wall Street Journal,* September 24, 1986.
63. Press release, Federal Election Commission, April 4, 1986.
64. *Federal Election Commission v. Democratic Senatorial Campaign Committee,* 454 U.S. 27 (1981).
65. Gary C. Jacobson, "Party Organization and Distribution of Campaign Resources: Republicans and Democrats in 1982," *Political Science Quarterly* 100 (Winter 1985-1986): 611.
66. Herbert E. Alexander, "Political Parties and the Dollar," *Society* 22 (January/February 1985): 49-58.
67. Norman J. Ornstein, Thomas E. Mann, Michael J. Malbin, Allen Schick, and John F. Bibby, *Vital Statistics on Congress, 1984-1985 Edition* (Washington, D.C.: American Enterprise Institute for Public Policy Research, 1984), 65-70.
68. Press release, Federal Election Commission, May 16, 1985.
69. Press release, Federal Election Commission, May 16, 1985.
70. According to Common Cause, 80 percent of the 248 House members who voted to weaken federal gun control laws in 1986 had received campaign gifts (averaging more than $4,000) from the National Rifle Association (NRA), while the 176 members who voted against the NRA position received no funds. Press release, Common Cause, May 1986. This evidence, however, does not prove anything conclusively about PAC influence on voting. Those who believe that PAC influence has been exaggerated can point out that PACs give money to members (or candidates) with whose policy positions they are in agreement. This is the argument that "money follows votes," and not the reverse.
71. For studies of the relationship between PAC contributions and congressional floor votes, see John R. Wright, "PAC's, Contributions, and Roll Calls: An Organizational Perspective," *American Political Science Review* 79 (June 1985): 400-414; W. P. Welch, "Campaign Contributions and Voting: Milk Money and Dairy Price Supports," *Western Political Quarterly* 35 (December 1982): 478-495; Henry W. Chappell, Jr., "Campaign Contributions and Voting on the Cargo Preference Bill: A Comparison of Simultaneous Models," *Public Choice* 36, no. 2 (1981): 302-312; and James B. Kau and Paul H. Rubin, *Congressmen, Constituents, and Contributors* (Boston: Martinus Nijhoff, 1982).
72. These observations on PACs by members of Congress are drawn from *Congressional Quarterly Weekly Report,* March 12, 1983, 504; *Time,* March 3, 1986; *Congressional Quarterly Weekly Report,* January 11, 1986, 99; *Congressional Quarterly Weekly Report,* December 7, 1985, 2568; *Congressional Quarterly Weekly Report,* March 12, 1983, 504; *Washington Post,* December 5, 1985.
73. S. 1806, 99th Cong., 1st sess., 1985, and memorandums from the office of Sen. David L. Boren.
74. Consider the observation of a New York representative: "When I ran for Congress, the first question asked me was whether I could finance my own

campaign. If I had said 'no, I cannot,' I would not have been the candidate. When you mention candidates for public office, you are only mentioning men of affluence." *Congressional Quarterly Weekly Report,* December 5, 1969, 2434.

75. 424 U.S. 1 (1976).

76. Struck down by the Court were provisions that limited the spending of personal funds by candidates ($35,000 for Senate candidates and $25,000 for House candidates) and those that limited total expenditures. Senate candidates were to be limited to total expenditures of no more than $100,000, or 8 cents per eligible voter (whichever is greater) in primaries, and $150,000, or 12 cents per voter (whichever is greater) in general elections. Fund-raising costs of up to 20 percent of the spending limit could be added to these amounts. House candidates were to be limited to no more than $70,000 in primaries and $70,000 in general elections (plus fund-raising costs of up to 20 percent of the spending limit).

77. *Congressional Quarterly Weekly Report,* October 12, 1974, 2865.

78. *Congressional Quarterly Weekly Report,* August 5, 1978, 2029.

79. Among the incumbent's advantages are the franking privilege, visibility gained through the media, a public record, a network of political allies, a structure of opportunities for helping constituents with their problems (casework), an established system for soliciting campaign funds, and a staff and offices.

80. For a discussion of some of these themes, see an insightful essay by F. Christopher Arterton, "Political Money and Party Strength," in *The Future of American Political Parties,* ed. Joel Fleishman (Englewood Cliffs, N.J.: Prentice-Hall, 1982), especially 116-122.

81. This paragraph is based largely on Ruth S. Jones and Warren E. Miller, "Financing Campaigns: Macro Level Innovation and Micro Level Response," *Western Political Quarterly* 38 (June 1985): 187-210, and Ruth S. Jones, "Campaign Contributions and Campaign Solicitations: 1980-1984," (Manuscript, Arizona State University, 1986). These studies rest on data drawn from the National Election Study.

82. Press release, Federal Election Commission, May 16, 1985.

83. Press release, Federal Election Commission, May 7, 1985.

84. *Federal Election Commission Record* (Washington, D.C.: Federal Election Commission, October 1985), 7.

85. Press release, Federal Election Commission, June 4, 1986.

86. *Wall Street Journal,* October 24, 1986. Using bundling money, the National Republican Senatorial Committee gave the campaign of Sen. James Abdnor (R-S.D.) nearly $1 million in 1986. Under FECA, direct national contributions to Abdnor were limited to $17,500 and coordinated expenditures to $43,620—pittances in terms of the actual money channeled into his campaign. A story in the *New York Times,* based on random telephone interviews, reported that many of the donors to the NRSC were unaware that their contributions had been designated for specific candidates. *New York Times,* October 29, 1986.

87. *New York Times,* October 29, 1986.

88. Alexander, "Political Parties and the Dollar," 48-58.

89. For insight into the reform question, see Michael J. Malbin, "Looking Back at the Future of Campaign Finance Reform: Interest Groups and American Elections," in *Money and Politics in the United States: Financing Elections in the 1980s,* ed. Michael J. Malbin (Washington, D.C.: American Enterprise Institute for Public Policy Research, 1984), 232-270.

Political Parties
and the Electorate

IT IS A nagging fact of American life that for a large proportion of the population politics carries no interest, registers no significance, and excites no demands. A vast array of evidence shows that the political role of the typical citizen is that of spectator, occasionally aroused by political events but more often inattentive to them. However tarnished this commonplace, it comes close to being the chief truth to be known about the political behavior of American citizens. Much less certain, however, is what this means. Whether it is necessary to have greatly interested and active citizens to have strong and responsible political institutions is by no means clear. No neat or simple formula exists for assessing public support for political institutions. Does the presence of a large nonvoting population reflect substantial disillusionment with the political system and its processes, or does it reflect a general satisfaction with the state of things? The answer is elusive.[1]

Whatever the consequences of low or modest turnouts for the vitality of a democratic political system, it is obvious that some American citizens use their political resources far more than others. Their political involvement is reflected not only in the fact that they vote regularly but also in the fact that they participate in politics in various other ways— perhaps by attempting to persuade other voters to support their candidates or party, by making campaign contributions, or by devoting time and energy to political campaigns. The net result of differential rates of participation is that some citizens gain access to political decision makers and can influence their decisions, while other citizens are all but excluded from the political process.

An important element in understanding the political behavior of the active members of the American electorate is the political party. More than any other agency, the party provides cues for the voters and gives shape and meaning to elections. Some voters elude party labeling, preferring the role of the independent. Their number has grown significantly in recent years. Even though their importance cannot be minimized, especially in presidential elections, their consistent impact on politics is less than that of party members. The reason for this is partly a matter of numbers: about two out of three voters classify themselves as members of one or the other of the two major parties. Before examining the behavior of partisans and nonpartisans, however, it is appropriate to consider the broad characteristics of citizen participation in politics.

Turnout: The Diminished Electorate

Few facts about American political behavior stand out more sharply than the comparatively low level of citizen involvement in politics. And there are clear signs that popular participation is declining.

Atrophy of the Electorate

In presidential elections during the last quarter of the nineteenth century, turnout was regularly high; in the presidential election of 1876, for example, over 85 percent of the eligible voters cast ballots (see Figure 4-1). Beginning around the turn of the century, however, a sharp decline in voting set in, reaching its nadir of 44 percent in 1920. A moderate increase in turnout occurred during the next several decades, with participation hovering around 60 percent during the 1950s and 1960s. But participation declined again in the 1970s, dropping to 54.3 percent in 1976 and to 53.2 percent in 1980—its lowest level since 1948. In the 1984 election between Ronald Reagan and Walter Mondale, turnout rose only fractionally, to 53.3 percent.[2] Thus in the most recent presidential elections, only slightly more than half of the eligible voters have turned out to vote.

Although these data on American voting participation are far from impressive, they may conceal more of the problem than they uncover. The hard truth is that turnout is much lower in nonpresidential elections. In off-year congressional elections from 1950 to 1970, turnout percentages ranged between 41 and 45 percent of the eligible voters. In the midterm election of 1974, turnout dropped to 36 percent; in 1978, it

FIGURE 4-1 Percentage of Voting-Age Population Casting Votes for the Office of President, 1856-1984

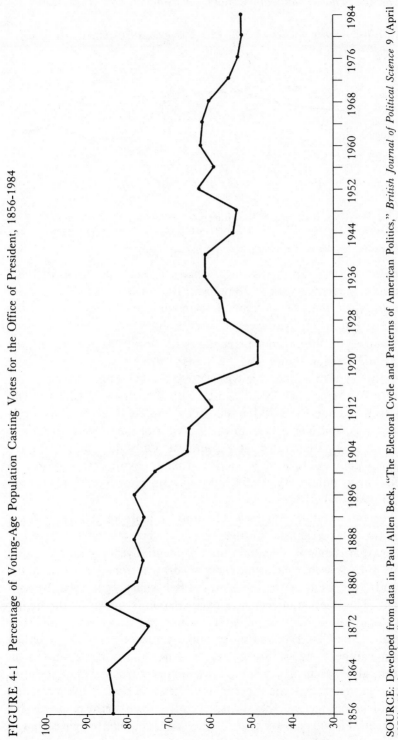

SOURCE: Developed from data in Paul Allen Beck, "The Electoral Cycle and Patterns of American Politics," *British Journal of Political Science* 9 (April 1979): 134 (as updated).

FIGURE 4-2   Voter Turnout in Off-year Elections, 1950-1986

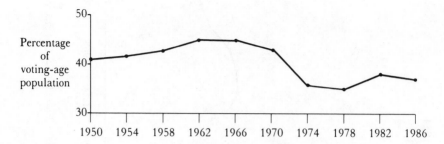

SOURCE: Developed from data in U.S. Bureau of the Census, *Statistical Abstract of the United States* (Washington, D.C.: U.S. Government Printing Office, 1986), 255.

NOTE: Estimated turnout for 1986.

fell to 35.5 percent. In the midst of a marked economic slump in 1982, the turnout percentage rose to 38 percent. But it eased off to 37.3 percent in 1986. More than 60 percent of all eligible voters do not take the trouble to vote in off-year elections (see Figure 4-2).

A survey of the turnout percentages in the fifty states in the 1984 presidential election shows that the highest turnout rates were achieved in certain western, upper midwestern, and New England states (see Figure 4-3). Minnesota led all states with a turnout of 68.5 percent, followed by Maine (65.2), Montana (65.0), South Dakota (63.9), Wisconsin (63.4), and North Dakota (62.9). Most of the states with unusually low participation rates were southern. Only 40.6 percent of the voting-age population voted in South Carolina; next lowest was Georgia (42.2). The populous states of California and New York had turnout rates of 49.9 and 51.1, respectively.

Turnout in state and local elections is more of the same story. Recent turnout percentages for the office of governor in the fifty states in off-year (that is, nonpresidential) and presidential years are presented in Figure 4-4. Several conclusions can be drawn from the data in the figure. In the first place, the states differ sharply in their turnout patterns. The relation of region to participation is shown by the higher voter participation rates in midwestern, western (especially plains and mountain), and New England states, and the lower rates of participation in most southern states. Second, those states that elect governors in presidential years nearly always have higher turnouts than those in which gubernatorial elections occur in off years. Third, notwithstanding major variations among the states, overall citizen performance is far from great. The median turnout for the states that elected governors in

FIGURE 4-3 Voting Participation Rates in 1984 Presidential Election

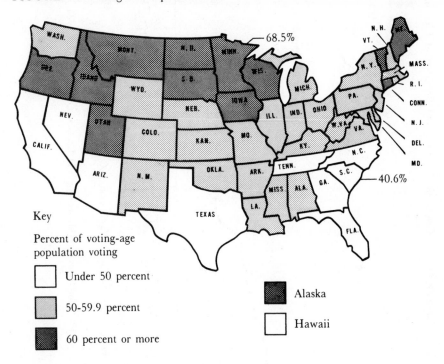

Key

Percent of voting-age
population voting

☐ Under 50 percent

▨ 50-59.9 percent

▩ 60 percent or more

■ Alaska

☐ Hawaii

SOURCE: Developed from data in U.S. Bureau of the Census, *Statistical Abstract of the United States* (Washington, D.C.: U.S. Government Printing Office, 1986), 255.

1982 was only 43 percent. In voting for governor in the 1984 presidential year, the median turnout was 57 percent.

The low point in participation is ordinarily plumbed in primary elections—a total primary vote of only 20 to 25 percent of the eligible electorate is not unusual. In certain southern states, however, participation in primary elections—often the "real" election in that region—is about as high as it is in general elections.[3] Primary turnout is highest in states where primaries are open (and particularly high in blanket or nonpartisan primaries), where the parties are most competitive, where presidential primaries coincide with other primaries, and where higher educational levels are present among voters. There is some evidence that closeness of election stimulates turnout and that incumbency diminishes it. Each state has a different mix of these factors, thus contributing to variations in turnout rates.[4]

It is a major and uncomfortable fact of American political life that a great many citizens—comprising almost half of the eligible electorate

FIGURE 4-4 Percentage of Voting-Age Population Casting Votes for the Office of Governor, Off-year and Presidential Elections, 1982 and 1984

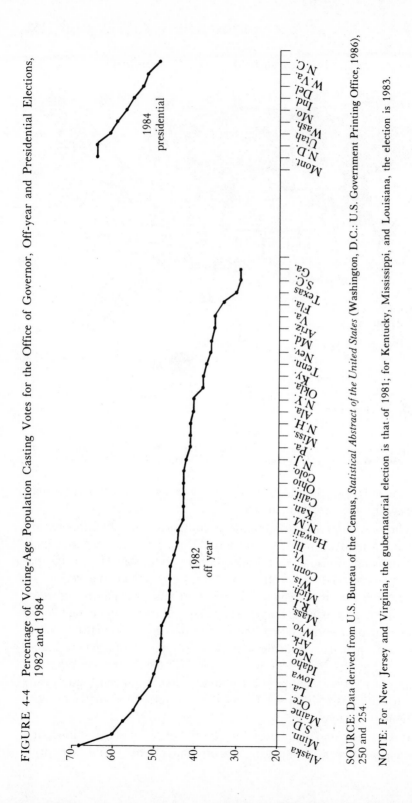

SOURCE: Data derived from U.S. Bureau of the Census, *Statistical Abstract of the United States* (Washington, D.C.: U.S. Government Printing Office, 1986), 250 and 254.

NOTE: For New Jersey and Virginia, the gubernatorial election is that of 1981; for Kentucky, Mississippi, and Louisiana, the election is 1983.

even in presidential years—are almost wholly detached from the political system and the processes through which its leadership is selected. What reasons help to account for the poor performance of twentieth century American electorates? In the case of southern states, limitations placed on black political participation shortly before the turn of the century drastically reduced turnout. A variety of legal abridgments and strategies, buttressed by social and economic sanctions of all kinds, effectively disfranchised all but the most persistent and resourceful black citizens. The ingenuity of southern white politicians during this era can scarcely be exaggerated. Poll taxes, literacy tests, understanding-the-Constitution tests, white primaries,[5] stringent residence and registration requirements, and discriminatory registration administration—all were consciously employed by dominant elites to maintain a white electorate and thus to settle political questions within the white community.

Another prime reason for the sharp contraction of the active electorate stems from the advent of one-party politics throughout large sections of the country. Democratic domination of the South began shortly after the Civil War Reconstruction governments were terminated. Nevertheless, even in the 1880s, the Republican presidential vote was at least half of the Democratic vote in all but a few southern states. The election of 1896, one of the most decisive elections in American history, culminated in the virtual disappearance of the Republican party in the South and in a precipitate drop in Democratic strength in the North. E. E. Schattschneider's analysis of this election is instructive:

> The 1896 party cleavage resulted from the tremendous reaction of conservatives in both major parties to the Populist movement, a radical agrarian agitation that alarmed people of substance all over the country. . . . Southern conservatives reacted so strongly that they were willing to revive the tensions and animosities of the Civil War and the Reconstruction in order to set up a one-party sectional southern political monopoly in which nearly all Negroes and many poor whites were disfranchised. . . . The northern conservatives were so badly frightened by the [William Jennings] Bryan candidacy that they adopted drastic measures to alarm the country. As a matter of fact, the conservative reaction to Bryanism in the North was almost as spectacular as the conservative reaction to Populism in the South. As a result the Democratic party in large areas of the Northeast and Middle West was wiped out, or decimated, while the Republican party consolidated its supremacy in all of the most populous areas of the country. The resulting party lineup was one of the most sharply sectional political divisions in American history. . . . Both sections became more conservative because *one-party politics tends strongly to*

vest political power in the hands of the people who already have enormous power. Moreover, in one-party areas (areas of extreme sectionalism) votes decline in value because the voters no longer have a valuable party alternative.[6]

The smothering effect of a noncompetitive environment on participation can be seen in election turnouts following the realignment of the 1890s. Consider this evidence: between 1884 and 1904, turnout in Virginia dropped 57 percent; in Mississippi, 51 percent; and in Louisiana, 50 percent. Part of the explanation for these drop-offs undoubtedly can be associated with the success of southern efforts to disfranchise blacks, but it is also clear that one-party politics had a decisive impact on the electorate. In the first place, the drop in participation was too large to be accounted for merely by the disappearance of black votes. Second, the impact of the new sectionalism was not confined simply to the South. Despite their growing populations, some fourteen northern states had smaller turnouts in 1904 than they did in 1896.[7]

The lower rate of turnout in the South in the twentieth century is partially attributable to diminished competition between the parties. If the outcome of an election is predictable, there is scant inducement for voters to pay in time, energy, and other costs that voting requires. Changes in the turnout of southern voters, however, are under way. Today, elections in the South (especially presidential) are substantially more competitive than they were a generation ago, and voter turnout rates have been increasing, here and there dramatically. Undoubtedly, the elimination of legal barriers to registration and voting (such as the poll tax and the literacy test) has also contributed to the expansion of southern electorates. In presidential elections, voters in some southern states now participate at a level only marginally lower than voters in other parts of the country.

Still other reasons have been advanced for the decline in mass political involvement in this century. One concerns woman suffrage. Although women were given the vote in 1920, large numbers of them were indifferent to their new right and did not use it immediately. In subsequent decades, a significantly larger proportion of women entered the active electorate; today, their rate of participation is about the same as that of men.

In the past, stringent registration laws undoubtedly served to keep many citizens away from the polls. During the latter part of the nineteenth century, when turnout was regularly between 75 and 85 percent of the eligible electorate, in many parts of the country voters were not required to register or automatic registration was in effect.

During the early twentieth century, registration laws became much more restrictive, making voting more difficult. Provisions were adopted, for example, requiring voters to register annually in person, purging voters' names from the registration rolls if they failed to vote within a particular period, and requiring that voters reside within a state at least a year (and sometimes two) before becoming eligible to register. In addition, poll taxes and literacy tests were used, particularly in the South, to disfranchise prospective voters. The effect of these legal barriers was to diminish turnout.

Major changes in the 1960s and 1970s, however, greatly relaxed registration laws. Poll taxes and literacy tests were eliminated. Periodic registration gave way virtually everywhere to permanent registration. As a result of an act passed by Congress in 1970, the residency requirement for federal elections is now limited to a maximum of thirty days before the election; moreover, for other elections, only a handful of states have closing dates earlier than thirty days. In about one-third of the states, registration is possible up to twenty days before the election. Finally, all states must now meet certain minimum national standards for absentee registration.[8]

Although states vary in their requirements, registration laws are no longer generally burdensome. Nonetheless, a study by Steven J. Rosenstone and Raymond E. Wolfinger has shown that if all states had registration laws as permissive as those found in the most permissive states, turnout would increase. If permissive laws had been in effect everywhere in the 1972 presidential election, turnout would have been about 9 percent higher. Their study shows that late closing dates have the largest impact on voting participation. Facilitative provisions for absentee registration also encourage turnout, as do provisions for registration during normal business hours, evenings, and Saturdays. What it comes down to is that in states where registration laws are permissive, the costs of voting in time, energy, and information are lower. It is simply easier to vote. Less restrictive provisions are particularly likely to increase the participation of persons with limited education and limited interest in politics.[9]

The evidence suggests that legal barriers to participation are no longer a key explanation for low turnout in American elections. One reason for the overall poor voting performance is that the number of potential voters has increased as a result of lowering the voting age to eighteen. Younger voters have the lowest participation rate of any group in American society.[10] In 1984 only a little more than one-third of those persons between eighteen and twenty-one turned out at the polls.

TABLE 4-1　The Decline in Voting in Presidential Elections, 1968-1984

Group	Percentage of persons reporting that they voted				
	1968	1972	1976	1980	1984
Nation	67.8	63.0	59.2	59.2	59.9
Men	69.8	64.1	59.6	59.1	59.0
Women	66.0	62.0	58.8	59.4	60.8
White	69.1	64.5	60.9	60.9	61.4
Black	57.6	52.1	48.7	50.5	55.8
Spanish origin	a	37.4	31.8	29.9	32.6
18-20 years old	33.3	48.3	38.0	35.7	36.7
21-24	51.1	50.7	45.6	43.1	43.5
25-34	62.5	59.7	55.4	54.6	54.5
35-44	70.8	66.3	63.3	64.4	63.5
45-64	74.9	70.8	68.7	69.3	69.8
65 and over	65.8	63.5	62.2	65.1	67.7
Metropolitan	68.0	64.3	59.2	58.8	a
Nonmetropolitan	67.3	59.4	59.1	60.2	a
North and West	71.0	66.4	61.2	61.0	a
South	60.1	55.4	54.9	55.6	a
8 years schooling or less	54.5	47.4	44.1	42.6	42.9
9-11 years	61.3	52.0	47.2	45.6	44.4
12 years	72.5	65.4	59.4	58.9	58.7
College, 4 years or more	a	83.6	79.8	79.9	79.1
Employed	71.1	66.0	62.0	61.8	61.6
Unemployed	52.1	49.9	43.7	41.2	44.0
Not in labor force	63.2	59.3	56.5	57.0	58.9

SOURCE: Derived from data in U.S. Bureau of the Census, *Statistical Abstract of the United States* (Washington, D.C.: U.S. Government Printing Office, 1969-1986).

NOTE: Actual turnout is lower than reported turnout. For elections prior to 1972, voting participation for persons 18-20 was confined to four states: Georgia and Kentucky (18 and over), Alaska (19 and over), and Hawaii (20 and over).

[a] Not available.

Youthful insensitivity and indifference to politics, however, is only part of the story. More important is the fact that turnout rates have declined for most major demographic groups (see Table 4-1).

Nonvoters offer a variety of reasons for their failure to vote (see Table 4-2). A growing number of people do not take the trouble to register—the explanation of 42 percent of the nonvoters in 1980 and of 31 percent in 1984. People who change residence are required to sign up again, and many fail to do so. Some people do not vote because they

TABLE 4-2   Reasons for Nonvoting in Presidential Elections, 1968-1984

Reason	1984	1980	1976	1972	1968
Not registered	31%	42%	38%	28%	34%
Didn't like candidates	10	17	14	10	12
Not interested in politics	8	5	10	4	7
Illness	7	8	7	11	15
Inconvenient	7	a	a	a	a
Working	7	3	2	7	3
Not a citizen	6	5	4	a	a
New resident	6	4	4	8	10
Out of town	5	3	3	5	6
Couldn't get to polls	3	1	2	a	a
Didn't get absentee ballot	1	a	1	1	2
No particular reason	8	10	10	13	8
All others	1	2	5	13	3

SOURCE: *Gallup Report,* November 1984, 11.

[a] Less than 1 percent.

disapprove of the candidates—at least 10 percent in election after election. And then there are those who are not interested in politics (8 percent in 1984), those who find voting inconvenient (7 percent), and those who have "no particular reason" (8 percent) for not voting.

A central explanation for nonvoting thus lies in the public's attitude toward politics and political institutions. It seems likely, for example, that participation has declined because an increasing number of citizens care less which party or which candidate wins, because they believe that their votes will not make much difference, because they believe that public officials are not concerned about what voters think, because they think that politicians cannot be trusted,[11] and because they believe public officials are unresponsive.[12] It also seems clear that the overall decline in the strength of voters' party identification has played a role in the decline of electoral participation.[13] Indifference, alienation,[14] declining party loyalty, and a generalized distrust of government combine to cut the turnout rate in elections. For many citizens, "voting simply isn't worth the effort." [15]

Turnout in other industrialized democracies averages about 80 percent of the eligible electorate, vastly higher than the average turnout in American presidential elections. A study by G. Bingham Powell, using aggregate and comparative survey data, finds that voter participation in the United States is "severely inhibited" by institutional factors such as voluntary registration (as opposed to automatic registration common in other nations), low levels of competition in many electoral districts, and weak linkages between parties and social groups (thus making the parties' task of voter mobilization more difficult). To approach the turnout levels of other democracies, Powell argues, the United States would need to adopt automatic registration laws and change the structure of party competition to mobilize lower-class voters. Obviously, changing registration laws would be easier to accomplish than changing party character and party competition.[16]

The Regulation of Voting

As stipulated in the U.S. Constitution, states have control over suffrage. The basic reference to suffrage in the Constitution appears in Article I, Section 2, which provides that for elections to the House of Representatives "... the electors [that is, voters] in each state shall have the qualifications requisite for electors of the most numerous branch of the state legislature." Until recently the major national intrusions involving suffrage came in the form of constitutional amendments. The Fifteenth Amendment (1870) forbade the states to deny citizens the right to vote on the grounds of race, and the Nineteenth Amendment (1920) provided that states could not deny citizens the ballot on account of sex. The Twenty-fourth Amendment (1964) outlawed poll taxes, and the Twenty-sixth Amendment (1971) lowered the voting age in all elections to eighteen.

In recent decades, the tradition of state control over suffrage has been significantly challenged by Congress through the passage of a series of civil rights acts (1957, 1960, 1964, and 1965). The acts of 1957 and 1960 were designed primarily to prevent discrimination against blacks seeking to register to vote. Individuals who were denied the right to register by local registrars could seek relief from the federal government through the attorney general and the federal court system. Where discriminatory practices affecting registration were found to exist, the court was empowered to appoint federal voting referees to enroll black voters. Although the overall impact of these early acts on black voting was marginal, due largely to the cumbersome procedural requirements involved in jury trials and in establishing patterns of discrimination, they were important for establishing the power of the federal government, through a legislative enactment, to intervene in state election systems.

Of much greater substantive significance has been the Civil Rights Act of 1964 and the Voting Rights Act of 1965. In its provisions concerning voting, the 1964 act made a sixth-grade education presumptive evidence of literacy and required that all literacy tests be administered in writing. In addition, registrars were required to administer registration procedures fairly and were forbidden to reject registration applications because of immaterial errors on registration forms.

With the support of strong majorities of both parties, Congress passed the Voting Rights Act of 1965. Under its terms, literacy tests or other voter qualification devices used for discriminatory purposes were suspended in any state or county in which less than 50 percent of the voting-age residents were registered to vote in November 1964 or less than 50 percent voted in the 1964 presidential election. Augmenting the federal government's power to supervise elections, the act called for the appointment of federal voting examiners with the authority to register persons who have been unable to register even though they meet state requirements for voting. Finally, the act provided that if a state or local governmental unit decides to change its voting regulations, the U.S. attorney general or the U.S. District Court for the District of Columbia must first certify that the new rules will not serve the purposes of racial discrimination. In 1975 this act was extended for another seven years, with its coverage expanded to include "language minorities" (including Spanish-speaking populations, American Indians, Alaskan natives, and Asian-Americans). The extension also placed a permanent ban on voter qualifying tests. Undoubtedly the most effective civil rights law ever adopted, the 1965 Voting Rights Act was again extended by Congress in 1982.

In its most important respects, the regulation of voting is today as much a matter of federal law as it is of state law. Had it not been for the civil rights movement in the 1950s and 1960s, it is doubtful that such fundamental changes would have occurred in the regulation of suffrage. What has been the impact of the new role of the national government in protecting the right to vote? For black political participation, the results have been dramatic (see Table 4-3). In 1960 only 29 percent of the blacks of voting age were registered to vote in the eleven states of the South. In 1984 66 percent of the blacks of voting age in these states were registered. In Mississippi, nearly fifteen times as many blacks were registered to vote in 1984 as there had been in 1960. The vast majority of these new voters in Mississippi and elsewhere were enrolled following the passage of the Voting Rights Act of 1965. In 1986 voters in the rural Mississippi Delta (Second Congressional District) elected the state's first black representative since the military occupation, or Reconstruction, following the Civil War.

Widespread black political participation is now a reality in south-

TABLE 4-3   Percentage of Voting-Age Population Registered to Vote in Eleven Southern States, by Race, 1960 and 1984

| | 1960 | | 1984 | |
State	White	Black	White	Black
Alabama	63.6	13.7	81.6	74.0
Arkansas	60.9	38.0	74.4	67.2
Florida	69.3	39.4	73.6	63.4
Georgia	56.8	29.3	68.5	57.9
Louisiana	76.9	31.1	76.3	65.7
Mississippi	63.9	5.2	96.7	77.1
North Carolina	92.1	39.1	74.3	65.4
South Carolina	57.1	13.7	59.8	58.5
Tennessee	73.0	59.1	73.8	69.9
Texas	42.5	35.5	81.7	71.5
Virginia	46.1	23.1	65.9	62.3
Total	61.1	29.1	75.3	66.2

SOURCE: Developed from data in U.S. Bureau of the Census, *Statistical Abstract of the United States* (Washington, D.C.: U.S. Government Printing Office, 1986), 257.

ern politics. To be sure, registration and voting will not solve all the problems of the black citizen. But political participation does give blacks much greater leverage in the political system. Race-baiting campaign ploys by white politicians are a thing of the past. The number of black elected officials has increased dramatically in recent years, and particularly in the South. The southern state electorates of today are vastly different from those of the 1950s. And it is a certainty that whatever the future shape of southern politics, black voters and black politicians will play a more important role in political decision making than at any time since Reconstruction.

Forms of Political Participation

The act of voting is an appropriate point of departure for exploring the political involvement of American citizens, but it is not the only form of participation. A comprehensive survey of political participation in America by Sidney Verba and Norman H. Nie shows the range and dimensions of citizen activities in politics (see Table 4-4). Several findings should be emphasized. Perhaps of most importance, the only political activity in which a majority of American citizens participates is voting in presidential elections. Voting regularly in local elections follows as a rather distant second.[17] The survey discloses that as political activity

TABLE 4-4   A Profile of the Political Activity of American Citizens

Form of activity	Percent of citizens
Report regularly voting in presidential elections	72
Report always voting in local elections	47
Acting in at least one organization involved in community problems	32
Have worked with others in trying to solve some community problems	30
Have attempted to persuade others to vote as they were	28
Have ever actively worked for a party or candidates during an election	26
Have ever contacted a local government official about some issue or problem	20
Have attended at least one political meeting or rally in last three years	19
Have ever contacted a state or national government official about some issue or problem	18
Have ever formed a group or organization to attempt to solve some local community problem	14
Have ever given money to a party or candidate during an election campaign	13
Presently a member of a political club or organization	8

SOURCE: Sidney Verba and Norman H. Nie, *Participation in America: Political Democracy and Social Equality* (New York: Harper and Row, 1972), 31.

requires more time, initiative, and involvement of the citizen—working to solve a community problem, attempting to persuade others how to vote, working for a party or candidate, contributing to political campaigns—participation levels drop even lower.

The impression most deeply conveyed by the data is that a relatively small group of citizens performs most of the political activities of the nation. There is obviously much more than a germ of truth to this. Yet, to some extent, the data underrepresent the political activity of citizens, since those citizens who perform one political act are not necessarily the same as those who perform another act. Verba and Nie indicate that, excluding voting from the analysis, less than a third of their sample reported engaging in no political activities.[18] Even so, this is a fairly large lump of the citizenry.

The evidence from a number of studies of political participation is that people do not get involved randomly in politics. Instead, there is a hierarchy of political involvement (see Figure 4-5).[19] Individuals who are politically active engage in a wide variety of political acts. A major characteristic of their participation is that it tends to be cumulative. The active members of a political party, for example, are likely to be found

The American Voter: Orientations . . .

Interest in Politics

How often do you discuss politics with your family or friends?

Every day	13%
Three or four times a week	18
Once or twice a week	35
Less often	34

Do you personally care a good deal about which party wins the presidential election this fall?

Care a great deal	65%
Don't care very much	33
Don't know	2

Ideology

When it comes to politics, do you usually think of yourself as a liberal, a conservative, a moderate, or what?

Liberal	19%
Moderate	30
Conservative	30
No preference or no understanding of term	21

Political Efficacy

Sometimes politics and government seem so complicated that a person like me can't really understand what's going on.

Agree	71%
Disagree	29

soliciting political funds, contributing time and money to campaigns, attending meetings, and so on. Individuals who are minimally involved in politics typically take part only in such limited activities as those grouped near the base of the hierarchy. At the very bottom are those persons who stand on the outskirts of the political world, scarcely, if at all, aware of the political forces that play on them or of the opportunities open to them to use their resources (including the vote) to gain political objectives.

...toward Politics and Political Activity

Political Activity

Did you talk with any people [during the campaign] and try to show them why they should vote for or against one of the parties or candidates?

Yes	32%
No	68

Did you wear a campaign button, put a campaign sticker on your car, or place a sign in your window or in front of your house?

Yes	9%
No	91

Did you go to any political meetings, rallies, speeches, dinners, or things like that in support of a particular candidate?

Yes	8%
No	92

Did you do any work for one of the parties or candidates?

Yes	4%
No	96

During the past year, did you give any money to an individual candidate, a political party organization, people supporting a ballot proposition, or to a particular issue or interest group?

Yes	12%
No	88

SOURCE: These questions are drawn from the 1984 presidential election survey, National Election Study, Center for Political Studies, University of Michigan.

The Active and Passive Citizenry

A number of social, demographic, and political variables are related to the act of voting. The data in Table 4-5 provide a profile of those citizens who are more likely to turn out at elections and those who are less likely to turn out. Some of the characteristics are closely related—for example, high income, high occupational status, and college education. Nevertheless, the high rate of participation by citizens of higher socioeconomic

FIGURE 4-5   Hierarchy of Political Involvement

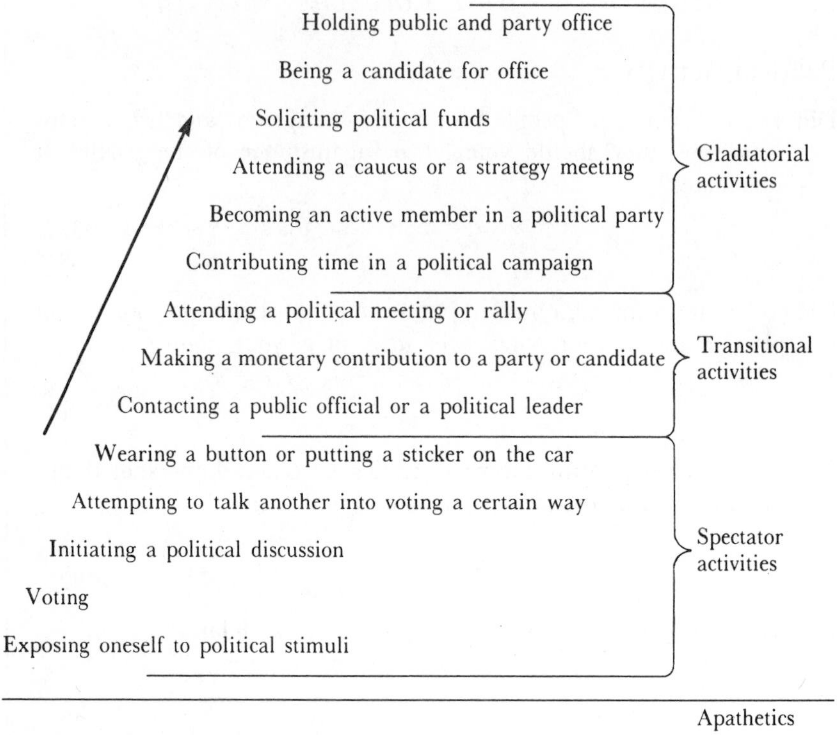

Holding public and party office	
Being a candidate for office	
Soliciting political funds	
Attending a caucus or a strategy meeting	Gladiatorial activities
Becoming an active member in a political party	
Contributing time in a political campaign	
Attending a political meeting or rally	
Making a monetary contribution to a party or candidate	Transitional activities
Contacting a public official or a political leader	
Wearing a button or putting a sticker on the car	
Attempting to talk another into voting a certain way	
Initiating a political discussion	Spectator activities
Voting	
Exposing oneself to political stimuli	

Apathetics

SOURCE: Lester W. Milbrath, *Political Participation* (Chicago: Rand McNally, 1965), 18.

status is not simply a function of status. The explanation lies in the civic orientations that are linked to upper-class status and environment. Upper-status citizens, for example, are more likely than citizens of lower status to belong to organizations and to participate in their activities, more likely to possess the resources and skills to be effective in politics, and more likely to be attentive to political problems and to feel efficacious in dealing with them.[20]

How much the factors that influence participation at the individual level can account for the differences among the states in voter turnout is not altogether clear. What is clear is that of all the sections of the country, the South ranks not only lowest in turnout but also lowest in terms of family income, levels of education, and other measures of economic well-being. Moreover, the legal structures (for example, election laws) in southern states typically do not encourage voting as much as those in northern states. The level of participation in southern states probably will increase as their sociodemographic characteristics change

TABLE 4-5   A Profile of the More Active and Less Active Citizenry

More likely to vote	Less likely to vote
High income	Low income
High occupational status	Low occupational status
College education	Grade school or high school education
Middle-aged	Young and elderly
White	Black and Hispanic
Metropolitan area resident	Small-town resident
Northern state resident	Southern state resident
Resident in competitive party environment	Resident in noncompetitive party environment
Union member	Nonunion labor
Homeowner	Renter
Married	Single, separated, divorced, widowed
Government employees	Private workers
Catholics and Jews	Protestants
Strong partisan	Independent

SOURCE: These findings were drawn from a large number of studies of the American electorate. For wide-ranging analyses, see Lester W. Milbrath, *Political Participation* (Chicago: Rand McNally, 1965); Raymond E. Wolfinger and Steven J. Rosenstone, *Who Votes?* (New Haven, Conn.: Yale University Press, 1980); and M. Margaret Conway, *Political Participation in the United States* (Washington, D.C.: CQ Press, 1985).

(for example, an improved economic position) or as their legal structures become more facilitative.[21]

For all their interest, the distinctions drawn from the data presented in Table 4-5 cannot be taken at face value. In the first place, the differences between voters and nonvoters are less apparent today than in the past. The participation rates of people who live in rural or urban areas are about the same today. Men and women now vote at about the same rate. Turnout in the South is on the rise, while it is decreasing in the North. A noticeable decline in voting by middle-aged persons has occurred.[22] What stands out most is that participation has declined along a broad demographic front.

The lower turnout of Protestants is also deceptive. It is undoubtedly due in part to the lower levels of participation of southern and of rural voters, who happen to be largely Protestant.

Finally, it should be stressed that the variables are not of equal importance. The best indicators of voting participation are those that reflect socioeconomic status: education, income, and occupation. And of these, education is clearly the most important (see Figure 4-6).

Citizens who show enthusiasm for voting and who participate regularly in elections can be distinguished by their psychological makeup as well as by their social and economic backgrounds. The prospect that

FIGURE 4-6   Education Levels and Participation of Voters in the 1984
Presidential Election

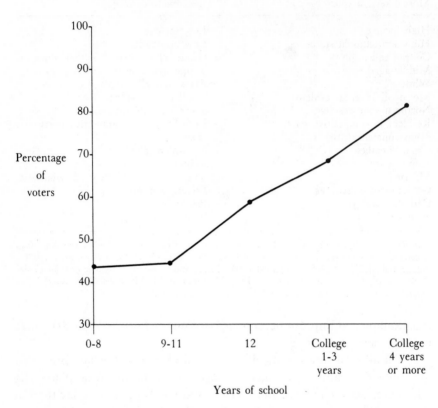

SOURCE: Data drawn from U.S. Bureau of the Census, *Statistical Abstract of the United States* (Washington, D.C.: U.S. Government Printing Office, 1986), 256.

persons will vote is clearly influenced by the intensity of their partisan preferences: the more substantial their commitments to a party, the stronger the probability that they will vote. Persons who have a strong partisan preference and who perceive the election as close are virtually certain to vote. Voters can also be distinguished by other indices of psychological involvement in political affairs. Survey research data show them to be more interested in campaigns and more concerned with election outcomes. They are also more likely than nonvoters to possess a strong sense of political efficacy; that is, a disposition to see their own participation in politics as important and effective. Finally, in contrast to nonvoters, voters are more likely to accept the norm that voting is a civic obligation. In sum, the evidence suggests that psychological involvement—marked by interest in elections, concern over their outcome, a sense of political efficacy, and a sense of citizen duty—increase the probability that a person will pay the costs in time and energy that voting requires.

Party Identification in the Electorate

Examining the distribution of party identification in the electorate from 1946 to 1986 is an interesting study in stability and change (see Figure 4-7). Throughout most of this forty-year period, the proportion of persons identifying themselves as Democrats remained stable. In the typical survey from 1950 to 1984, between 42 and 48 percent of the respondents identified themselves as Democrats, with the remainder reflecting changing divisions between Republicans and independents. At certain intervals during the 1960s and 1970s, Democratic identifiers outnumbered Republican identifiers by a margin of two-to-one.

Of greater interest are the changes that have occurred in party identification. According to Gallup polls, during the late 1970s only about 21 to 24 percent of the voters saw themselves as Republicans—the smallest proportion of Republican partisans since the first surveys were taken in 1940. The election of Ronald Reagan was followed by a sharp increase in the number of Republican partisans, reaching 35 percent in early 1985 (to the Democrats' 37 percent), before settling back to 32 percent in 1986 (to the Democrats' 39 percent). And of major significance, by the mid-1980s more younger voters (under thirty years of age) were claiming allegiance to the Republican party than to the Democratic.

An especially interesting change in partisan affiliation has occurred along racial lines. Since 1952 the commitment of black voters to the Democratic party has grown markedly. Current surveys disclose that about 70 to 75 percent of all blacks see themselves as Democrats, with independents outnumbering Republicans about two-to-one among the remainder. The overall growth in Republican identifiers in recent years is due almost entirely to a shift of white voters, particularly in the South. Thus it can be argued that the nation in reality has two electorates: "a white majority that is somewhat more Democratic than Republican . . . and a black minority that is overwhelmingly Democratic." [23] (Data revealing significant changes in party identification among groups are presented in Table 4-6.)

Perhaps no change in party identification is more important than the growth in the number of persons who perceive themselves as inde-

FIGURE 4-7 The Distribution of Party Identification in the Electorate, 1946-1986

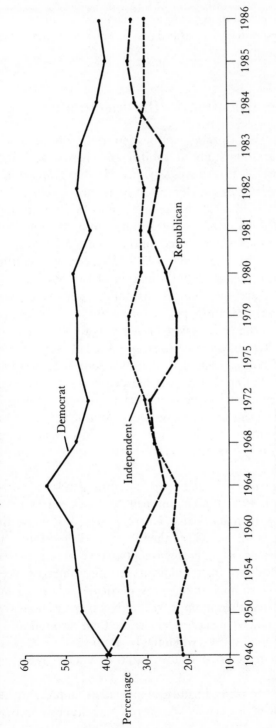

SOURCE: Developed from data in *Gallup Report*, July 1986, 21.

TABLE 4-6   Major Changes in Party Identification among Groups, from 1952 to 1985

	Party identification	
	1952	1985
White southern Protestants		
Democratic	66%	34%
Republican	17	41
White southerners		
Democratic	62	36
Republican	19	39
Blacks		
Democratic	55	73
Republican	20	10
Youth (18-21 years old)		
Democratic	40	30
Republican	25	40
White northern Catholics		
Democratic	48	38
Republican	23	30
Jews		
Democratic	52	48
Republican	13	22

SOURCE: Developed from data in *Public Opinion,* October/November 1985, 21-31.

pendents.[24] In 1940 one out of five persons was classified as an independent; currently the proportion is almost one out of three. The outcomes of recent elections confirm that independents have been at the center of American elections, holding the balance of power between the major parties. Republican presidents in particular have benefited from their support.

Declining partisanship appears throughout the electorate. The loyalty of older voters to the parties is not as firm as in the past. Of greater significance, many younger voters who entered the electorate as partisans have deserted their parties in favor of independence. But the most important factor in partisan dealignment has been the entry of new voters with low levels of partisanship. The new voters and the younger voters who have abandoned their partisan ties, one study shows, account for about 75 percent of the decline in partisanship in the electorate.[25] In sum, the broad picture is one of younger persons who are less partisan than their parents and hence more volatile in their voting behavior. As these younger voters succeed older ones, Kent Jennings and Gregory Markus observe, "the role of political parties in mass politics may be substantially redefined." [26]

The Voting Behavior of Independents . . .

	1952		1956		1960		1964	
	D	R	D	R	D	R	D	R
National vote	45%	55%	42%	58%	50.1%	49.9%	61%	39%
Independents	36	65	30	70	43	57	56	44

SOURCE: Developed from data in *Gallup Report,* November 1984, 8-9.

The American public is composed of partisans, independents, and apoliticals. The number of independents has grown significantly in recent decades. All candidates and political analysts take them seriously today, and much more is known about their behavior:

Independents are a varied lot. They are not simply civic misfits who reside on the outskirts of politics, as they have sometimes been portrayed. Like other citizens, independents are both attentive and inattentive to politics, involved in elections and indifferent to them, well informed and uninformed, ideological and nonideological. There are "pure" independents, whose voting behavior is especially volatile, and "leaners," who tilt toward one party or the other and whose voting behavior resembles that of partisans. Typically, about one-third of the electorate classifies itself as independent, with leaners much more numerous than the pure variety. Whites are twice as likely to be independents as blacks.

Independents like winners, independents produce winners, or both. In seven of the nine presidential elections between 1952 and 1984, independents voted on the side of the winner and contributed substan-

The Significance of Party Identification

The distribution of underlying partisan loyalties in the electorate is plainly an advantage for the Democratic party. Over most of the last four decades, the Democratic party has launched each national campaign with at least 60 percent of all partisans affiliated in one degree or another with it. When the party has received relatively strong support from those who identify themselves as Democrats and made a reasonably good showing among independents, it has won. The Republican party has faced a more formidable task. It has had to hold its own partisans, carry a major share of the independents, and attract a significant number of Democrats. One factor that has helped Republicans to win is that the turnout rate of Democratic partisans is always lower than that of

... in Presidential Elections, 1952-1984

1968		1972		1976		1980		1984	
D	R	D	R	D	R	D	R	D	R
43.0%	43.4%	38%	62%	50%	48%	41%	51%	41%	59%
31	44	31	69	38	57	29	55	33	67

NOTE: D = Democrat; R = Republican.

tially to these victories. But in 1960 independents voted decisively for Nixon over Kennedy, and in 1976, decisively for Ford over Carter.

When the nation has favored a Republican candidate for president (and with no third party or independent candidates in the race), independents have voted for him emphatically—averaging about 8 percent more Republican than the national average (elections of 1952, 1956, 1972, 1980, and 1984). "Hidden" Republicans among self-identified independents are apparently more numerous than "hidden" Democrats. A majority of independents supported the Democratic presidential nominee only once (1964) between 1952 and 1984.

Independents are more likely than partisans to vote for a nonmajor party candidate. In 1968 25 percent of all independents voted for George C. Wallace, presidential candidate of the American Independent party. In 1980 14 percent of independents voted for the self-styled independent candidate, John B. Anderson, a former Republican representative from Illinois who began his presidential quest in Republican presidential primaries.

Republicans.[27]

Despite its electoral disadvantage, the Republican party has done remarkably well in presidential elections, beginning with the election of Dwight D. Eisenhower in 1952. In 1956 one out of four Democrats and three out of four independents joined a united Republican party to reelect Eisenhower by a comfortable margin. Following the Kennedy and Johnson interlude, Republicans again captured the presidency with Richard Nixon's narrow victory in 1968 and his decisive reelection in 1972. The predictive value of party identification suffered again in the presidential elections of 1980 and 1984, each won easily by Ronald Reagan despite the Democrats' superior position among party identifiers. The Republican party has won six out of the last nine presidential elections and four out of the last five.

Straight- and Split-Ticket Voters

Most likely to vote straight ticket		Most likely to vote split ticket	
Voters	Percent	Voters	Percent
Blacks	69	Independents	76
Income under $10,000	59	Age 18-24 years	66
Nonlabor force	57	Income $20,000-$29,999	63
Grade school education	55	Professional and business	62
Democrats	54	Income $40,000 and over	61
Age 25-29 years	49	Age 50-64 years	60
Southerners	48	College graduates	59
Age 30-49 years	47	Midwesterners	58
Easterners	46	Westerners	58
Republicans	46	Whites	57
Protestants	46	Income $30,000-$39,999	57
National average	43	National average	54

SOURCE: Developed from data in *Gallup Report,* November 1984, 14.

In three respects, party identification is less important today than it was two or three decades ago. First, fewer persons now choose to identify with a party. During the 1950s and early 1960s, nearly 80 percent of all persons classified themselves as either Democrats or Republicans. During the 1980s, the proportion has hovered around 70 or 71 percent. Second, the proportion of strong party identifiers has declined, particularly in the Democratic party. For white voters during the 1950s and early 1960s, the percentage of strong Democrats ranged between 20 and 26 percent; the high point for this group during the 1980s was only 16 percent. Strong Republicans are somewhat less numerous today (11 to 14 percent in the 1980s) than in the 1950s and early 1960s (12 to 17 percent). Only about one-third of all voters now profess to be strong, rain-or-shine partisans. And third, the influence of party identification on voting is less pronounced today than earlier, though it is by no means inconsequential. (Party loyalties clearly influenced the vote for president in 1984, especially in the case of (white) strong Democrats and strong Republicans—88 percent Democratic, 98 percent Republican, respectively.)[28]

Although party identification is less significant today in explaining voter decisions, it is nevertheless an important factor in voting and in other respects.[29] First, party identification continues to be the best single explanation for the vote decision on candidates, and particularly for

Split-Ticket Voting and Split-Party Victories

A major result of declining partisanship in American politics is split-ticket voting and split-party victories.

Year	Number of states electing governor and senator at same time	Number of states electing governor and senator of different parties	Percentage of split victories
1950	19	3	16
1952	20	6	30
1954	25	5	20
1970	23	11	48
1972	12	6	50
1974	26	11	42
1976	10	3	30
1978	24	10	42
1980	9	5	56
1982	22	6	27
1984	7	3	43
1986	26	11	42

SOURCE: Data drawn from Richard M. Scammon, ed., *America Votes 1* (New York: Macmillan, 1956); and various issues of *Congressional Quarterly Weekly Report.*

offices less visible than the presidency. The ability of the Democratic party to win congressional elections year in and year out is due in no small degree to its dominant position in party affiliation. Party identification generally plays a bigger role in congressional elections than in presidential; typically, between 70 and 80 percent of party identifiers vote for the congressional candidate of their party.[30] Second, party loyalty is closely associated with political involvement. Strong partisans are more likely than weak partisans or independents to be interested in political campaigns, to vote, and to express concern over election outcomes. Third, and most important, despite the overall decline in party identification, it continues to be salient for a great many voters, serving to orient them to candidates, issues, and political events and to simplify and order their electoral choices.[31]

Party Identification and National Election Outcomes

Traditionally, presidential elections have been classified in broad contour by examining the relationship between election outcomes and the pattern of party loyalties present in the electorate. Three basic types of elections have been identified: *maintaining, deviating,* and *realigning.*[32] A maintaining election is described as one in which the pattern of party attachments in the electorate fixes the outcome; the winning party owes its victory to the fact that more voters identify with it than with any other party. A deviating election, by contrast, is one in which existing party loyalties are temporarily displaced by short-term forces, enabling the minority (or second) party to win the presidency. In a realigning election the majority party in the electorate not only loses the election but also finds that many of its previous supporters have abandoned their loyalties and moved into the ranks of the other party. So fundamental is the transformation of partisan affiliation that the second party becomes the majority party.

From a historical perspective, the most common form of presidential election has been that in which the party dominant in the electorate wins the presidency—that is, a maintaining election. The dynamics of a maintaining election are furnished by the majority party; the minority party loses because it has been unable to develop either issues or candidates sufficiently attractive to upset the prevailing pattern of party affiliation. Most of the Republican victories during the last half of the nineteenth century and the first quarter of the twentieth century would be classified as maintaining elections. Recent elections of this type occurred in 1948, 1960, 1964, and 1976. The 1976 election is of special interest. After a period of party decline, party identification assumed much of its earlier importance, as a significantly larger proportion of party identifiers cast votes in accordance with their partisan predispositions. As Warren E. Miller and Teresa E. Levitan observed, "the 1976 election was as much a party election as those elections from the 1950s or early 1960s in which party was acknowledged to be a major determinant of voters' decisions." [33]

Deviating elections are those in which the party that occupies minority status in terms of electoral preferences wins the presidential office. Although the Republicans held an electoral majority in the early twentieth century, Democrat Woodrow Wilson was twice elected president—in 1912, when the Republican party was split between Theodore Roosevelt and William Howard Taft, and in 1916, when Wilson's incumbency and the war issue were sufficient to give him a slight edge. More recent examples are the elections of 1952, 1956, 1968, 1972, 1980, and 1984. Both victories of Dwight D. Eisenhower in the 1950s were achieved in the face of heavy Democratic majorities in the electorate, as were Richard Nixon's victories in 1968 and 1972. And Ronald Reagan won decisive victories in 1980 and 1984 despite Democratic dominance in party identification—a pronounced advantage in 1980 and a marginal advantage in 1984. Despite the appeal of the minority party's presidential candidate, the coattail effect rarely has been strong enough to give the candidate's party control of Congress. Hence, deviating elections are likely to result in control of the presidency by one party and control of Congress by the other.

The familiar terrain of American politics is sharply changed as a result of realigning elections. Large numbers of voters move out of the majority party and into the minority party, switching not only their vote but their party allegiance. Major changes in public policy are likely to result.[34] The most recent examples of realigning elections are those of 1896 and 1932. In the former, a great many Democrats left their party following the financial panic of 1893, voted for William McKinley in 1896, and became part of the strong Republican majority that dominated the country until 1932. An even sharper upheaval in the electorate occurred in the election of 1932, when the normal Republican majority collapsed as a result of the Great Depression. Franklin D. Roosevelt was swept into office, and millions of Republicans shifted into the ranks of the Democratic party. And even more important, the new voters entering the electorate during the realignment era were predominantly Democratic.[35]

Based on party identification, the categories of elections currently are less useful in analyzing presidential elections than they are in analyzing congressional and subnational elections. In the first place, for many voters party identification has lost its saliency, and this is especially true in presidential elections. It is not at all unusual for one-third of the partisans to abandon their party to vote for the presidential candidate of the other party (elections of 1964, 1972, and 1980).[36] In fact, when less than 20 percent of the Democrats defect in presidential elections, as in 1976, it is something of a surprise. And second, voters' evaluations of presidential candidates have increasingly focused on "personality" characteristics rather than on parties or issues. Thus in judging presidential contenders, a recent study suggests, many people use broad categories, assessing candidates in terms of *competence* (political experience, ability, intelligence), *integrity* (honesty, sincerity, trustworthiness), *reliability* (dependable, hardworking, decisive), *charisma* (leadership, dignity, ability to communicate and inspire), and *personal features* (age, health, smile, religion, and the like). By far the most important of these dimensions is competence, followed by integrity and reliability.[37] For voters who use the personality mode of organizing information about candidates, in the process of making assessments of them, party identification is obviously of slight significance.

Voting in presidential and other elections can also be examined in terms of *prospective* and *retrospective* perspectives. In prospective voting, voters consider the platforms, policy positions, and promises of the candidates and seek to assess which one is closest to their own view of what is important and what should be done, and vote accordingly. In retrospective voting, a less demanding form of evaluation, voters simply judge how well things have been going—how well the party or incumbent has done in the past—and vote accordingly. Incumbents (or the parties or both) are rewarded if they have been successful and punished if they have been unsuccessful. Thus Jimmy Carter was defeated in 1980 primarily because voters evaluated his performance as largely unsatisfactory.[38] Ronald Reagan was reelected in 1984 primarily because of positive retrospective evaluations of his administration. The evidence is persuasive that retrospective voting has played a major role in all recent presidential elections. Interestingly, partisanship is closely related to restrospective evaluations.[39]

The Voting Behavior of Social Groups

The role of social groups needs to be examined in explaining the behavior of the American electorate. It has long been known that the voting behavior of individuals is influenced not only by their personal values[40] and predilections but also by their affiliations with social groups.[41]

The most important conclusion to be drawn from a study of the relationships between social categories and voting behavior in the six presidential elections between 1964 and 1984 is that each party has enjoyed a set of relatively loyal followings within the electorate—at least until recently (see Table 4-7). In most elections since the advent of the New Deal, the Democratic party has received strong, sometimes overwhelming, support from the poor, members of the working class, union households, blacks, Catholics, Jews, voters with limited formal education, central-city voters, and younger voters. In contrast, the Republican party has received disproportionate support from the nonpoor, nonunion families, whites, Protestants, voters with college educations and professional and business backgrounds, white-collar workers, older voters, and voters from outside central cities.[42] These party-group linkages have contributed to the stability of the political system.

TABLE 4-7 Vote by Groups in Presidential Elections, 1964-1984

	1964		1968			1972		1976		1980			1984	
	D	R	D	R	Wallace	D	R	D	R	D	R	Anderson	D	R
National	61.3%	38.7%	43.0%	43.4%	13.6%	38%	62%	50%	48%	41%	51%	7%	41%	59%
Men	60	40	41	43	16	37	63	53	45	38	53	7	36	64
Women	62	38	45	43	12	38	62	48	51	44	49	6	45	55
White	59	41	38	47	15	32	68	46	52	36	56	7	34	66
Nonwhite	94	6	85	12	3	87	13	85	15	86	10	2	87	13
College	52	48	37	54	9	37	63	42	55	35	53	10	39	61
High school	62	38	42	43	15	34	66	54	46	43	51	5	43	57
Grade school	66	34	52	33	15	49	51	58	41	54	42	3	51	49
Professional and business	54	46	34	56	10	31	69	42	56	33	55	10	34	66
White collar	57	43	41	47	12	36	64	50	48	40	51	9	47	53
Manual	71	29	50	35	15	43	57	58	41	48	46	5	46	54
Farmers	53	47	29	51	20	—	—	—	—	—	—	—	—	—
Under age 30	64	36	47	38	15	48	52	53	45	47	41	11	40	60
30-49 years	63	37	44	41	15	33	67	48	49	38	52	8	40	60
50 years and older	59	41	41	47	12	36	64	52	48	41	54	4	41	59
Protestant	55	45	35	49	16	30	70	46	53	39	54	6	39	61
Catholic	76	24	59	33	8	48	52	57	42	46	47	6	39	61
Republicans	20	80	9	86	5	5	95	9	91	8	86	5	4	96
Democrats	87	13	74	12	14	67	33	82	18	69	26	4	79	21
Independents	56	44	31	44	25	31	69	38	57	29	55	14	33	67
East	68	32	50	43	7	42	58	51	47	43	47	9	46	54
Midwest	61	39	44	47	9	40	60	48	50	41	51	7	42	58
South	52	48	31	36	33	29	71	54	45	44	52	3	37	63
West	60	40	44	49	7	41	59	46	51	35	54	9	40	60
Members of labor union families	73	27	56	29	15	46	54	63	36	50	43	5	52	48

SOURCE: *Gallup Report*, November 1984, 12-13.

NOTE: D = Democrat; R = Republican.

But change is in the air. The Democrat's majority status in the electorate is much less imposing. Republican support among younger voters has surged. Independents are numerous. Split-ticket voting is widespread. An extraordinary number of voters ignore elections altogether. And the Democrats' hold over the groups composing the New Deal coalition has eased substantially.[43] In the presidential elections of the 1980s, blue-collar workers, members of labor union families, and Catholics became more supportive of the Republican party. The shift of white southerners to the Republican party, beginning earlier, has been nothing short of spectacular.[44] Of course the extent to which these changes will endure in the post-Reagan era remains to be seen, but it seems altogether unlikely that the traditional Democratic majority coalition can be restored intact.

Both loyalties and group ties to the parties have weakened, particularly in presidential elections. Longstanding religious, regional, and class differences between the parties have lost their vitality or vanished. Political affiliation for many voters is casual at best, and for some, simply irrelevant. An electorate characterized by stable, deep-rooted party loyalties no longer exists. Whatever else may be said about these conditions, they are fully consistent with a period of party dealignment and electoral volatility.

What do these changes mean for the future of American politics and parties? Is the nation now in the early stages of a critical realignment that will culminate in a major transformation of the party system and a period of sustained Republican dominance? Or is the present condition merely a state of dealignment that itself might persist on a long-term basis (and thus not necessarily serve as a precursor to a new and durable partisan alignment)?

These are hard questions to answer. But several general observations can be made. First, scholars themselves do not agree on the answers to these questions;[45] nor do politicians. Second, it helps to remember that "we cannot be sure realignment has occurred until after it has ended." [46] Third, although the Republican party has thoroughly dominated recent presidential elections, it has not been able to capture the House or to retain control of the Senate (which it won in 1980 and lost in 1986). And clearly of most importance, it thus far has not made solid gains at the state and local levels. Most of the governorships won by Republicans in 1986 were open seats. At the state legislative level in 1986, Democrats continued their dominance. In 1987 Democrats controlled more than twice as many state governments (both executive and legislative branches) as the Republicans. But the real "winner," as usual, in a

Group Basis of the 1986 Congressional Vote

The data presented below reflects the behavior of traditional party groups, groups worth noticing, and groups that significantly exceeded the national average in support of Democratic or Republican 1986 House candidates. The 1986 congressional vote was not a carbon copy of the 1984 presidential vote.

| | Democratic | | | Republican | |
Group	Percent Democratic	Percent more Democratic than national average	Group	Percent Republican	Percent more Republican than national average
Blacks	86	34	White Funda-		
Hispanics	75	23	mentalist or		
Jews	70	18	Evangelical		
Unemployed	63	11	Christian	69	21
Union			White		
household	63	11	Protestants	57	9
Government			High income[a]	53	5
employees	62	10	First-time		
Southerners	56	4	voters	51	3
Low income[a]	56	4	Whites	51	3
Catholics	55	3	Professionals		
Blue-collar			or managers	50	2
workers	55	3			

SOURCE: Developed from *New York Times*/CBS exit poll data in 1986, as reported in *American Political Science Association Legislative Studies Newsletter* (November-December 1986), 42-43.

NOTE: Democratic national average was 52%; Republican national average, 48%.

[a] Low income: under $12,500; high income: over $50,000.

period of electoral party decomposition, was divided party government—the governorship and the legislative chambers split between the parties, a condition present in six out of ten states in 1987 (see Table 2-1).

What the Republican party has demonstrated convincingly in the last two decades is that, in presidential voting, it stands a good chance of winning, irrespective of its minority position in the electorate.[47] But it has not become the nation's majority party, either by virtue of its lopsided victories in 1980 and 1984 or by virtue of a critical alignment. And it has not gained a lock on the presidency. No durable voting alignment exists in a politics largely without omen. Probably the best

Change and Continuity . . .

More than 92 million individuals cast ballots in the 1984 presidential election. Their voting decisions were influenced by their independent judgments, political party affiliation, and membership in various groups.

The most important factor in voter decisions is political party affiliation. Although the impact of party identification on voting behavior is clearly less significant today than it was several decades ago, it is nevertheless true that about two out of three Americans still hold attachments to the Democratic or Republican parties. The great majority of these partisans vote in keeping with their identification. Party has declined but not disappeared in the voting calculus.

Group membership historically has also had a major effect on voting. Each party has been distinguished by group-based loyalties. The Republican party has carried special appeal for upper-income groups, while the Democratic party has appealed to the relatively disadvantaged in the process of assembling a coalition of minorities. Today, these loyalties are in flux. The accompanying graphs reflect the voting behavior of key groups in the Democratic and Republican coalitions over the last forty years. As a vote predictor, group membership, like party identification, is less reliable than in the past.

Social class does not explain much about voting behavior in the presidential elections of the current era. Voters from the ranks of the professions and business do not vote much more Republican than the national Republican average, while manual workers are less committed to the Democratic party.

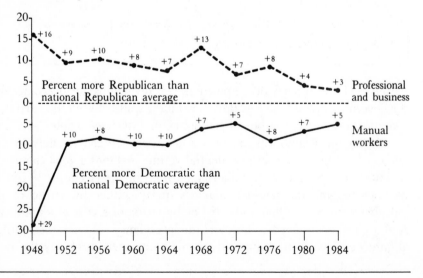

... in Voting Behavior

Nor does Catholic or Protestant religious affiliation. The voting behavior of Catholics and Protestants is becoming increasingly similar; Catholics much less Democratic in their preference, Protestants somewhat less Republican.

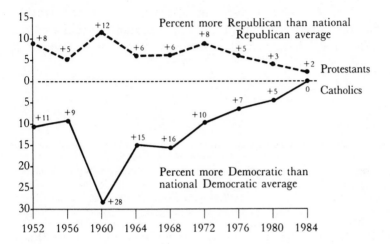

But blacks and Jews continue to have a distinct preference for Democratic presidential candidates.

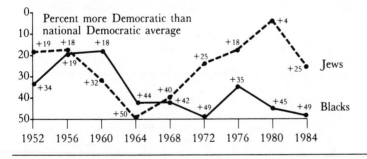

SOURCE: Calculated from data in *Gallup Report,* November, 1984, 7; *New York Times*/CBS News poll, as reported in *New York Times,* November 8, 1984. For social class vote in 1948, see Robert R. Alford, *Party and Society* (Chicago: Rand McNally, 1963), 352. Data on Jewish vote, for 1952-1968, drawn from Mark R. Levy and Michael S. Kramer, *The Ethnic Factor* (New York: Simon and Schuster, 1972), 103; for 1972-1980, Robert J. Huckshorn, *Political Parties in America* (Monterey, Calif.: Brooks/Cole, 1984), 214; for 1984, *New York Times*/CBS News poll.

NOTE: In 1980 14% of the Jewish vote was cast for John B. Anderson.

guess about the future, or at least the near future, is for a continuation of dealignment—marked by loose ties between the public and the parties, voter ambivalence, and voting behavior that reflects ticket-splitting, a preference for incumbents in legislative elections, and an inclination to switch parties at the drop of a hat. Faithful to this pattern, voting decisions are likely to be heavily influenced by voter inferences concerning presidential candidates' qualities (competence, integrity, and reliability in particular) and their retrospective appraisals of the performance and success of presidents, administrations, and parties in promoting the nation's well-being. Nothing in this picture suggests the emergence of tidy and predictable politics.

Notes

1. Among the studies that can be consulted on the meaning of modest rates of turnout are the following: E. E. Schattschneider, *The Semisovereign People* (New York: Holt, Rinehart and Winston, 1975), especially Chapter 6; Heinz Eulau, "The Politics of Happiness," *Antioch Review* 16 (September 1956): 259-264; Arthur T. Hadley, *The Empty Polling Booth* (Englewood Cliffs, N.J.: Prentice-Hall, 1978); William H. Flanigan and Nancy H. Zingale, *Political Behavior of the American Electorate* (Boston: Allyn and Bacon, 1979), especially Chapter 1; and, of a different order, Everett Carll Ladd, Jr., *Where Have All the Voters Gone?* (New York: Norton, 1982).
2. Paul R. Abramson and William Claggett, "Race-Related Differences in Self-Reported and Validated Turnout in 1984," *Journal of Politics* 48 (May 1986): 413. The U.S. Bureau of the Census showed reported turnout in 1984 to be 59.9 percent, nearly 7 percent higher than the actual turnout.
3. The explanation for this is well known: often the only significant choice among candidates available to southern voters is to be found in Democratic primaries. As the Republican party gains competitive strength in the South, participation in general elections is virtually certain to increase.
4. Patrick J. Kenney, "Explaining Primary Turnout: The Senatorial Case," *Legislative Studies Quarterly* 11 (February 1986): 65-73. Also see Malcolm E. Jewell, "Northern State Gubernatorial Primary Elections: Explaining Voter Turnout," *American Politics Quarterly* 12 (January 1984): 101-116, and Malcolm E. Jewell and David M. Olson, *American State Political Parties and Elections* (Homewood, Ill.: Dorsey Press, 1982). For evidence that perceived closeness of an election is not an independent variable in influencing turnout, see Kenneth D. Wald, "The Closeness-Turnout Hypothesis: A Reconsideration," *American Politics Quarterly* 13 (July 1985): 273-296. Also see several studies that deal with the question of whether election night forecasts decrease turnout: Raymond E. Wolfinger and Peter Linquiti, "Tuning In and Tuning Out," *Public Opinion* 4 (February/March 1981): 56-60; John E. Jackson, "Election Night Reporting and Voter Turnout," *American Journal of Political Science* 27 (November 1983): 615-635; and Michael X. Delli Carpini, "Scooping the Voters?: The Consequences of the Networks' Early Call of the 1980 Presidential Race," *Journal of Politics* 46 (August 1984): 866-885.
5. The white primary in southern states resulted from the exclusion of blacks from

membership in the Democratic party, which was held to be a "private" organization. Since the real election at this time in most southern states occurred in the Democratic primaries, there was little opportunity for blacks to make their influence felt. After many years of litigation, the Supreme Court in 1944 held that the white primary was in violation of the Fifteenth Amendment. The Court's position in *Smith v. Allwright* was that the primary is an integral part of the election process and that political parties are engaged in a public, not a private, function in holding primary elections. After the white primary was held unconstitutional, southern states turned to the development of literacy and understanding tests, along with discriminatory registration systems, to bar black access to the polls.

6. From *The Semisovereign People* by E. E. Schattschneider. Copyright © 1975 by E. E. Schattschneider. Reprinted by permission of Holt, Rinehart and Winston, 78-80.

7. Schattschneider, *The Semisovereign People*, 84.

8. Steven J. Rosenstone and Raymond E. Wolfinger, "The Effect of Registration Laws on Voter Turnout," *American Political Science Review* 72 (March 1978): especially 25-30. The most facilitative laws on closing dates, apart from North Dakota, which requires no registration, are those of Idaho and Vermont. Voters in these states may register up to three days before the election. Maine provides for eight days and New Hampshire for nine.

9. Rosenstone and Wolfinger, "The Effect of Registration Laws on Voter Turnout," 31-36.

10. See an article by Stephen D. Shaffer, "A Multivariate Explanation of Decreasing Turnout in Presidential Elections, 1960-1976," *American Journal of Political Science* 25 (February 1981): 68-93.

11. But see a study that shows that persons who have low levels of trust in government vote at about the same level as those persons who have high trust in government. Jack Citrin, "Comment: The Political Relevance of Trust in Government," *American Political Science Review* 68 (September 1974): 973-988.

12. See Paul R. Abramson and John H. Aldrich, "The Decline of Electoral Participation in America," *American Political Science Review* 76 (September 1982): 502-521.

13. Abramson and Aldrich, "The Decline of Electoral Participation in America," 504-510, and Shaffer, "A Multivariate Explanation of Decreasing Turnout in Presidential Elections, 1960-1976," 68-93. Also see James DeNardo, "Turnout and the Vote: The Joke's on the Democrats," *American Political Science Review* 74 (June 1980): 406-420; and Harvey J. Tucker, Arnold Vedlitz, and James DeNardo, "Does Heavy Turnout Help Democrats in Presidential Elections?" *American Political Science Review* 80 (December 1986): 1291-1304.

14. For a study that finds alienation to be a major factor in nonvoting, see Priscilla L. Southwell, "Alienation and Nonvoting in the United States: A Refined Operationalization," *Western Political Quarterly* 38 (December 1985): 663-674.

15. Richard A. Brody, "The Puzzle of Political Participation in America," in *The New American Political System*, ed. Anthony King (Washington, D.C.: American Enterprise Institute for Public Policy Research, 1978), 306.

16. G. Bingham Powell, Jr., "American Voter Turnout in Comparative Perspective," *American Political Science Review* 80 (March 1986): 17-43.

17. Actual turnout is clearly lower than the voting percentages reported in Table 4-1. Survey respondents sometimes forget whether or not they voted or else

exaggerate their participation.

18. The findings of these paragraphs are drawn from Sidney Verba and Norman H. Nie, *Participation in America: Political Democracy and Social Equality* (New York: Harper and Row, 1972), 25-43.

19. Lester W. Milbrath, *Political Participation* (Chicago: Rand McNally, 1965), 17-21. The holding that political participation involves a hierarchy of political acts—under which the citizen who performs a difficult political act, such as forming an organization to solve a local community problem, is virtually certain to perform less demanding acts—can be overstated. See Verba and Nie, *Participation in America,* especially Chapters 2 and 3. Their general position is that "the citizenry is not divided simply into more or less active citizens. Rather there are many types of activists engaging in different acts, with different motives, and different consequences." Quotation on p. 45.

20. See Verba and Nie, *Participation in America,* 133-137.

21. Milbrath, *Political Participation,* 43-44.

22. See Hadley, *The Empty Polling Booth,* especially Chapter 1.

23. Paul R. Abramson, John H. Aldrich, and David W. Rohde, *Change and Continuity in the 1984 Elections* (Washington, D.C.: CQ Press, 1986), 214.

24. For a view that strengthened partisanship within the electorate depends on convincing people that the two parties are different in policy orientations and that these differences affect peoples' well-being, see Patrick R. Cotter, "The Decline of Partisanship: A Test of Four Explanations," *American Politics Quarterly* 13 (January 1985): 51-78.

25. Helmut Norpoth and Jerrold G. Rusk, "Partisan Dealignment in the American Electorate: Itemizing the Deductions since 1964," *American Political Science Review* 76 (September 1982): 522-537.

26. M. Kent Jennings and Gregory B. Markus, "Partisan Orientations over the Long Haul: Results from the Three-Wave Political Socialization Panel Study," *American Political Science Review* 78 (December 1984): 1000-1018 (quotation on p. 1016). See an analysis of young adults that suggests that they are active in adjusting their partisan affiliation to coincide with their views on preferred policies: Charles H. Franklin, "Issue Preferences, Socialization, and the Evolution of Party Identification," *American Journal of Political Science* 28 (August 1984): 459-478.

27. A disposition to participate in elections is related to high interest, information, and involvement. The Democratic vote regularly suffers because citizens who might be expected to vote Democratic—those in the lower socioeconomic strata—are often not sufficiently interested or involved in the election to turn out on election day.

28. The data for this paragraph are drawn from Abramson, Aldrich, and Rohde, *Change and Continuity in the 1984 Elections,* 211-215.

29. For evidence on the significance of party identification for different offices over time, see Stephen D. Shaffer, "Voting in Four Elective Offices: A Comparative Analysis," *American Politics Quarterly* 10 (January 1982): 5-30.

30. Norman J. Ornstein, Thomas E. Mann, Michael J. Malbin, Allen Schick, and John F. Bibby, *Vital Statistics on Congress, 1984-1985 Edition* (Washington, D.C.: American Enterprise Institute for Public Policy Research, 1984), 59. As a result of its ascendant position in the House of Representatives, the Democratic party also benefits heavily from the voters' preference for incumbents.

31. See a study that finds that the American electorate is changing in three significant ways: becoming more "ideologically constrained and sophisticated," more rational in behavior, and less stable in its behavior (or consistent in its support of parties). Michael X. Delli Carpini, "Political Distallation: The

Changing Impact of Partisanship on Electoral Behavior," *American Politics Quarterly* 11 (April 1983): 163-180.

32. Angus Campbell, Philip E. Converse, Warren E. Miller, and Donald E. Stokes, *The American Voter* (New York: Wiley, 1960), 531-538.

33. Warren E. Miller and Teresa E. Levitan, *Leadership and Change: Presidential Elections from 1952 to 1976* (Cambridge, Mass.: Winthrop, 1976), 211.

34. The major effect of a realignment, David W. Brady argues, is the creation of a unified majority party in Congress that is capable of bringing about significant changes in public policy. See David W. Brady, "A Reevaluation of Realignments in American Politics: Evidence from the House of Representatives," *American Political Science Review* 79 (March 1985): 28-49; David W. Brady and Joseph Stewart, Jr., "Congressional Party Realignment and Transformations of Public Policy in Three Realignment Eras," *American Journal of Political Science* 26 (May 1982): 333-360; and Barbara Sinclair, "Party Realignment and the Transformation of the Political Agenda: The House of Representatives, 1925-1938," *American Political Science Review* 71 (September 1977): 940-953.

35. James E. Campbell, "Sources of the New Deal Realignment: The Contributions of Conversion and Mobilization to Partisan Change," *Western Political Quarterly* 38 (September 1985): 357-376.

36. It is interesting to find that *partisan defectors* (those who identify with one party but vote for the other party's presidential candidate) are much more likely to cast a negative or anticandidate vote than persons who vote in keeping with their party identification. See Michael M. Gant and Lee Sigelman, "Anti-Candidate Voting in Presidential Elections," *Polity* 18 (Winter 1985): 329-339.

37. Arthur H. Miller, Martin P. Wattenberg, and Oksana Malanchuk, "Schematic Assessments of Presidential Candidates," *American Political Science Review* 80 (June 1986): 521-540. Interestingly, college-educated voters place particular emphasis on these characteristics. Party competence evaluations are also important in explaining the congressional vote. See Albert D. Cover, "Party Competence Evaluations and Voting for Congress," *Western Political Quarterly* 39 (June 1986): 304-312.

38. President Carter's relations with Congress were also unsatisfactory. See Charles O. Jones, "Keeping Faith and Losing Congress: The Carter Experience in Washington," *Presidential Studies Quarterly* 14 (Summer 1984): 437-445.

39. See the analysis and evidence of Abramson, Aldrich, and Rohde, *Change and Continuity in the 1984 Elections,* especially Chapters 6 and 7, and Morris P. Fiorina, *Retrospective Voting in American National Elections* (New Haven, Conn.: Yale University Press, 1981).

40. For an analysis of the importance of friends and family in influencing voter decisions, see John G. Geer, "Voting and the Social Environment," *American Politics Quarterly* 13 (January 1985): 3-27.

41. Studies of electoral behavior that bear too heavily on the group as the unit of analysis may do some injustice to the individual voter, making him appear as an object to be managed by skillful propagandists or as the victim of social determinants (for example, occupation, race, or education). Preoccupation with the gross characteristics of voters may lead the analyst to minimize the individual's awareness and concern over issues. V. O. Key, Jr., has argued that ". . . the electorate behaves about as rationally and responsibly as we should expect, given the clarity of the alternatives presented to it and the character of the information available to it." By and large, in Key's study, the American voter emerges as a rational and responsible person concerned about matters of public policy, governmental performance, and executive personality. See V. O.

Key, Jr., (with Milton C. Cummings), *The Responsible Electorate* (New York: Vintage Books, 1966), 7.

42. For an analysis of the characteristics of the Democratic and Republican party coalitions between 1952 and 1984, focusing on the importance of each group to the total party vote, see Robert Axelrod, "Presidential Election Coalitions in 1984," *American Political Science Review* 80 (March 1986): 281-284.

43. See an analysis of shifting group loyalties by Harold W. Stanley, William T. Bianco, and Richard G. Niemi, "Partisanship and Group Support Over Time: A Multivariate Analysis," *American Political Science Review* 80 (September 1986): 970-976. They conclude that "journalistic and party obituaries for the New Deal coalition appear harsher than the reality warrants. Native southern whites had a strong, prolonged decline in their incremental partisan impact, but the milder declines for most groups [such as Catholics and working-class members], coupled with the increases for females, Jews, and blacks, suggest the New Deal group basis of Democratic identification may not be dazzling, but is far from dead." (Quotation on p. 975.)

44. See the thesis of Edward G. Carmines and James A. Stimson that the rapid change in behavior of blacks and native southern whites in the mid-1960s constituted a *racial realignment*. "Racial Issues and the Structure of Mass Belief Systems," *Journal of Politics* 44 (February 1982): 2-20.

45. For instruction on the dealignment-realignment question, see James L. Sundquist, *Dynamics of the Party System: Alignment and Realignment of Political Parties in the United States* (Washington, D.C.: The Brookings Institution, 1983); Paul A. Beck, "The Dealignment Era in America," in *Electoral Change in Advanced Industrial Democracies: Realignment or Dealignment,* ed. Russell J. Dalton, Scott C. Flanagan, and Paul A. Beck (Princeton, N.J.: Princeton University Press, 1984), 240-266; Herbert B. Asher, *Presidential Elections and American Politics* (Homewood, Ill.: Dorsey Press, 1984), 281-302; Abramson, Aldrich, and Rohde, *Change and Continuity in the 1984 Elections,* 281-305; Theodore J. Lowi, "An Aligning Election, A Presidential Plebiscite," in *The Elections of 1984,* ed. Michael Nelson (Washington, D.C.: CQ Press, 1985), 277-301; Raymond E. Wolfinger, "Dealignment, Realignment, and Mandates in the 1984 Election," in *The American Elections of 1984,* ed. Austin Ranney (Durham, N.C.: Duke University Press, 1985), 277-296; John E. Chubb and Paul E. Peterson, "Realignment and Institutionalization," in *The New Direction in American Politics,* ed. John E. Chubb and Paul E. Peterson (Washington, D.C.: The Brookings Institution, 1985), 1-30; and Everett Carll Ladd, "On Mandates, Realignments, and the 1984 Presidential Election," *Political Science Quarterly* 100 (Spring 1985): 1-25.

46. Paul A. Beck, "Realignment Begins: The Republican Surge in Florida," *American Politics Quarterly* 10 (October 1982): 421-438 (quotation on p. 433).

47. The importance of Republican victories in presidential elections should not be exaggerated, writes Gerald M. Pomper. "It is possible that the presidency has now become completely nonpartisan, individualized and distinct from the general political system, so that elections for the chief executive have no larger import." "The Presidential Election," in *The Election of 1984: Reports and Interpretations,* ed. Gerald M. Pomper (Chatham, N.J.: Chatham House, 1985), 86.

c h a p t e r   f i v e

The Congressional Party and the Formation of Public Policy

THE TASKS that confront the American major party are formidably ambitious. From one perspective, the party is a wide-ranging electoral agency organized to make a credible bid for power. Here and there a party organization is so stunted and devitalized that it is seldom able to make an authentic effort to win office. Where it is not taken seriously, the party finds it difficult to develop and recruit candidates, to gain the attention of the media, and to attract financial contributors. Elections may go by default to the dominant party as the second party struggles merely to stay in business. But throughout most of the country the parties compete on fairly even terms—if not for certain offices or in certain districts, at least for some offices or in a state at large. Presidential elections, of course, are vigorously contested virtually everywhere. As electoral organizations, the parties recruit candidates, organize campaigns, develop issues, and mobilize voters. Typical voters get their best glimpse of the workings of party when they observe the "party in the electorate" during political campaigns.

From another perspective, the party is a collection of officeholders who share in some measure common values and policy orientations. In the broadest sense, its mission is to take hold of government, to identify national problems and priorities, and to work for their settlement or achievement. In a narrower sense, the task of the "party in the government" is to consolidate and fulfill promises made to the electorate during the campaign. How it is organized to do this and how it does it is the concern of this chapter. The focus centers on the party in Congress.

Congressional Elections

The two most important variables in the election of members of Congress are incumbency status and party affiliation. Congressional incumbents have numerous advantages in elections. The offices and staffs of members are basic units in their campaign organizations. Voters are much more likely to recognize the name of the incumbent than that of the challenger. Some voters will have benefited from the many services that members regularly perform for their constituents. The franking privilege permits members to send mail to their constituents at government expense. And of major importance, incumbents ordinarily find it much easier than challengers to raise campaign funds, particularly from the political action committees of interest groups. Thus, it is not surprising that incumbents are frequently reelected. Typically, more than 90 percent of all House incumbents seeking reelection are successful. In 1986 the number reached a record 98 percent. Although Senate incumbents usually face stronger competition, they also win much more often than they lose. In 1982 93 percent of the Senate incumbents on the general election ballot were reelected; in 1986 the proportion dropped to 75 percent.

Party affiliation is also a key factor in congressional elections. In the typical state there are districts that nearly always elect Democratic legislators and districts that nearly always elect Republican legislators. Some districts are so thoroughly dominated by one party that the second party has virtually no chance of winning. With few exceptions, for example, House districts in major cities are securely Democratic, irrespective of the incumbency factor. In other suburban, small-town, and rural districts Democratic candidates may face insurmountable odds in election after election.

Incumbency and party combine to yield a great many one-sided elections, especially in the House. Seventy percent of all House elections from 1970 to 1986 were won by margins of 60 percent or more (see Figure 5-1). By contrast, only 14 percent of all elections were marginal—that is, won by less than 55 percent of the vote. In 1986 an extraordinary 81 percent of all House elections were won by 60 percent or more of the vote.

Close elections sometimes carry large consequences for the parties and public policy. Increasingly, they have determined which party controls the Senate. In 1980 Republican senatorial candidates won nine of twelve Senate elections in which the winner received 52 percent or less of the vote, and in the process captured the Senate for the first time in more

FIGURE 5-1   Marginal and One-sided House Elections, 1970-1986

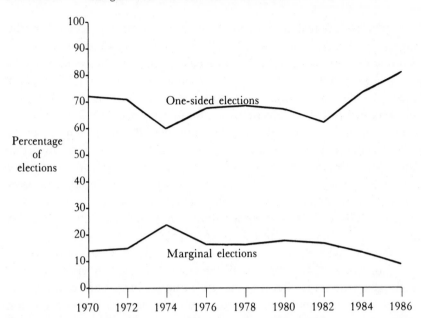

SOURCE: Developed from data in various issues of *Congressional Quarterly Weekly Report.*

NOTE: One-sided elections were won by 60 percent or more of the vote; marginal elections were won by less than 55 percent of the vote. All other elections fell in the 55-59.9 percent range.

than two decades. Some argue, with reason, that the "Reagan [policy] Revolution" turned on these Senate victories. In 1982 Republicans continued their Senate control by winning all six elections in which the winner gained 52 percent or less of the vote. From this set of very close elections in 1984, Democratic candidates won three of five. And in 1986 the Senate shifted back to Democratic control as Republican candidates lost nine of eleven races settled by a margin of 52 percent or less. The way the votes break is thus paramount. With a shift of only 28,000 votes in five states (Alabama, Colorado, Nevada, North Dakota, and South Dakota) the Republicans would have maintained control of the Senate for the last two years of the Reagan administration. Instead they suffered a spectacular loss.

On the whole, the level of competitiveness for congressional seats is not high. Safe seats abound, thus fostering a relatively stable membership. Exactly how public policy is thus affected is hard to say. Conventional wisdom holds that opportunities for major policy change are limited by a membership that remains largely intact election after election.

Party Representation in Congress

Two central conclusions emerge from a study of the parties in the congressional races from 1932 to 1986 (see Figures 5-2 and 5-3). First, with few exceptions since 1932, the Democratic party has held comfortable majorities in Congress. Second, the capacity of the Republican party to win presidential elections has not extended to Congress. The Republican party controlled the House by a slim margin from 1952 to 1954 and broke even in the Senate during the same period. Since then the party has controlled only the Senate—for six years during the Reagan presidency. Given the prevailing pattern of party allegiance in the electorate and the Democrats' continuing incumbency advantage, Republican presidents can expect to face Democratic majorities in one or both houses of Congress. The success of their legislative programs usually depends on their ability to develop effective biparty coalitions.

Party membership is a major factor not only in determining who is elected to Congress but also in influencing members' behavior once they have taken office. The fact that party cohesion collapses on certain issues that come before Congress does not alter the general proposition that party affiliation is a major explanation of voting behavior. Party cues are not taken lightly by most members. An examination of party voting follows an analysis of congressional party organization.

Party Organization in Congress

Party Conferences

The central agency of each party in each chamber is the conference or caucus. All those elected to Congress automatically become members of their party's caucus. During the early twentieth century, and particularly during the Wilson administration, the House majority party caucus was exceptionally powerful. Following World War I, disillusionment with the caucus became manifest, and members came to question the right of the caucus to bind them to a course of action. The power of the caucus declined sharply in the 1920s and soon its functions were limited to the selection of party leaders such as the Speaker of the House, the floor leaders, and the whips.

For all intents and purposes, the caucus was moribund for the next half century. In 1969, after years of somnolence, the Democratic caucus began to hold regular monthly meetings to examine proposals for reforming the House. In the early 1970s, the caucus made several modifi-

FIGURE 5-2   Democratic Strength in Senate Elections, 1932-1986

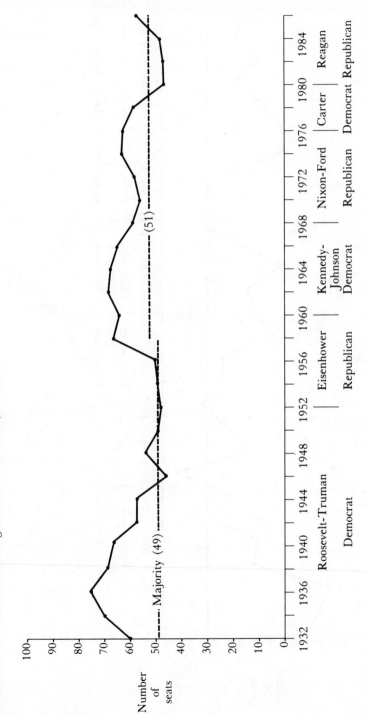

FIGURE 5-3 Democratic Strength in House Elections, 1932-1986

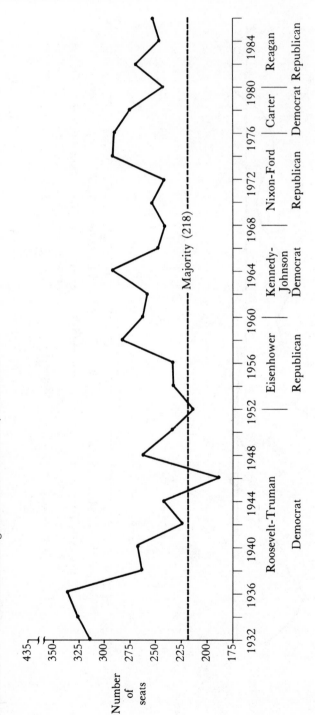
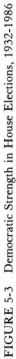

cations of the seniority system, the most important of which provided for secret ballots on nominees for committee chairmen. A Steering and Policy Committee was created by the caucus in 1973 to formulate legislative programs and to participate in the scheduling of legislation for floor consideration.

The power of the Democratic caucus was dramatically demonstrated at the opening of the Ninety-fourth Congress in 1975 when, among other things, the caucus voted to remove three committee chairmen from their positions, transferred to the Steering and Policy Committee the power to make committee assignments from the Democratic members of the Ways and Means Committee, and made a number of changes involving nominations and subcommittee procedures. Included in these changes was a provision to empower the Speaker, subject to caucus approval, to nominate the Democratic members of the powerful Rules Committee. The key test in filling vacancies on this committee now appears to be the member's allegiance to the Speaker. Major disciplinary action by the Democratic caucus occurred again at the start of the Ninety-eighth Congress (1983-1984). In an unusual action, the caucus voted to remove a Texas representative from the Budget Committee because he had worked closely with the administration in the design of President Reagan's budget strategy in the previous Congress.

The revitalization of the Democratic caucus has weakened the hold of the seniority system and strengthened the positions of party leaders, particularly the Speaker. But to what extent can the caucus influence the behavior of party members on major policy proposals? Caucus power collides with the nagging reality of all legislative politics: the individual member's electoral security, and thus his primary interest, lies in the constituency. For many members of the House, the attractions of a cohesive party are not nearly so great as the attractions of independence, with all the opportunities it affords the legislator to concentrate on constituency interests and problems. Party leaders and committee leaders, moreover, usually take a dim view of caucus involvement in policy questions. As Speaker Thomas P. "Tip" O'Neill, Jr., (1977-1986) observed: "I don't like any of these [policy] matters coming from the caucus on a direct vote." A similar view was expressed by Richard Bolling (D-Mo.) during his long tenure in the House: "I think [members] would have an awful time if they tried [to set party policy in the caucus]. It's better left to the committee system." [1] The cards are stacked against centralized power in any form. The independence of today's members makes a return to the earlier days when "King Caucus" reigned over the House all but impossible.

Party Leaders and Committees. . .

House Democrats

Party Leaders

Speaker
majority leader
majority whip
caucus chairman
caucus vice
  chairman
chief deputy whip
deputy whips
at-large whips

Party Committees

Steering and Policy: assigns Democratic members to committees and helps to develop party policy. Speaker serves as chairman, majority leader as vice chairman.

Democratic Congressional Campaign Committee: provides campaign support for Democratic House candidates.

Personnel Committee: supervises the party's patronage positions.

House Republicans

Party Leaders

minority leader
minority whip
conference chairman
conference vice
  chairman
conference secretary
chief deputy whip
deputy whips

Party Committees

Policy: helps to develop Republican policy positions.

Committee on Committees: assigns Republican members to committees.

National Republican Congressional Committee: provides campaign support for Republican House candidates.

Personnel Committee: supervises the party's patronage positions.

The Speaker of the House

The most powerful party leader in Congress is the Speaker of the House.[2] In the early twentieth century, the Speaker's powers were almost beyond limit, the House virtually his private domain. It is scarcely an exaggeration to say that legislation favored by the Speaker was adopted and that legislation opposed by him was defeated. The despotic rule of Speaker "Uncle Joe" Cannon eventually proved his undoing. A coalition of Democrats and rebellious Republicans was formed in 1910 to challenge the leadership of Cannon. After a struggle

---

... *in One-hundredth Congress (1987-1988)*

Senate Democrats

Party Leaders

president pro tempore
majority leader
majority whip
conference chairman
conference secretary
chief deputy whip
deputy whips

Party Committees

Policy: helps to develop party policy and advises on the scheduling of legislation. Majority leader serves as chairman.

Steering: assigns Democratic members to committees. Majority leader serves as chairman.

Legislative Review Committee: analyzes legislative proposals and makes recommendations.

Democratic Senatorial Campaign Committee: provides campaign support for Democratic Senate candidates.

Senate Republicans

Party Leaders

minority leader
assistant minority
    leader
conference chairman
conference secretary

Party Committees

Policy: helps to develop party policy and advises on the scheduling of legislation.

Committee on Committees: assigns Republican members to committees.

National Republican Senatorial Committee: provides campaign support for Republican Senate candidates.

---

of many months, it succeeded in instituting a number of rules changes to curb the Speaker's powers. He was removed from membership on the Rules Committee (of which he had been chairman), his power to appoint and remove members and chairmen of the standing committees was eliminated, and his power to recognize (or not to recognize) members was limited. Although the "revolution of 1910-1911" fundamentally altered the formal powers of the Speaker, it did not render the office impotent. Since then, a succession of Speakers—men disposed to negotiate rather than to command—has helped to rebuild the powers of the office. What a Speaker like Joseph G. Cannon (1903-1911) secured through autocratic rule, today's Speakers secure through persuasion and the astute exploitation of the bargaining advantages inherent in their positions.

Each Speaker leaves his imprint on the office. Changes in the times and in the character of politics also help to shape the speakership. Speaker Tip O'Neill once observed:

> Old Sam Rayburn [Speaker for seventeen years between 1940 and 1961] couldn't name 12 new members of Congress, and he was an institution that awed people. Only on the rarest of occasions could a Congressman get an appointment to see him. And when he called the Attorney General and said, "You be in my office at 3 in the afternoon," that Cabinet officer was there at 3 in the afternoon. Politics has changed. I have to deal in dialogue, in openness; if someone wants to see me, they see me. And of course they're highly independent now. You have to talk to people in the House, listen to them. The whole ethics question has changed. Years ago you'd think nothing of calling Internal Revenue and saying that this case has been kicking around for a couple of years, and it ought to be civil instead of criminal. You'd think nothing of calling a chairman of a committee and saying, "Put this projet in, put this dam in." Well, you can't do that now.[3]

The Speaker's formal powers are wide ranging, though not especially significant in themselves.[4] He is the presiding officer of the House, and in this capacity he announces the order of business, puts questions to a vote, refers bills to committees, rules on points of order, interprets the rules, recognizes members who desire the floor, and appoints members to select and conference committees. He also has the right to vote and enter floor debate. Ordinarily he exercises these rights only in the case of major, closely contested issues.

Although difficult to delineate with precision, the informal powers of the Speaker are far more impressive. As the foremost leader of his party in Congress, he is at the center of critical information and policy-making systems. No one is in a better position than the Speaker to obtain and disseminate information, to shape strategies, or to advance or frustrate the careers of members. Perhaps the principal "tangible preferment" the Speaker has at his disposal is the influence he can exert to secure favorable committee assignments for members of the majority party. Having the good will of the Speaker is important to members of his party anxious to move ahead in the House. The following analysis by Randall B. Ripley describes the structure of the Speaker's influence:

> His personal traits influence his ability to deal with members of his party. The one constant element is the importance of his showing trust

in and respect for individual members of his party. A smile or nod of the head from the Speaker can bolster a member's ego and lead him to seek further evidences of favor. Being out of favor hurts the individual's pride, and may be noticed by his colleagues. Most Speakers have had an instinct for knowing their loyal followers on legislative matters. Others have either kept records themselves or made frequent use of whip polls and official records to inform themselves about the relative loyalty of their members. Speakers have been able to convey critical information to members on a person-to-person basis, often with the help of the Parliamentarian. They have also encouraged their floor leaders and whip organizations to become collectors and purveyors of information on a larger scale. Particularly useful to a number of Speakers has been an informal gathering of intimates and friends of both parties to discuss the course of business in the House. Through such discussions, Speakers have been able to keep themselves informed of developments in the House and, at the same time, convey their desires to other members invited to attend.[5]

Another way of viewing the Speaker and other party officials is provided by Joseph Cooper and David W. Brady. Today's party leaders, they write, "function less as the commanders of a stable party majority and more as brokers trying to assemble particular majorities behind particular bills." [6]

The Floor Leaders

In addition to the Speaker of the House, the key figures in the congressional party organizations are the House and Senate floor leaders, who are chosen by party caucuses in their respective chambers. The floor leaders serve as the principal spokespersons for party positions and interests and as intermediaries in both intraparty and interparty negotiations. The floor leaders of the party that controls the presidency also serve as links between the president and his congressional party. Because floor leaders are obliged to play several roles at the same time—for example, representatives of both the congressional party and the president—it is not surprising that role conflicts develop. Serving the interests of their congressional party colleagues or perhaps those of their constituents is anything but a guarantee that they will be serving presidential interests.

Floor leaders have a potpourri of informal, middling powers. Their availability, however, does not ensure that they can lead their colleagues or strongly shape the legislative program. By and large, their influence is based on their willingness and talent to exploit these powers steadily and imaginatively in their relations with other members. They can, if they choose, (1) influence the allocation of committee assignments (not only rewarding individual members but also shaping the ideological makeup of the committees); (2) help members to advance legislation of particular interest to them; (3) assist members in securing larger appropriations for their committees or subcommittees; (4) play a major role in debate; (5) intercede with the president or executive agencies on behalf of members (perhaps to assist their efforts to secure a federal project in their state or district); (6) make important information available to members; (7) help members to secure campaign money from a congressional campaign committee or from the political action committee of an interest group; (8) campaign on behalf of individual members; and (9) focus the attention of the communications media on the contributions of members. Much of the influence of floor leaders, like that of the Speaker, is derived from informal powers, in particular from opportunities afforded them to advance or protect the careers of party colleagues. In solving problems for them and in making their positions more secure, floor leaders increase the prospects of gaining their support on critical questions. By the same token, floor leaders can in some measure hamper the careers of those members who continually refuse to go along with them. At the center of active floor leaders' powers is the capacity to manipulate rewards and punishments.

An important function and a major source of power for the majority floor leader, particularly in the Senate, is that of controlling the scheduling of bill consideration on the floor. In the House, the Rules Committee dominates the process of controlling the agenda. However pedestrian the scheduling function may sound, it is a surprisingly important source of power. The majority leader who fails to keep his lines of communication clear, who misjudges the sentiments of members, who neglects to consolidate his majority by winning over undecided members or by propping up wavering members, or who picks the wrong time to call up a bill, can easily go down to defeat. Prospective majorities are much more tenuous and much more easily upset than might be supposed. Support can be lost rapidly as a result of poor communications, missed opportunities for negotiation and compromise, and bad timing. The effective leader builds his power base by tending to the shop, by ordering priorities, by having a sense of detail that overlooks nothing, by taking account of the demands placed on members, by sensing the mood of congressional opinion (especially that of key members), and by exhibiting skill in splicing together the legislative elements necessary to fashion a majority.

The principal power of the floor leader is the power of persuasion.

As a former Democratic leader of the Senate, Lyndon Johnson, once observed, ". . . the only real power available to the leader is the power of persuasion. There is no patronage; no power to discipline; no authority to fire Senators like a President can fire his members of Cabinet." [7] Jim Wright (D-Texas), current Speaker and former majority leader, expressed a similar view of the leader's role: "The majority leader is a conciliator, a mediator, a peacemaker. Even when patching together a tenuous majority he must respect the right of honest dissent, conscious of the limits of his claims upon others." [8] And as a House Republican leader has observed: "Everyone has a different idea as to how the leadership is supposed to operate. I think that's perfectly healthy. But I think everybody also understands that you can't please everybody on everything. To please the majority, you have to keep from going too far to the left or to the right." [9]

To be persuasive, a leader must know the members well, know what they want and what they will settle for, and what concessions they can make and what concessions they cannot make, given their constituencies. The critical importance of such information requires the leader to develop a reliable communications network within his party. But more than that, he requires good lines of communication into the other party to pick up support when elements of his own party appear likely to wander off the reservation. Members prefer to support their leader and the party position rather than the opposing forces. The task of the leader is to find reasons for them to do so and conditions under which they can.

The development of a legislative program requires the majority leader to work closely with the key leaders in his party, particularly the chairmen of the major committees. As Lyndon Johnson observed during his tenure as Senate majority leader, "You must understand why the committee took certain actions and why certain judgments were formed." [10] His successor, Mike Mansfield, observed: "I'm not the leader, really. They don't do what I tell them. I do what they tell me. . . . The brains are in the committees." [11] The effective leader works with the resources available—in essence, the power of persuasion. Relations between the leader and the committee chairmen are never characterized by a one-way flow of mandates. On the contrary, the leader must be acutely sensitive to the interests of the chairmen, adept at recognizing their political problems, and flexible in his negotiations with them. Bargaining is the key characteristic of the relationships between the majority leader and the committee chairmen.

Party management in Congress has become increasingly difficult in recent years. Several reasons help to explain this situation. In the first place, the adoption of "sunshine" rules in both houses has made Congress a much more "open" institution. For the most part, committee, subcommittee, and even party caucus meetings are now open to the public. Second, combined with the new visibility of congressional actions, the growing power of interest groups, stemming particularly from their campaign contributions, has made members more vulnerable to outside pressures and, at the same time, increasingly resistant to the influence of party leaders. Third, the weakening of the electoral parties has been accompanied by an extraordinary growth in candidate-centered campaigns. Members who are elected to Congress largely on their own efforts have less reason to concern themselves with party objectives, less reason to defer to the wishes of party leaders. Independence and freewheelingness have become the modus vivendi of many members of Congress. Finally, internal changes have contributed to the further decentralization of congressional power. Subcommittees have grown both in number and in independence.[12] The influence of committee chairmen has declined while that of subcommittee chairmen has grown. In addition, both chambers now limit the number of committee and subcommittee chairmanships that a member may hold, the effect of which has been to spread leadership positions (and thus power) among more members. The presence of a large number of specialized policy caucuses may also have made it more difficult for the parties to integrate policy making. Singly and in combination, these changes have diminished the capacity of the parties to build majorities and to mobilize their members for concerted action.

A prominent New Yorker, Emanuel Celler, who served fifty years in the House (nearly twenty-five years as chairman of the Judiciary Committee), made these comments on the devolution of congressional power:

> When I was in Congress, we had strong chairmen. . . . They ruled the roost. . . . Then came along the so-called young Turks, insisting upon lessening the power of the chairmen. And you have all these youngsters clamoring for power and more power and more help, so that there's a tremendous proliferation of [staff] assistants to the subcommittees. And they are yammering and hollering for more and more power, which results in the combined efforts of Congress shouting and trying to make itself heard above the power of the president. . . .[13]

The more individualistic Congress becomes, the more difficult it becomes for the party leadership to play a decisive role. Senate majority whip Alan Cranston (D-Calif.) has observed: "A lot of leadership is just housekeeping now. Occasionally you have an opportunity to provide leadership, but not that often. The weapons to keep people in line just aren't there." [14]

What has been said thus far suggests that several important constraints shape the position of the floor leader. The leader is not free to fashion his role as he might like to see it. The limited range of powers available to him, his personality, his relationship to the president, and his skills in bargaining—all affect in some measure the definition of his role. Moreover, no two leaders are likely to perceive the leader role in exactly the same light. In addition, the nature of the leader's position is strongly influenced by the nature of the legislative parties. The evidence is that the persistent cleavages present within both parties make it necessary for a leader to occupy the role of middleman. The leader is a middleman in the sense that he is more or less steadily involved in negotiations with all major elements within the party, and also in terms of his voting record. [15] In the passage of much legislation the test is not so much the wisdom of the decision as it is its political feasibility. A leader identified with an extreme group within his party would find it difficult to work out the kinds of compromises necessary to put together a majority. The leader is first and foremost a broker. Candidates for leadership positions whose voting records place them on the ideological edges of their party are less likely to be elected than those whose voting records fall within the central range of party opinion.

The Whips

Another unit in the party structure of Congress is the whip organization. Party whips are selected in each house by the floor leaders or by other party agencies. Many assistant whips are required in the House because of the large size of the body. Working to enhance the efforts of the leadership, the whips carry on a number of important functions. They attempt to learn how members intend to vote on legislation, relay information from party leaders to individual members, work to ensure that a large number of "friendly" members will be present at the time of voting, and attempt to win the support of those party members who are in opposition, or likely to be in opposition, to the leadership. The influence of the Speaker and the majority leader supplements the pressure of the whips. As described by the chief staff assistant to the majority whip, they apply "the heavy party loyalty shtick. Then it's more personalities than issues. There are some members who can only be gotten by the Speaker or the majority leader." [16]

The central importance of the whip organization is that it forms a communications link between the party leadership and rank-and-file members. The whips are charged with discovering why members are opposed to certain legislation and how it might be changed to gain their support. The intelligence the whips supply is sometimes the difference between victory and defeat on a major issue. The decentralization of Congress has made the whip function indispensable to all efforts to achieve party unity.[17] On some issues no amount of activity on the part of the leadership can bring recalcitrant members into the fold. If the outlook for a bill looks unpromising following a whip check of members' sentiments, the leadership will often postpone its floor consideration. Whip checks can thus protect the leadership from embarrassing losses.

The Policy Committees

Few proposals for congressional reform have received as much attention as those designed to strengthen the role of political parties in the legislative process. The Joint Committee on the Organization of Congress recommended in its 1946 report that policy committees be created for the purpose of formulating the basic policies of the two parties. Although this provision was later stricken from the reorganization bill, the Senate independently created such committees in 1947. The House Republicans established a policy committee in 1949, though it did not become fully active for another decade.[18] Rounding out the list, the rejuvenated House Democratic caucus voted to establish a policy committee in 1973.

The high promise of the policy committees as agencies for enhancing party responsibility for legislative programs has never been realized. Neither party leaders nor rank-and-file members have been agreed on the functions of the policy committees. The policy committees are "policy" committees in name only. The policy committees in the Senate ". . . have never been 'policy' bodies, in the sense of considering and investigating alternatives of public policy, and they have never put forth an overall congressional party program. The committees do not assume leadership in drawing up a general legislative program . . . and only rarely have the committees labeled their decisions as 'party policies.' " [19]

It is not surprising that the policy committees have been unable to function effectively as agencies for the development of overall party programs. An authoritative policy committee would constitute a major threat to the scattered and relatively independent centers of power within Congress. The seniority leaders who preside over the committee system would undoubtedly find their influence over legislation diminished if the policy committees were to assume a central role in defining party positions. Not only would the independence of the committee system be affected adversely, but many individual members would suffer an erosion of power. If the policy committees had functioned as planned, a major reshuffling of power in Congress would have resulted. To those who hold the keys to congressional power, this is scarcely an appealing idea. However attractive the proposal for centralized committees empowered to speak for the parties in Congress, these committees are altogether unlikely to emerge so long as the parties themselves are decentralized and fragmented, composed of members who represent a wide variety of constituencies and ideological positions.

Although the lack of internal party agreement prevents the policy committees from functioning in a policy-shaping capacity, it does not render them useless. Both parties require forums for the discussion of issues and for the negotiation of compromises, and for these activities the policy committees are well designed. Moreover, the staffs of the committees have proved helpful for individual members seeking research assistance. Most important, the policy committees have served as a communications channel between the party leaders and their memberships. The policy committees are an ambitious attempt to deal with the persistent problem of party disunity. If they have generally failed in this respect, they have nonetheless succeeded in other respects. As clearinghouses for the exchange of party information and as agencies for the reconciliation of at least some intraparty differences, they have made useful contributions.

Informal Party Groups and Specialized Congressional Caucuses

In addition to the formal party units in Congress, several informal party organizations meet more or less regularly to discuss legislation, strategy, and other questions of common interest. Among these organizations are the Democratic Study Group (DSG) (liberal), Conservative Democratic Forum, United Democrats of Congress (conservative), Republican Study Committee (conservative), and Wednesday Group (Republican, liberal). Formed to promote the policy positions of a faction within the party, these groups are major sources of information for their members. They focus primarily on the congressional agenda, drafting and introducing legislation and amendments as well as seeking to attract the interest and support of other members and outside forces. Extending their reach, some of these groups have sought to influence the content of party platforms. The largest and best known of these groups is the Democratic Study Group, formed in 1959 by liberal Democrats as a counterbloc to the southern wing of the party. Today the DSG has a membership of more than two hundred, an elected chairman and executive committee, a professional staff, and a whip system that functions on important legislation. Issuing fact sheets and weekly legislative reports, the DSG focuses its efforts on meeting the information problems of its members and in encouraging them to turn out for floor votes.

Informal party groups compete and cooperate with dozens of other specialized policy caucuses organized to advance particular interests. These relatively narrow-gauge groups are formed around geographic, economic, race, gender, and assorted concerns. Included in this far-flung policy network are such caucuses as the Steel Caucus, Coal Caucus, Textile Caucus, Travel and Tourism Caucus, Farm Crisis Caucus, Wine Caucus, Mushroom Caucus, Port Caucus, Human Rights Caucus, Black Caucus, Blue Collar Caucus, Hispanic Caucus, Sunbelt Caucus, Northeast-Midwest Congressional Coalition, Border Caucus, Congress-women's Caucus, Rural Caucus, Suburban Caucus, Crime Caucus, Arts Caucus, and Drug Enforcement Caucus. Groups such as these have come to play a significant role in the policy process through problem identification, member mobilization, and coalition building. They are centers for information exchange.[20] At the same time, they reflect the fragmentation of power in Congress. Whether they enhance or inhibit the capacity of party leaders to control the policy-making process is an empirical question. But whatever the answer, it is not likely that these representative mechanisms will disappear.

Factors Influencing the Success of Party Leaders

The cohesiveness of the parties in Congress can never be taken for granted. The independence of the committees and their chairmen, the rudimentary powers of elected leaders, the importance of constituency pressures, the influence of political interest groups, and the disposition of members to respond to parochial impulses—all, at one time or another, contribute to the fragmentation of power in Congress and to the erosion of party unity. The member who ignores leadership cues and requests or is oblivious to them, or who builds a career as a party maverick, is far more common than might be supposed. There are few weapons in the leadership arsenal that can be used to bring refractory members into line.

Research on the Democratic party in the House by Lewis Froman and Randall Ripley identifies a number of conditions under which leadership influence on legislative decisions will either be promoted or inhibited.[21] In the first place, leadership success is likely to be contingent on a high degree of agreement among the leaders themselves. Ordinarily the Speaker, majority leader, and whip will be firm supporters of their president's legislative program; frequently, however, other key leaders, such as committee chairmen will be allied with opponents. When unity among the leaders breaks down, prospects for success fall sharply. Second, leadership success in gathering the party together tends to be affected by the nature of the issue under consideration—specifically, whether it is procedural or substantive. On procedural issues (for example, election of the Speaker, adoption of rules, motions to adjourn), party cohesion is ordinarily much higher than on issues that involve substantive policy. Third, the efforts of party leaders are most likely to be successful on issues that do not have high visibility to the general public. In the usual pattern, conflicting pressures emerge when issues gain visibility, and the leaders must commit greater resources to keep party ranks intact.

In the fourth place, the visibility of the action to be taken will have bearing on the inclination of members to follow the leadership. Not all forms of voting, for example, are equally visible. Roll-call votes on final passage of measures are highly visible—the member's "record" on a public question is firmly established at this point. Voting with the leadership on the floor may seem to the member to pose too great a risk. On the other hand, supporting the leadership in committee or on a key amendment is less risky, because the actions are not as easily brought into public focus. Fifth, and perhaps most important, members are most likely to vote with their party when the issue at stake does not stir up opposition in their constituencies. Party leaders know full well that they cannot count on the support of members who feel that they are under the thumb of constituents on a particular issue—for example, southern members on certain questions relating to civil rights. Finally, support for the leadership is likely to be dependent upon the activity of the state delegations. Leadership victories are more likely to result when individual state delegations are not involved in bargaining with leaders over specific demands.

These conditions, then, constitute the background against which leadership efforts to mold their party as a unit are made. Party loyalty, it should be emphasized, is more than a veneer. By and large, members prefer to stay "regular," to go along with their party colleagues. But they will not queue up in support of their leaders if the conditions appear wrong, if apparently more is to be lost than gained by following the leadership. Members guard their careers by taking frequent soundings within their constituencies and among their colleagues and by making careful calculations of the consequences that are likely to flow from their decisions.

National Party Agencies and the Congressional Parties

In theory, the supreme governing body of the party between one national convention and the next is the national committee, which is composed of representatives from each state. In the best of all worlds, from the perspective of those who believe in party unity and responsibility, there would be close and continuing relationships between the national committee of each party and fellow party members in Congress. Out of such associations, presumably, would come coherent party policies and a heightened sense of responsibility among members of Congress for developing a legislative program consistent with the promises of the party platform. The tone and mood that dominate relations between the national committees and the congressional parties, however, are as likely to be characterized by suspicion as by cooperation. Congressional leaders in particular are little disposed to follow the cues that emanate from the national committees or, for that matter, from any other national party agency.

Not only do national party leaders have a minimal impact on congressional decision making, but they are also largely excluded from the process of nominating congressional candidates. Although the National Republican Congressional Committee sometimes enters House primary fights, giving funds to the Republican candidate it prefers, the practice is not common. "We don't look for fights, which would do both us and [the candidates] damage," the NRCC campaign director said. "The thing we look for is whether a candidate has [local] support." The Democratic Congressional Campaign Committee does not make funds available to primary candidates.[22]

The reason that national party leaders seldom become involved in the congressional nominating process is that state and local leaders are likely to resent it. Occasionally an intrepid president has sought to influence congressional nominations, as Franklin D. Roosevelt did in 1938. Disturbed by mounting opposition to his program in Congress, Roosevelt publicly endorsed the primary opponents of certain prominent anti-New Deal incumbent Democrats. As it turned out, nearly all of the lawmakers marked for defeat won easily, much to the chagrin of the president. Twelve years later President Harry S Truman met the same fate when he endorsed a candidate in the Democratic senatorial primary in Missouri. The state party organization rallied to the other side, and the president lost. Although a few presidential "purges" have succeeded, most attempts have failed. The lesson seems evident: congressional nominations are regarded as local matters, to be decided in terms of local preferences.

The national party is concerned with the election of members who are broadly sympathetic to its traditional policy orientations and its party platform. In counterpoise, local party organizations aim to guarantee their own survival as independent units. Occasional conflict between the two is predictable. The principal consequence of local control over congressional nominations is that all manner of men and women get elected to Congress, those who find it easy to accept national party goals and those who are almost wholly out of step with the national party. The failure of party unity in Congress is due as much as anything to the folkway that congressional nominations are local questions to be settled by local politicians and voters according to preferences they alone establish.

Do the Parties Differ on Public Policies?

Party affiliation is the cutting edge of congressional elections. Ordinarily there are few surprises on election day: Democratic candidates win where they are expected to win, and Republican candidates win where they are expected to win. The public at large may continue to believe that each election poses an opportunity for the outs to replace the ins, but in fact this occurs infrequently. The chief threat to an incumbent legislator is a landslide presidential vote for the other party, one so great that congressional candidates on the winning presidential ticket are lifted into office on the strength of the presidential candidate's coattails. Even landslide votes, however, do not disturb the great majority of congressional races.

If party affiliation largely determines which men and women go to Congress, does it also significantly influence their behavior once in office? The answer for most legislators—for majorities within each party—is yes. Party affiliation is the most important single variable in predicting how members will respond to questions that come before them. Indeed, the key fact to be known about any member is the party to which he belongs—it influences his choice of friends, his membership in groups, his relations with lobbies, his relations with other members and the leadership, and, most important, his policy orientations. Party loyalty does not govern the behavior of members; neither is it a factor taken lightly.

The proportion of roll-call votes in Congress in which the parties are firmly opposed to each other is not particularly large. A study of selected congressional sessions between 1921 and 1967 shows that the number of "party votes" that occur in the House has declined markedly over the years. Between 1921 and 1948, about 17 percent of the House roll-call votes were party votes—votes in which 90 percent of the voting membership of one party opposed 90 percent of the voting membership of the other party. In the usual House sessions since 1950, party votes have numbered about 6 or 7 percent of the total.[23] The "90 percent versus 90 percent" standard is, of course, an exceedingly rigorous test of party voting. If the standard is relaxed to "50 percent versus 50 percent," the proportion of party votes rises sharply. Between 1981 and 1987, for example, about 48 percent of all congressional roll-call votes found party majorities arrayed against each other. From 1977 to 1980, during the time of the Carter administration, party voting appeared on 42 percent of all roll-call votes.[24]

One of the main reasons that party voting is not greater is found in the behavior of the wings of each party. A study of voting patterns in the House from the Eighty-sixth Congress through the Ninety-first revealed not only a sharp decline in party voting but also a growing tendency for eastern Republicans to join forces with northern Democrats against an alliance of noneastern Republicans and southern Democrats. Throughout this period the majority elements of the two parties—northern Democrats and noneastern Republicans—steadily opposed each other on issues involving some degree of controversy. Defections among the minority segments of each party—eastern Republicans and southern Democrats—is traced to a growing responsiveness among members to constituency preferences.[25]

Although party voting is less common today than it was some decades ago, important issues are often at stake when party lines form. In general, Democrats have been much more likely than Republicans to support federal programs to assist agriculture, expanded health and welfare programs, legislation advantageous to labor and low-income groups, government regulation of business, reductions in the defense budget, and a larger role for the federal government. Recently, interparty conflict has become more common on certain kinds of foreign policy questions, such as aid to anticommunist guerrillas. Data in Table 5-1 reflect how the parties lined up on major issues in the House during the first two years of President Reagan's second term (Ninety-ninth Congress, Second Session).

The Parties and Liberal-Labor Legislation

The current policy orientations of the parties in Congress are not distinctly different from those they have held over the last half century. The positions of the parties (and the wings within them) on proposals of interest to the AFL-CIO in the Second Session of the Ninety-ninth Congress are presented in Figures 5-4 and 5-5. A member voting in agreement with the AFL-CIO would have supported such measures as liberalized benefits for the long-term unemployed, various education and training programs (Head Start, guaranteed student loans), U.S. subsidies for Amtrak, a minimum federal income tax on corporate earnings, general revenue sharing, import quotas on textiles and apparel, postal subsidies for charitable and religious organizations, greater Medicare and Medicaid funding, expanded benefit and eligibility levels for food stamps, the use of compulsory union dues for political activities, the Democratic alternative to the Reagan budget, and economic sanctions against South Africa.

Inspection of Figures 5-4 and 5-5 will show two broad patterns of congressional voting on legislation of central interest to organized labor. First, it is plain that the parties are not cohesive units in voting on liberal-labor legislation. Second, despite noticeable intraparty splits, there are substantial differences between the parties. The two largest groups in each house—northern Democrats and northern Republicans— view liberal-labor legislation from vastly different perspectives. The only Republicans who are found at the highest support level—voting in agreement with AFL-CIO positions between 76 and 100 percent of the time—are a few members from eastern states. Northern Democrats, by contrast, give overwhelming support to labor objectives. Only a handful of northern Democrats are markedly out of step, voting less than half the time with the AFL-CIO.

The strongest opponents of liberal-labor legislation in both houses are southern Republicans. Noneastern Republicans are close behind. Although southern Democrats are arrayed at all points, a clear-cut majority in each house supports the objectives of the AFL-CIO. Indeed, about one-fourth of the southern Democratic House members and more than 40 percent of the southern Democratic senators have voting records

TABLE 5-1 Congressional Party Behavior: Key Differences between the Parties during the Reagan Administration

| Legislation | Bipartisan[a] | Party conflict | |
		Moderate[b]	Significant[c]
Relaxation of gun control law	R-support (91%) D-support (53%)		
Adoption of Tax Reform Act of 1986	D-support (70%) R-support (65%)		
Override of Reagan veto of South Africa sanctions	D-support (98%) R-support (51%)		
Shift in emphasis in federal housing policy from construction of low-income public housing units toward repair and modernization of existing dwellings		R-support (89%) D-oppose (68%)	
Override of Reagan veto of bill restricting textile and apparel imports		D-support (83%) R-oppose (60%)	
Relaxation of 55 mph speed limit		R-support (67%) D-oppose (67%)	
Pesticide control—amendment to increase the discretion of the Environmental Protection Agency in setting uniform national standards for pesticide residues on foods		R-oppose (84%) D-support (68%)	
Immigration reform		D-support (73%) R-oppose (63%)	
Provision for military and nonmilitary aid for "contra" guerrillas in Nicaragua			R-support (94%) D-oppose (80%)
Reduction in defense budget			D-support (89%) R-oppose (78%)
Provision for one-year nuclear test ban except for smallest weapons			D-support (87%) R-oppose (78%)

Legislation	Bipartisan[a]	Party conflict Moderate[b]	Significant[c]
Reduction of Strategic Defense Initiative ("star wars") spending by 40 percent			D-support (86%) R-oppose (81%)
Amendment to block production of new chemical weapons			R-oppose (78%) D-support (70%)
Revival of automatic budget-cutting device in Gramm-Rudman-Hollings antideficit law, which Supreme Court declared unconstitutional			D-oppose (92%) R-support (85%)
Covert U.S. aid to antigovernment guerrillas in Angola			R-support (96%) D-oppose (74%)
End-of-session continuing appropriations for 1987 fiscal year (largest money bill in history with bans on nuclear testing and nerve gas production, affirmation of SALT II, and limits on farm program payments; "nay" vote agrees with president's position)			R-oppose (91%) D-support (81%)

SOURCE: Developed from data in *Congressional Quarterly Weekly Report,* November 1, 1986, 2761-2765.

NOTE: R = Republican; D = Democrat. Conflict between the congressional parties ranged from limited to moderate during President Reagan's first term. But during his second term, Democratic resistance heightened. The data in this table show how the parties voted in the House (controlled by the Democrats) on sixteen major issues (as designated by Congressional Quarterly) during the second session of the Ninety-ninth Congress (1985-1986). On fully half of these key policy questions, sharp party divisions emerged, with at least 70 percent of the voting members of one party opposed to at least 70 percent of the voting members of the other party. Only three issues reflected bipartisan agreement (gun control, tax reform, South Africa sanctions). Interparty conflict in the Senate (controlled by the Republicans) on key issues was less intense, but still prominent. Party membership clearly has a significant impact on members' voting, perhaps especially on major issues.

[a] Bipartisan: majorities of both parties in agreement.
[b] Moderate party conflict: party majority against party majority.
[c] Significant party conflict: at least 70 percent of the voting members of one party aligned against at least 70 percent of the voting members of the other party.

FIGURE 5-4   House Support for Labor Legislation by Party and Region,
Ninety-ninth Congress, Second Session

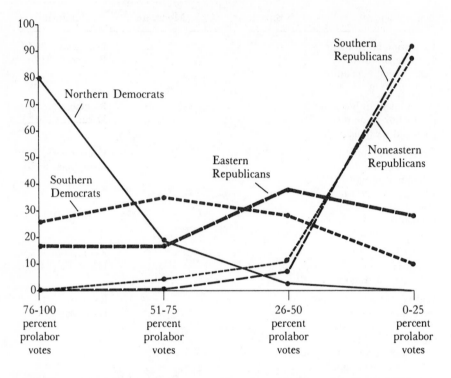

SOURCE: Developed from data in *Congressional Quarterly Weekly Report,* November 22,
1986, 2959-2966.

NOTE: House members are ranked by the percentage of votes they cast in accord with the
positions of the AFL-CIO. The South is defined as the eleven states of the Confederacy plus
Kentucky and Oklahoma. Noneastern Republicans are all northern members except those
from eastern states.

on labor legislation that are about the same as those of their liberal
northern colleagues. Southern Democrats and southern Republicans are
not peas in the same pod.

Another way of looking at the policy orientations of the congressional parties is to examine the range of attitudes in the Senate in the
Ninety-ninth Congress, Second Session, on issues deemed important by
the liberal-oriented Americans for Democratic Action (ADA) and the
conservative-oriented American Conservative Union (ACU) (see Figure
5-6). Senators are located on the diagram according to the percentage of
votes that they cast in agreement with the positions of each political
interest group. Senators Gary Hart (D-Colo.), Howard M. Metzen-
baum (D-Ohio), Paul S. Sarbanes (D-Md.), Alan Cranston (D-Calif.),

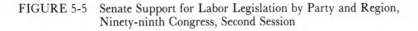

FIGURE 5-5   Senate Support for Labor Legislation by Party and Region, Ninety-ninth Congress, Second Session

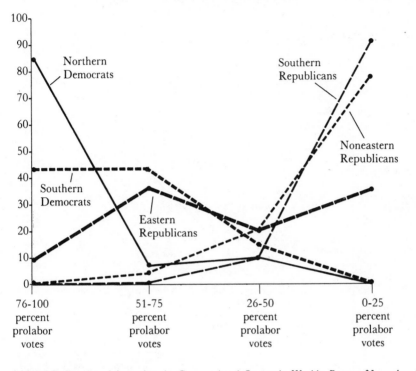

SOURCE: Developed from data in *Congressional Quarterly Weekly Report*, November 22, 1986, 2959-2966.

NOTE: Senate members are ranked by the percentage of votes they cast in accord with the positions of the AFL-CIO. The South is defined as the eleven states of the Confederacy plus Kentucky and Oklahoma. Noneastern Republicans are all northern members except those from eastern states.

and Tom Harkin (D-Iowa) emerge as the most liberal members of the upper house. At the conservative pole are such senators as James A. McClure (R-Idaho), Steve Symms (R-Idaho), Chic Hecht (R-Nev.), John P. East (R-N.C.), Jesse Helms (R-N.C.), and Jake Garn (R-Utah).

The data in Figure 5-6 reinforce the conclusions reached earlier. Despite the party-in-disarray quality that appears in the Senate scatter-gram, it is nevertheless clear that significant differences separate the majorities of the two parties. A strong majority of the Republican senators are found on the right-hand side of the diagram, indicating their agreement with the ACU, while most Democratic senators are lodged on the left-hand side, showing their agreement with ADA policy objectives.

FIGURE 5-6   Support for Positions Held by Americans for Democratic Action (ADA) and by American Conservative Union (ACU) by Each Senator, Ninety-ninth Congress, Second Session

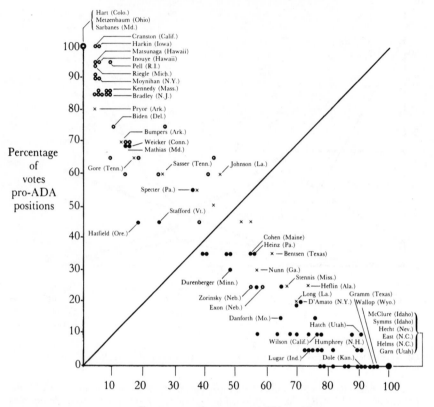

Percentage of votes pro-ACU positions

SOURCE: Developed from data in *Congressional Quarterly Weekly Report,* November 22, 1986, 2966.
NOTE: ○ = Northern Democrats;   × = Southern Democrats;   ● = Republicans.

The "deviant" behavior of party members is largely confined to certain wings in each party—in particular, southern Democrats and eastern Republicans.

Biparty Coalitions

Of all the problems that confront the legislative party, none is more persistent or difficult than that of maintaining party unity. Some members assiduously ignore the requests and entreaties of leaders; others cling tenaciously to constituency lines without pausing to consider the requirements of party; still others seek to tailor party measures to the specifications of those parochial interests to which they respond. The party is a repository for divergent claims and preferences. Getting it to act as a collectivity is no mean feat.

The disruption of party lines leads to the formation of biparty coalitions. The most durable biparty coalition in the history of Congress has been the so-called conservative coalition—an informal league of southern Democrats and northern Republicans. Data in Table 5-2 provide a statistical picture of the power held by the coalition since 1961, or from the Kennedy presidency to the Reagan presidency. In recent years, the coalition has come to life on about one-sixth of the roll-call votes held during a session. And the success of the coalition often has been spectacular. In only two sessions (1965 and 1966, the first two years of Lyndon Johnson's Great Society) did the coalition win less than 50 percent of the roll calls on which it appeared. In seventeen of the twenty-six sessions, the batting average of the coalition exceeded 60 percent. In 1981, the first year of the Reagan administration, the coalition won 92 percent of the time it appeared. The coalition's success rate fell off somewhat during the following years of the Reagan administration.

The conservative coalition is a potent force in Congress. A wide range of issues engages its attention. Year in and year out it can be counted on (1) to resist new federal spending on education and welfare or to attempt to cut the level of this spending; (2) to support proposals to transfer federal programs to the states; (3) to support the military and the Department of Defense; (4) to support major business interests; (5) to oppose legislation that would strengthen the position of organized labor; (6) to favor military instead of economic aid to foreign countries; and, recently, (7) to provide financial support for anticommunist rebels (as in Nicaragua).

The President and the Congressional Party

Presidential power appears more awesome at a distance than it does at close range. Although the Constitution awards the president a number of formal powers—for example, the power to initiate treaties, to make certain appointments, and to veto legislation—his principal everyday power is simply the power to persuade. The president who opts for an active role in the legislative process, who attempts to persuade members

TABLE 5-2   The Conservative Coalition in Congress, Appearances and Victories, 1961-1986

Year	Percentage of roll calls in which the coalition appeared in Congress	Percentage of coalition victories		
		Congress	House	Senate
1961	28	55	74	48
1962	14	62	44	71
1963	17	50	67	44
1964	15	51	67	47
1965	24	33	25	39
1966	25	45	32	51
1967	20	63	73	54
1968	24	73	63	80
1969	27	68	71	67
1970	22	66	70	64
1971	30	83	79	86
1972	27	69	79	63
1973	23	61	67	54
1974	24	59	67	54
1975	28	50	52	48
1976	24	58	59	58
1977	26	68	60	74
1978	21	52	57	46
1979	20	70	73	65
1980	18	72	67	75
1981	21	92	88	95
1982	18	85	78	90
1983	15	77	71	89
1984	16	83	75	94
1985	14	89	84	93
1986	16	87	78	93

SOURCE: *Congressional Quarterly Weekly Report,* November 15, 1986, 2908.

NOTE: A "coalition roll call" is defined as any roll call on which the majority of voting southern Democrats and the majority of voting Republicans are opposed to the majority of voting northern Democrats. Congressional Quarterly considers these states in the southern wing of the Democratic party: Alaska, Arkansas, Florida, Georgia, Kentucky, Louisiana, Mississippi, North Carolina, Oklahoma, South Carolina, Tennessee, Texas, and Virginia. The other thirty-seven states are classified as northern in this analysis.

of Congress to accept his leadership and his program, runs up against certain obstacles in the structure of American government. Foremost among these is the separation of powers. This arrangement of "separated institutions sharing powers" [26] not only divides the formal structure of government, thus creating independent centers of legislative and executive authority, but it also contributes to the fragmentation of the national parties. The perspectives of those elements of the party for

Party "Loyalists" and "Irregulars" in the Senate, Ninety-ninth Congress, Second Session

High party loyalty		High party loyalty	
Democratic senators	Votes cast with own party against majority of other party	Republican senators	Votes cast with own party against majority of other party
Riegle (Mich.)	96%	Hecht (Nev.)	95%
Sarbanes (Md.)	96	Gramm (Texas)	95
Levin (Mich.)	91	Helms (N.C.)	95
Harkin (Iowa)	91	Quayle (Ind.)	94
Simon (Ill.)	89	Wallop (Wyo.)	94
Sasser (Tenn.)	87	Dole (Kan.)	92
Burdick (N.D.)	87	Hatch (Utah)	92
Metzenbaum (Ohio)	86	Thurmond (S.C.)	91
Melcher (Mont.)	86	McConnell (Ky.)	90
Cranston (Calif.)	85	Simpson (Wyo.)	90
Kerry (Mass.)	85	Lugar (Ind.)	89
Byrd (W.Va.)	84	Rudman (N.H.)	89
Mitchell (Maine)	84	Domenici (N.M.)	80
Average Democratic senator	72	Average Republican senator	76

Limited party loyalty		Limited party loyalty	
Democratic senators	Votes cast in opposition to own party majority	Republican senators	Votes cast in opposition to own party majority
Long (La.)	64%	Specter (Pa.)	68%
Heflin (Ala.)	57	Mathias (Md.)	55
Zorinsky (Neb.)	55	Andrews (N.D.)	50
Boren (Okla.)	54	Weicker (Conn.)	44
Stennis (Miss.)	52	Hatfield (Ore.)	43
Bentsen (Texas)	50	Heinz (Pa.)	41
Hollings (S.C.)	46	Packwood (Ore.)	36
Chiles (Fla.)	43	Chafee (R.I.)	34
Nunn (Ga.)	43	Cohen (Maine)	33
		Stafford (Vt.)	33
Average Democratic senator	25	Average Republican senator	19

SOURCE: Adapted from data in *Congressional Quarterly Weekly Report,* November 15, 1986, 2901-2906.

NOTE: Members are ranked according to their behavior on party unity votes, which are defined as those recorded votes that split the parties, with a majority of voting Democrats opposing a majority of voting Republicans. Failures to vote lower both party unity and opposition-to-party scores.

whom the president speaks are not necessarily the same as those for whom members of his congressional party speak. Policy that may suit one constituency may not suit another. Indeed, the chances are high that the presidential constituency and the constituencies of individual members of his party in Congress will differ in many important respects, thus making inevitable a certain amount of conflict between the branches.

The separation of powers is not the only constraint that faces the activist president who hopes to move Congress to adopt his program. The lack of centralized party leadership in Congress, the relatively independent position of committees and their chairmen, the paucity of sanctions to apply to wayward legislators, and the parochial cast in congressional perceptions of policy problems all converge to limit presidential influence. Moreover, electoral arrangements and electoral behavior may make executive leadership difficult. Off-year elections are nearly always more damaging to the president's party than they are to the out party. In off-year elections from 1926 to 1986, for example, the president's party gained seats in only one House election (1934) and in only three Senate elections (1934, 1962, and 1970). Losses are often severe. The Democratic party emerged from the 1966 election with forty-seven fewer seats in the House, and the Republican party lost forty-three House seats in the 1974 election. Following the first two years of the Reagan administration, the Republicans lost twenty-six seats in the House while holding their margin in the Senate. In 1986 the Republicans lost eight seats in the Senate but only five in the House. Over the sixty-year period from 1926 to 1986, the administration party had an average loss of thirty-two House seats in off-year elections. The president has every reason to fear the worst when these elections roll around; the next two years are certain to be more difficult.

Finally, the root of the president's legislative difficulties may lie with the voters themselves. The election that produces a president of one party may yield a Congress dominated by the other party or one influenced by a different ideological coloration. James Sundquist's analysis of John F. Kennedy's congressional miseries is instructive:

> [It] is neither fair nor accurate to blame the failure of the Kennedy domestic program in the Eighty-seventh Congress primarily upon congressional organization or procedure—the power of the reformed House Rules Committee, the seniority system, or any other of Congress' internal processes. The failure of Congress to enact the Kennedy program is chargeable, rather, to the simple fact that the voters who elected Kennedy did not send to Congress enough supporters of his program. His razor-thin popular majority was reflected in a

Congress formally Democratic but actually narrowly balanced between activists and conservatives. If the machinery of both houses had been entirely controlled by supporters of the Kennedy program, that in itself would not have changed the convictions of the members so as to produce a dependable administration majority. The machinery might have been used more effectively to coerce Democratic congressmen into voting in opposition to their convictions—but that is another matter.[27]

A measure of the legislative success enjoyed by presidents from 1953 (the Eisenhower administration) to 1986 (the second term of the Reagan administration) is presented in Figure 5-7. This analysis shows how frequently Congress voted in accordance with positions taken by each president during his administration. The highest rate of success of any of these seven presidents was achieved by Lyndon B. Johnson; in 1965 his position prevailed 93 percent of the time. The major reason for his success was undoubtedly that the Democratic party controlled both houses by such large margins that even the defections of southern members had minimal impact on outcomes. Ronald Reagan's 82 percent success rate in 1981 ranks third highest in the preceding thirty years. In the process of winning numerous legislative victories, Reagan received unusually strong support from Republican members in both houses, but especially in the Senate. His overall party support scores were higher than those of any other president since 1953.[28] And, as expected, his support declined after the honeymoon period. By 1986 Reagan's success rate had slipped to 56 percent, a level lower than for any year of the Carter administration. Most of Reagan's losses occurred in the Democratically-controlled House. When the opposition party controls one or both houses of Congress, presidential influence is difficult to sustain. Republican presidents understand this better than anyone. The last four Republican presidents—Eisenhower, Nixon, Ford, and Reagan—were confronted more or less steadily by this nagging party problem.

So many words have been written about the role of the president as "chief legislator" that it is easy to lose sight of the fact that members of Congress have power in their own right. Although in recent decades the initiative for generating legislation has shifted to the president, Congress remains one of the world's most powerful legislative bodies. There are a good many conditions that are inimical to presidential domination of Congress. Congress may adopt what the president proposes, but in the process may change the accent and scope. Sometimes it merely disposes of what he proposes. Nothing in the president's plans is inviolable. No certainty exists that Congress will share his perceptions or succumb to

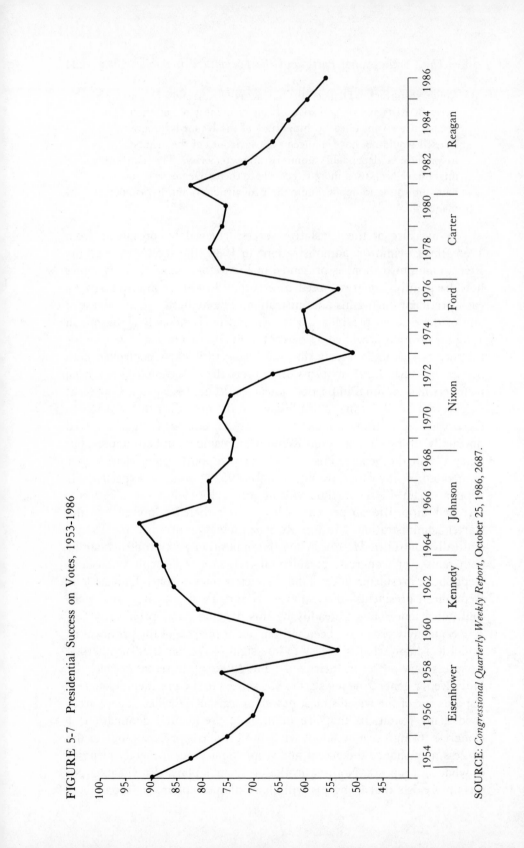

FIGURE 5-7 Presidential Success on Votes, 1953-1986

SOURCE: *Congressional Quarterly Weekly Report*, October 25, 1986, 2687.

his influence. The careers of individual legislators are not tightly linked to the president's, except perhaps for those members from marginal districts, and even here the link is firm only when the president's popularity is high.[29] Indeed, some members of Congress have made their careers more secure through the visibility that comes from opposing the president and his program. Notwithstanding the worldwide trend toward executive supremacy, Congress remains a remarkably independent institution—a legislature almost as likely to resist executive initiatives as to embrace them.

The president and Congress get along as well as they do because of one element that the president and some members of Congress have in common: party affiliation. In substantial measure, party provides a frame of reference, an ideological underpinning, a rallying symbol, a structure for voting, and a language for testing and discussing ideas and policies. The member's constituency has never been the only valid criterion for assessing the wisdom of public policies. Legislators prefer to ride along with their party if it is at all possible, if the costs do not loom too large. Moreover, the president and his legislative leaders are not at liberty to strike out in any direction they feel may be immediately popular with the voters. They are constrained by party platforms, by previous policy commitments, by interest group involvement, and by the need to consult with party officials and members at all levels, particularly with those who compose the congressional wing. Consensus politics is the essence of party processes.

The President and Legislative Leaders

A study of majority party leadership in Congress indicates that many alternatives are open to the president and party leaders in Congress in structuring their relations with one another. Typically, when the president and the majority leadership in Congress are of the same party and the president assumes the role of chief legislator, relations between the two branches have been characterized by cooperation. Within this pattern leaders tend to see themselves as lieutenants of the president, of necessity sensitive to his initiatives and responsible for his program. On the other hand, even though his party controls Congress, the president may decline to play a central role in the legislative process. In this situation, relations between the president and congressional leaders tend to be mixed and nonsupportive. Collegial rather than centralized leadership usually emerges as Congress generates its own legislative program instead of relying on presidential initiative. Finally, when the president and the majority in Congress (at least in one house) are of opposing parties (a so-called truncated majority), relations between the president and congressional leaders are often characterized by conflict and opposition. Leadership tends to be highly centralized, but legislative successes are usually few in number. "The leader of a truncated majority has great room for maneuver in the tactics of opposition and embarrassment on the domestic front, if his followers are willing to go along with him, but he must necessarily remain partially frustrated by his inability to accomplish much of his program domestically." [30]

David Truman has described the relationship between the president and the elective leaders of his congressional party as one of "functional interdependence." There are mutual advantages in this interdependence. The president needs information to make intelligent judgments, and the leaders can supply it. Moreover, they can offer him policy guidance. At the same time, the leaders can do their jobs better if bolstered by the initiatives and leverage of the president. They have no power to give orders. They can only bargain and negotiate, and their effectiveness in doing this, in notable measure, is tied to the president's prestige and political assets. The nature of their jobs makes it important for the president's program to move through Congress. If the president wins, they win; if he loses, they lose. [31]

The Role of the Minority Party in Congress

A study by Charles O. Jones identifies a number of political conditions that individually and in combination help to shape the role that the minority party plays in mobilizing congressional majorities and in shaping public policy. Some of these conditions originate outside Congress; others manifest themselves inside Congress. The principal external forces are the temper of the times (for example, the presence of a domestic or an international crisis), the relative political strength of the minority party in the electorate, the degree of unity within the parties outside Congress, and the power of the president and his willingness to use the advantages that are inherent in his office. Conditions within Congress that affect minority party behavior are legislative procedures, the majority party's margin over the minority, the relative effectiveness of majority and minority party leadership, the time the party has been in a minority status (perhaps contributing to a "minority party mentality"), and the relative strength of the party in the other house. [32]

The important point to recognize about the behavior of the minority party is that the strategies open to it are determined not simply by the preferences of the leadership or the rank-and-file members, by idiosyncratic circumstances, or by opportunities thrust up from time to time. Rather, what it does is influenced to a significant extent by conditions of varying importance over which it has little or no control. By and large, the conditions most likely to affect the minority party's behavior and shape its strategies are, among the external group, party unity and presidential power, and among the internal group, the size of the margin and the effectiveness of party leaders in both parties. Although restrictive political conditions depress the range of alternatives available to the minority party, a resourceful minority leadership can occasionally overcome them, enabling the minority party to assume an aggressive, creative role in the legislative process. Among twentieth-century Congresses, however, this has been the exception, not the rule.[33]

The Party in Congress

It is about as difficult to write about congressional parties without revealing uncertainty as it is to pin a butterfly without first netting it. The party is hard to catch in a light that discloses all its qualities or its basic significance. Party is the organizing mechanism of Congress, and Congress could not do without it. It is hard to imagine how Congress could assemble itself for work, process the claims made on it, lend itself to majority coalition building, or be held accountable in any fashion without a wide range of party activities in its midst. Moreover, there are some sessions of Congress in which the only way to understand what Congress has done is to focus heavily on the performance of the majority party. But that is only part of the story. In the critical area of policy formation, majority party control often slips away, to be replaced by enduring biparty alliances or coalitions of expediency. Party counts, but not altogether predictably—hence the reason for the uncertainty in assessing the role of the congressional party.

Summary arguments may help to establish a perspective in the analysis. The indifferent success that sometimes characterizes party efforts in Congress is easy to explain. The odds are stacked against the party. In the first place, members of Congress are elected under a variety of conditions in a variety of constituencies: they are elected in environments where local party organizations are powerful and where they are weak; where populations are homogeneous and where they are heterogeneous; where competition is intense and where it is absent; where the level of voter education is relatively high and where it is relatively low;

where income is relatively high and where it is relatively low; and where one or a few interests are dominant and where a multiplicity of interests compete for the advantages government can confer. The mix within congressional parties is a product of the mix within the nation's constituencies. It could scarcely be otherwise. The net result of diversity is that the men and women who make their way to Congress see the world in different ways, stress different values, and pursue different objectives. A vast amount of disagreement inevitably lurks behind each party's label.

In the second place, the salient fact in the life of the legislator is his career. If he fails to protect it, no one else will. The representative or senator knows that his party can do very little to enhance his security in office or, conversely, very little to threaten it. As a member of Congress puts it, "If we depended on the party organization to get elected, none of us would be here." [34] Each member is on his own. Whether he is reelected or not will depend more on the decisions he makes than on those his party makes, more on how he cultivates his constituency than on how his party cultivates the nation, more on the credit he is able to claim for desirable governmental action than on the credit his party is able to claim,[35] more on the electoral coalition he puts together or benefits from than on the electoral coalition his party puts together or benefits from. A sweeping electoral tide may, of course, carry him out of office. Though this is to be feared from time to time, there is not much he can do about it. Hence, the typical member concentrates on immediate problems. He takes his constituency as it is; if he monitors and defends its interests carefully, he stands a good chance of having a long career in Congress, no matter what fate deals to his party.

The growing importance of party campaign expenditures on behalf of congressional candidates (coordinated expenditures) may ultimately increase the members' dependence on the party and, accordingly, be reflected in their voting behavior in Congress. But there is no current evidence that members vote one way or another in response to party pressures linked to financial aid in campaigns. Parties are in business to win elections, and each prefers the election of its own mavericks to the election of members of the opposition. The ability of members to attract sizable PAC contributions, moreover, gives them additional political space in which to maneuver, free from party controls. What interest groups may extract from them is another question.

Third, party efforts are confounded by the fragmentation of power within Congress. The seniority leaders who chair major committees and subcommittees are as likely to have keys to congressional power as the elected party leaders. Committees go their separate ways, sometimes in harmony with the party leadership and sometimes not. Powerful committees are sometimes under the control of party elements that are out of step with the leadership and with national party goals. No power to command rests with the party leadership, and there is not a great deal it can do to bring into line those members who steadily defy the party and oppose its objectives. Two former, well-known members of the House comment on the problems that confront party leaders:

> In order for the Speaker to twist arms he has to have power, and we haven't recovered from the revolt against Uncle Joe Cannon which stripped power from a dictatorial Speaker nearly 65 years ago. (James O'Hara, D-Mich.)

> We Democrats are all under one tent. In any other country we'd be five splinter parties. Years ago we had patronage. The Speaker doesn't have any goodies to hand out. The President can promise judgeships, public works and fly [members] around in the airplanes. There's nothing like having the White House.[36] (Thomas P. "Tip" O'Neill, former Speaker of the House)

In addition, the party caucuses and the policy committees have never in any real sense functioned as policy-shaping agencies. "Parties" within parties, such as the House Democratic Study Group, bear witness to the lack of party agreement on public policy. Numerous specialized caucuses (steel, coal, textiles, cotton, sunbelt, New England, and the like) also contribute to the decentralization of power in Congress.

Fourth, the intricacies of the legislative process make it difficult for the parties to function smoothly and effectively. For the party to maintain firm control, it must create majorities at a number of stages in the legislative process: first in the standing committee, then on the floor, and last in the conference committee. In the House a majority will also be needed in the Rules Committee. Failure to achieve a majority at any stage is likely to mean the loss of legislation. Even those bills that pass through the obstacle course may be so sharply changed as to be scarcely recognizable by their sponsors. In contrast, the opponents of legislation have only one requirement: to splice together a majority at one stage in the decision-making process. Breaking the party leadership at some point in the chain requires neither great resources nor imagination. For these reasons, the adoption of a new public policy is immeasurably more difficult than the preservation of an old one. All the advantages, it seems, rest with those legislators bent on preserving existing arrangements.

Finally, the congressional party functions as it does because, by and large, it is a microcosm of the party in the electorate, beset by the same internal conflicts. The American political party is an extraordinary collection of diverse, conflicting interests and individuals brought together for the specific purpose of winning office. The coalition carefully put together to make a bid for power comes under heavy stress once the election is over and candidates have become officeholders. Differences ignored or minimized during the campaign soon come to the surface. Party claims become only one input among many the member considers in shaping his positions on policy questions. Not surprisingly, for reasons already noted, national party objectives may be disregarded as the member sorts out his own priorities and takes account of those interests, including his local party organization, whose support he deems essential to his election the next time around.

The astonishing fact about the congressional parties is that they perform as well as they do. One reason for this is the phenomenon of party loyalty—the typical member is more comfortable when he votes in league with his party colleagues than when he opposes them. Another reason is that most members within each party represent constituencies that are broadly comparable in makeup; in "voting their district" they are likely to be in harmony with the general thrust of their party.[37] A third reason is found in the informal powers of the elected leaders. Members who respond to their leadership may be given assistance in advancing their pet legislation, awarded with an appointment to a prestigious committee, or armed with important information. There are advantages to getting along with the leadership. Lastly, there is a great deal of evidence that presidential leadership serves as a unifying force for his congressional party. Members may not go along with the president gladly, but many of them do go along, and even those who do not, give his requests more than a second thought.

Notes

1. *Congressional Quarterly Weekly Report*, April 15, 1978, 875-876.
2. For instructive studies of the congressional leadership, including patterns of leadership change, see Robert L. Peabody, *Leadership in Congress* (Boston: Little, Brown, 1976); and Garrison Nelson, "Partisan Patterns of House Leadership Change, 1789-1977," *American Political Science Review* 71 (September 1977): 918-939.
3. *New York Times*, April 5, 1977. In discussing President Carter's many difficulties with Congress, Speaker O'Neill observed, "Maybe the President ought to go the route I go. I just come into a congressman's office and get down on bended knees." *U.S. News & World Report*, June 11, 1979, 17.
4. The Speaker's formal counterpart in the Senate is the vice president. His role is simply that of presiding officer, since he is not a member of the body, cannot

enter debate, and is permitted to vote only in the case of a tie. His influence on the legislative process is ordinarily insignificant.

5. Randall B. Ripley, *Party Leaders in the House of Representatives* (Washington, D.C.: The Brookings Institution, 1967), 23-24.
6. Joseph Cooper and David W. Brady, "Institutional Context and Leadership Style: The House from Cannon to Rayburn," *American Political Science Review* 75 (June 1981): 417.
7. "Leadership: An Interview with Senate Leader Lyndon Johnson," *U.S. News & World Report,* June 27, 1960, 88. Reprinted from *U.S. News & World Report,* copyright 1960 by U.S. News & World Report. See also Ralph K. Huitt, "Democratic Party Leadership in the Senate," *American Political Science Review* 55 (June 1961): 333-344.
8. *Congressional Quarterly Weekly Report,* December 11, 1976, 3293.
9. *Congressional Quarterly Weekly Report,* July 7, 1979, 1345.
10. "Leadership: An Interview with Senate Leader Lyndon Johnson," 90.
11. *New York Times,* July 17, 1961, 11.
12. Changes in committee-subcommittee relations in the 1970s, including the adoption of a Subcommittee Bill of Rights, have had a major impact on decision making in the House. Subcommittees now have relatively clear-cut policy jurisdictions and, of more importance, substantial control over their own budgets, staffs, and agendas. Subcommittee chairmen commonly manage legislation on the floor. For analysis of the new role of subcommittees, see Norman J. Ornstein, *Congress in Change: Evolution and Reform* (New York: Praeger, 1975), 88-114; and David W. Rohde, "Committee Reform in the House of Representatives and the Subcommittee Bill of Rights," *The Annals* 411 (January 1974): 39-47.
13. *Pittsburgh Press,* September 23, 1978.
14. *Congressional Quarterly Weekly Report,* September 4, 1982, 2181.
15. Concerning the middleman role of the floor leader, see these studies: David B. Truman, *The Congressional Party* (New York: Wiley, 1959), 106-116 and 205-208; Barbara Hinckley, "Congressional Leadership Selection and Support: A Comparative Analysis," *Journal of Politics* 32 (May 1970): 268-287; and William E. Sullivan, "Criteria for Selecting Party Leadership in Congress," *American Politics Quarterly* 3 (January 1975): 25-44.
16. *Congressional Quarterly Weekly Report,* May 27, 1978, 1304.
17. See a study by Randall B. Ripley, "The Party Whip Organizations in the United States House of Representatives," *American Political Science Review* 58 (September 1964): 561-576.
18. For a detailed study of this committee, see Charles O. Jones, *Party and Policy-Making: The House Republican Policy Committee* (New Brunswick, N.J.: Rutgers University Press, 1964).
19. Hugh A. Bone, "An Introduction to the Senate Policy Committees," *American Political Science Review* 50 (June 1956): 352. Also see Peabody, *Leadership in Congress,* 337-338.
20. Among the studies to consult on this subject are Susan Webb Hammond, Daniel P. Mulhollan, and Arthur G. Stevens, Jr., "Informal Congressional Caucuses and Agenda Setting," *Western Political Quarterly* 38 (December 1985): 583-605; Arthur G. Stevens, Jr., Daniel P. Mulhollan, and Paul S. Rundquist, "U.S. Congressional Structure and Representation: The Role of Informal Groups," *Legislative Studies Quarterly* 6 (August 1981): 415-437; Burdett A. Loomis, "Congressional Caucuses and the Politics of Representation," in *Congress Reconsidered,* 2d ed., ed. Lawrence C. Dodd and Bruce I. Oppenheimer (Washington, D.C.: CQ Press, 1981), 204-220; Arthur G. Ste-

vens, Jr., Arthur H. Miller, and Thomas E. Mann, "Mobilization of Liberal Strength in the House, 1955-1970: The Democratic Study Group," *American Political Science Review* 68 (June 1974): 667-681; and Kenneth Kofmehl, "The Institutionalization of a Voting Bloc," *Western Political Quarterly* 17 (June 1964): 256-272. Of related interest, see Barbara Sinclair, "State Party Delegations in the U.S. House of Representatives: A Comparative Study of Group Cohesion," *Journal of Politics* 34 (February 1972): 199-222; Richard Born, "Cue-Taking within State Party Delegations in the U.S. House of Representatives," *Journal of Politics* 38 (February 1976): 71-94; and Jeffrey E. Cohen and David C. Nice, "Changing Party Loyalty of State Delegations to the U.S. House of Representatives, 1953-1976," *Western Political Quarterly* 36 (June 1983): 312-325.

21. See Lewis A. Froman, Jr., and Randall B. Ripley, "Conditions for Party Leadership: The Case of the House Democrats," *American Political Science Review* 59 (March 1965): 52-63.

22. *Congressional Quarterly Weekly Report,* November 1, 1980, 3235.

23. See Edward V. Schneier's revised version of a classic study by Julius Turner, *Party and Constituency: Pressures on Congress* (Baltimore, Md.: Johns Hopkins Press, 1970), especially Chapters 2 and 3, from which certain data in this paragraph were drawn.

24. *Congressional Quarterly Weekly Report,* November 15, 1986, 2902.

25. Barbara Sinclair, "Political Upheaval and Congressional Voting: The Effects of the 1960s on Voting Patterns in the House of Representatives," *Journal of Politics* 38 (May 1976): 326-345. Also see David W. Brady and Barbara Sinclair, "Building Majorities for Policy Change in the House of Representatives," *Journal of Politics* 46 (November 1984): 1033-1060.

26. Richard E. Neustadt, *Presidential Power: The Politics of Leadership* (New York: Wiley, 1960), 33.

27. James Sundquist, *Politics and Policy: The Eisenhower, Kennedy, and Johnson Years* (Washington, D.C.: The Brookings Institution, 1968), 478-479.

28. *Congressional Quarterly Weekly Report,* January 2, 1982, 20-21.

29. There is additional evidence that a member's support for the president's policy proposals is influenced by how well the president ran in his district. In essence, the stronger the president runs in the member's district, the more policy support he will receive from that member. Presidential elections thus do more than select winners; they help to shape support patterns in Congress for presidential initiatives. See George C. Edwards III, "Presidential Electoral Performance as a Source of Presidential Power," *American Journal of Political Science* 22 (February 1978): 152-168.

30. From Randall B. Ripley, *Majority Party Leadership in Congress,* 175. Copyright © 1969, Little, Brown and Company Inc. Reprinted by permission.

31. See Truman, *The Congressional Party,* especially 279-319. *The Congressional Party* is required reading for an understanding of the role of party in the contemporary Congress. Its central conclusions continue to ring true. To examine congressional parties from other perspectives, see these recent studies: Keith T. Poole and R. Steven Daniels, "Ideology, Party, and Voting in the U.S. Congress, 1959-1980," *American Political Science Review* 79 (June 1985): 373-399; Sara Brandes Crook and John R. Hibbing, "Congressional Reform and Party Discipline: The Effects of Changes in the Seniority System on Party Loyalty in the U.S. House of Representatives," *British Journal of Political Science* 15 (April 1985): 207-226; Ross K. Baker, "Party and Institutional Sanctions in the U.S. House: The Case of Congressman Gramm," *Legislative Studies Quarterly* 10 (August 1985): 315-337; David W. Brady, "A Reevalua-

tion of Realignments in American Politics: Evidence from the House of Representatives," *American Political Science Review* 79 (March 1985): 28-49; Burdett A. Loomis, "Congressional Careers and Party Leadership in the Contemporary House of Representatives," *American Journal of Political Science* 28 (February 1984): 180-202; David W. Brady and Barbara Sinclair, "Building Majorities for Policy Changes in the House of Representatives," *Journal of Politics* 46 (November 1984): 1033-1060; Donald A. Gross, "Changing Patterns of Voting Agreement among Senatorial Leadership: 1947-1976," *Western Political Quarterly* 37 (March 1984): 120-142; Jeffrey E. Cohen and David C. Nice, "Changing Party Loyalty of State Delegations to the U.S. House of Representatives, 1953-1976," *Western Political Quarterly* 36 (June 1983): 312-325; Charles S. Bullock III and David W. Brady, "Party, Constituency, and Roll-Call Voting in the U.S. Senate," *Legislative Studies Quarterly* 8 (February 1983): 29-43; Thomas H. Hammond and Jane M. Fraser, "Baselines for Evaluating Explanations of Coalition Behavior in Congress," *Journal of Politics* 45 (August 1983): 635-656; Robert G. Brookshire and Dean F. Duncan III, "Congressional Career Patterns and Party Systems," *Legislative Studies Quarterly* 8 (February 1983): 65-78; Richard A. Champagne, "Conditions for Realignment in the U.S. Senate, or What Makes the Steamroller Start?" *Legislative Studies Quarterly* 8 (May 1983): 231-249; William R. Shaffer, "Party and Ideology in the U.S. House of Representatives," *Western Political Quarterly* 35 (March 1982): 92-106; Thomas E. Cavanagh, "The Dispersion of Authority in the House of Representatives," *Political Science Quarterly* 97 (Winter 1982-1983): 623-637; Walter J. Stone, "Electoral Change and Policy Representation in Congress," *British Journal of Political Science* 12 (January 1982): 95-115; and Patricia A. Hurley, "Predicting Policy Change in the House," *British Journal of Political Science* 12 (July 1982): 375-384.

32. Charles O. Jones, *The Minority Party in Congress* (Boston: Little, Brown, 1970), especially 9-24.

33. This study by Charles O. Jones identifies eight strategies open to the minority party in the overall task of building majorities in Congress: support of the majority party by contributing votes and possibly leadership, inconsequential opposition, withdrawal, cooperation, innovation, consequential partisan opposition, consequential constructive opposition, and participation (this strategy representing a situation in which the minority party controls the White House and thus is required to participate in constructing majorities). Strategies may vary within a single session of Congress and from one stage of the legislative process to the next. Jones, *The Minority Party in Congress,* 19-24 and Chapters 4-8.

34. Charles L. Clapp, *The Congressman: His Work as He Sees It* (Washington, D.C.: The Brookings Institution, 1963), 30-31.

35. For an analysis of the "credit claiming" activities of members, see David R. Mayhew, *Congress: The Electoral Connection* (New Haven, Conn.: Yale University Press, 1974), 52-61. The basic assumption of this remarkable little book is that reelection to Congress is the singular goal of members, and the relentless pursuit of it steadily influences not only their behavior but also the structure and functioning of the institution itself.

36. *Washington Post,* June 17, 1975, 12.

37. The typical northern Democrat is elected from a district with these characteristics: higher proportion of nonwhite population, lower owner-occupancy of dwellings, higher population density, and higher percentage of urban population. The typical northern Republican represents a district whose characteristics

are just the opposite. Constituency characteristics undoubtedly have an important impact on congressional voting. See Lewis A. Froman, Jr., "Inter-Party Constituency Differences and Congressional Voting Behavior," *American Political Science Review* 57 (March 1963): 57-61.

c h a p t e r   s i x

The American Party System: Problems and Perspectives

EXTOLLING the virtues of the American party system is something of an anomaly in popular commentary and scholarship. To be sure, a few scholars have found merit in the party system, particularly in its contributions to unifying the nation, fostering political stability, reconciling social conflict, aggregating interests, and institutionalizing popular control of government. But the broad thrust in evaluations of this basic political institution has been heavily critical. American parties, various indictments contend, are too much alike in their programs to afford voters a meaningful choice; are dominated by special interests; are unable to deal imaginatively with public problems; are beset by a confusion of purposes; are ineffective because of their internal divisions; are short on discipline and cohesion; are insufficiently responsive to popular claims and aspirations; and are deficient as instruments for assuming and achieving responsibility in government.

The Doctrine of Responsible Parties

The major ground for popular distress over the parties may be simply that most people are in some measure suspicious of politicians and their organizations (machines). The criticism of scholars, on the other hand, has focused mainly on the lack of party responsibility in government. The most comprehensive statement on behalf of the doctrine of party responsibility is found in a report of the Committee on Political Parties of the American Political Science Association (APSA), *Toward a More*

Responsible Two-Party System, published in 1950. The report argues that what is required is a party system that is "democratic, responsible, and effective." In the words of the committee:

> Party responsibility means the responsibility of both parties to the general public, as enforced in elections. Party responsibility to the public, enforced in elections, implies that there be more than one party, for the public can hold a party responsible only if it has a choice. . . . When the parties lack the capacity to define their actions in terms of policies, they turn irresponsible because the electoral choice between the parties becomes devoid of meaning. . . . An effective party system requires, first, that the parties are able to bring forth programs to which they commit themselves and, second, that the parties possess sufficient internal cohesion to carry out these programs.[1]

Two major presumptions underlie the doctrine of responsible parties. The first is that the essence of democracy is to be found in popular control over government rather than in popular participation in the immediate tasks of government. A nation such as the United States is far too large and its government much too complex for the general run of citizens to become steadily involved in its decision-making processes. But this fact does not rule out popular control over government. The direction of government can only be controlled by the people as long as they are consulted on public matters and possess the power to replace one set of rulers with another set, the "opposition." The party, in this view, becomes the instrument through which the public—or more precisely, a majority of the public—can decide who will run the government and for what purposes. Government by responsible parties is thus an expression of majority rule.

The second tenet in this theory holds that popular control over government requires that the public be given a choice between competing, unified parties capable of assuming collective responsibility to the public for the actions of government. A responsible party system would make three contributions. One, it "would enable the people to choose effectively a general program, a general direction for government to take, as embodied in a set of leaders committed to that program." Two, it would help to "energize and activate" public opinion. Three, it would increase the prospects for popular control by substituting the collective responsibility of an organized group, the party, for the individual responsibility assumed, more or less inadequately, by individual office-holders.[2]

The responsible parties model proposed by the Committee on Political Parties is worth examination because it presents a sharp contrast to the contemporary party system. Disciplined and programmatic parties, offering clearer choices to voters, would replace the loose and inchoate institutions to which Americans are accustomed. The committee's report deals with national party organization, party platforms, congressional party organization, intraparty democracy, and nominations and elections.

National Party Organization

The national party organizations envisaged by the committee would be much different from those existing today. The national convention, for example, would be composed of not more than five hundred or six hundred members, over half of whom would be elected by party voters. Ex officio members drawn from the ranks of the national committee, state party chairmen, and congressional leaders, along with certain prominent party leaders outside the party organizations, would make up the balance of the convention membership. Instead of meeting every four years, the convention would assemble regularly at least once every two years and perhaps in special meetings. Reduced in size, more representative of the actual strength of the party in individual states, and meeting more frequently and for longer periods, the "new" convention would gain effectiveness as a deliberative body for the development of party policy and as a more representative assembly for reconciling the interests of various elements within the party.

The most far-reaching proposal for restructuring national party organization involves the creation of a party council of perhaps fifty members, composed of representatives from such units as the national committee, the congressional parties, the state committees, and the party's governors. Meeting regularly and often, the party council would examine problems of party management, prepare a preliminary draft of the party platform for submission to the national convention, interpret the platform adopted by the convention, screen and recommend candidates for congressional offices, consider possible presidential candidates, and advise such appropriate party organs as the national convention or national committee "with respect to conspicuous departures from general party decisions by state or local party organizations." Empowered in this fashion, the party council would represent a firm break with familiar and conventional arrangements that contribute to the dispersion of party authority and the elusiveness of party policy. The essence of the council's task would be to blend the interests of national, congressional, and state organizations to foster the development of an authentic national party, one capable of fashioning and implementing coherent strategies and policies.

Party Platforms

Party platforms, the report holds, are deficient on a number of counts. At times the platform "may be intentionally written in an ambiguous manner so as to attract voters of any persuasion and to offend as few voters as possible." State party platforms frequently espouse principles and policies in conflict with those of the national party. Congressional candidates and members of Congress may feel little obligation to support platform planks. No agency exists to interpret and apply the platform in the years between conventions. There is substantial confusion and difference of opinion over the binding quality of a platform—that is, whether party candidates are bound to observe the commitments presumably made in the adoption of the platform. Such are the principal shortcomings of this instrumentality.

To put new life back into the party platform, the report recommends that it should be written at least every two years to take account of developing issues and to link it to congressional campaigns in off-year elections; that it should "emphasize general party principles and national issues" that "should be regarded as binding commitments on all candidates and officeholders of the party, national, state and local"; that state and local platforms "should be expected to conform to the national platform on matters of general party principle or on national policies"; and that the party council should take an active role in the platform-making process, both in preparing tentative drafts of the document in advance of the convention and in interpreting and applying the platform between conventions. In sum, the report argues that party platforms and the processes through which they are presently formulated and implemented are inimical to the development of strong and responsible parties.

Congressional Party Organization

One of the most vexing problems in the effort to develop more responsible parties has been the performance of the congressional parties. The proliferation of leadership committees in Congress, the weakness of the caucus (or conference), the independence of congressional committees, and the seniority system have combined to limit possibilities for the parties to develop consistent and coherent legislative records. To tighten up congressional party organization would require a number of changes.

First, each party in both the Senate and the House should consolidate its various leadership groups (for example, policy committees, committees on committees, House Rules Committee) into a single leadership group; its functions would be to manage legislative party affairs, submit policy proposals to the membership, draw up slates of committee assignments, and assume responsibility for scheduling legislation.

Second, there should be more frequent meetings of the party caucuses, their decisions to be binding on legislation involving the party's principles and programs. Moreover, members of Congress who ignore a caucus decision "should not expect to receive the same consideration in the assignment of committee posts or in the apportionment of patronage as those who have been loyal to party principles."

Third, the seniority system should be made to work in harmony with the party's responsibility for a legislative program. The report states:

> The problem is not one of abolishing seniority and then finding an alternative. It is one of mobilizing the power through which the party leadership can successfully use the seniority principle rather than have the seniority principle dominate Congress. . . . Advancement within a committee on the basis of seniority makes sense, other things being equal. But it is not playing the game fairly for party members who oppose the commitments in their party's platform to rely on seniority to carry them into committee chairmanships. Party leaders have compelling reason to prevent such a member from becoming chairman—and they are entirely free so to exert their influence.

Fourth, the assignment of members of Congress to committees should be a responsibility of the party leadership committees. "Personal competence and party loyalty should be valued more highly than seniority in assigning members to such major committees as those dealing with fiscal policy and foreign affairs." At the same time, committee assignments should be reviewed at least every two years by the party caucus. A greater measure of party control over committee assignments is essential, if the party is to assume responsibility for a legislative program.

Finally, party leaders should take over the function of scheduling legislation for floor consideration. In particular, the power held by the House Rules Committee over legislative scheduling should be vested in the party leadership committee. If the party cannot control the flow of legislation to the floor and shape the agenda, there is little chance that it can control legislative output, which is the essence of responsible party performance in Congress.

Intraparty Democracy

The achievement of a system of responsible parties demands more than the good intentions of the public and of party leaders. It requires widespread and meaningful political participation by grass-roots members of the party, democratic party processes, and an accountable leadership. According to the report:

> Capacity for internal agreement, democratically arrived at, is a critical test for a party. It is a critical test because when there is no such capacity, there is no capacity for positive action, and hence the party becomes a hollow pretense. It is a test which can be met only if the party machinery affords the membership an opportunity to set the course of the party and to control those who speak for it. The test can be met fully only where the membership accepts responsibility for creative participation in shaping the party's program.

There is nothing easy about the task of developing an active party membership capable of creative participation in the affairs of the party. Organizational changes at both the summit and the base of the party hierarchy are required. "A national convention, broadly and directly representative of the rank and file of the party and meeting at least biennially, is essential to promote a sense of identity with the party throughout the membership as well as to settle internal differences fairly, harmoniously, and democratically." Similarly, at the grass-roots level, there is need for the development of local party groups that will meet frequently to generate and discuss ideas concerning national issues and the national party program. The emergence and development of local issue-oriented party groups can be facilitated by national party agencies engaged in education and publicity and willing to undertake the function of disseminating information and research findings.

A new concept of party membership is required—one that emphasizes "allegiance to a common program" rather than mere support of party candidates in elections. Its development might take this form:

> The existence of a national program, drafted at frequent intervals by a party convention both broadly representative and enjoying prestige, should make a great difference. It would prompt those who identify themselves as Republicans and Democrats to think in terms of support of that program, rather than in terms of personalities, patronage, and local matters. . . . Once machinery is established which gives the party member and his representative a share in framing the party's objectives, once there are safeguards against internal dictation by a few in positions of influence, members and representatives will feel

readier to assume an obligation to support the program. Membership defined in these terms does not ask for mindless discipline enforced from above. It generates the self-discipline which stems from free identification with aims one helps to define.

Nominations and Elections

The report's recommendations for changing nomination and election procedures fit comfortably within its overall political formula for strengthening the American party system. It endorses the direct primary—"a useful weapon in the arsenal of intraparty democracy"—while expressing preference for the closed rather than the open version. The open primary is incompatible with the idea of a responsible party system, since by permitting voters to shift from one party to the other between primaries, it subverts the concept of membership as the foundation of party organization. Preprimary meetings of party committees should be held for the purpose of proposing and endorsing candidates in primary elections. Selection of delegates to the national conventions should be made by the direct vote of party members instead of by state conventions. Local party groups should meet prior to the convention to discuss potential candidates and platform planks.

Three major changes should be made in the election system. The electoral college should be changed to give "all sections of the country a real voice in electing the president and the vice-president" and to help develop a two-party system in areas now dominated by one party. Second, the term of members of the House of Representatives should be extended from two to four years, with coinciding election of House members and the president. If this constitutional change is made, prospects would be improved for harmonizing executive and legislative power through the agency of party. Finally, the report recommends a variety of changes in the regulation of campaign finance, the most important of which calls for a measure of public financing of election campaigns.

The Promise of Responsible Parties

In the broadest sense, the publication of *Toward a More Responsible Two-Party System* was an outgrowth of increased uneasiness among many political scientists over the performance of the nation's party system and the vitality of American government. Specifically, the report sought to deal with a problem that is central to the overall political system: the weakness of political parties as instruments for governing in a democratic and responsible fashion. The report is not a study in political feasibility. It does not offer a blueprint depicting where the best opportunities lie for making changes in the party system. What it does offer is a set of wide-ranging prescriptions consonant with a particular model of political organization. If the model sketched by the committee were to come into existence, the American party system would bear only modest resemblance to that which has survived for well over a century. The key characteristics of the new parties would be the national quality of their organization, a much greater degree of centralization of party power, a tendency for party claims to assume primacy over individual constituency claims in public policy formation, a heightened visibility for the congressional parties and their leadership and for the president's role as party leader, and a greater concern over party unity and discipline.

To its credit, the report was not accompanied by the usual somnolence that settles over prescriptive efforts of this kind. Nor, on the other hand, did queues of reformers form in the streets, in the universities, or elsewhere to push for its implementation. What occurred instead is that the report gave substantial impetus to the study of American political parties and helped to foster a concern for reform that, in one respect or another, continues to the present.

The goal of advocates of party responsibility is to place the parties at the creative center of policy making in the United States. That is what party responsibility is all about. Voters would choose between two disciplined and cohesive parties, each distinguished by relatively clear and consistent programs and policy orientations. Responsibility would be enforced through elections. Parties would be retained in power or removed from power depending upon their performance and the attractiveness of their programs. Collective responsibility for the conduct of government would displace the individual responsibility of officeholders. Such are the key characteristics of the model party system.

How well responsible parties would mesh with the American political system is another matter.[3] Critics have contended that disciplined parties might contribute to an erosion of consensus, to heightened conflict between social classes, to the formation of splinter parties (and perhaps to a full-blown multiple-party system), and to the breakdown of federalism. Moreover, the voting behavior and attitudes of the American people would have to change markedly to accommodate to the model of centralized parties, since many voters are more oriented to candidates than they are to parties or issues. The indifference of the public to the idea of programmatic parties would appear to be a major obstacle to rationalizing the party system along the lines of the responsible parties model.

Responsible Parties and Party Reform

The reform wave of the last two decades has produced a number of organizational and procedural changes in the American party system and in Congress. Perhaps as much by accident as by design, a surprising number of these changes are largely or fully compatible with the recommendations of the APSA report.

Intraparty Democracy

Consider the steps that have been taken to foster intraparty democracy. No feature of the reform movement of the Democratic party, beginning with the guidelines of the Commission on Party Structure and Delegate Selection (the McGovern-Fraser Commission), stands out more sharply than the commitment to make the party internally democratic and more responsive to its grass-roots elements.

Commenting on the overall process by which delegates were selected to the 1968 convention, the McGovern-Fraser Commission[4] observed that "meaningful participation of Democratic voters in the choice of their presidential nominee was often difficult or costly, sometimes completely illusory, and, in not a few instances, impossible." For example, the commission found that (1) in nearly half the states, rules governing the selection process were either nonexistent or inadequate, "leaving the entire process to the discretion of a handful of party leaders"; (2) more than one-third of the convention delegates had, in effect, been chosen prior to 1968—well before all the possible presidential candidates were known and before President Johnson had withdrawn from the race; (3) "the imposition of the unit rule from the first to the final stage of the nominating process, the enforcement of binding instructions on delegates, and favorite-son candidacies were all devices used to force Democrats to vote against their stated presidential preferences"; (4) in primary, convention, and committee delegate selection systems, "majorities used their numerical superiority to deny delegate representation to the supporters of minority presidential candidates"; (5) procedural irregularities, such as secret caucuses, closed-slate making, and proxy voting, were common in party conventions from the precinct to the state level; (6) the costs of participating in the delegate selection process, such as filing fees for entering primaries, were often excessive; and (7) certain population groups—in particular blacks, women, and youth—were substantially underrepresented among the delegates.

To eliminate these practices and conditions, the commission adopted a series of guidelines to regulate the selection of delegates for future conventions. Designed to permit all Democratic voters a "full, meaningful, and timely" opportunity to take part in the presidential nominating process, the guidelines set forth an extensive array of reforms to be implemented by state parties.

The initial step required of state Democratic parties was the adoption of a comprehensive set of rules governing the delegate selection process to which all rank-and-file Democrats would have access. Not only were these rules to make clear how all party members can participate in the process but they were also to be designed to facilitate their "maximum participation." In addition, certain procedural safeguards were specified. Proxy voting and the use of the unit rule were outlawed. Party committee meetings held for the purpose of selecting convention delegates were required to establish a quorum of not less than 40 percent of the members. Mandatory assessments of convention delegates were prohibited. Adequate public notice of all party meetings called to consider delegate selection was required, as were rules to provide for uniform times and dates of meetings.

The commission enjoined state parties to seek a broad base of support. Standards eliminating all forms of discrimination against the participation of minority group members in the delegate selection process were required. To overcome the effects of past discrimination, moreover, each state was expected to include in its delegation blacks, women, and young people in numbers roughly proportionate to their presence in the state population.

A number of specific requirements for delegate selection were adopted by the commission. For example, provisions must be made for the selection of delegates in a "timely manner" (within the calendar year in which the convention is held), for selection of alternates in the same manner as delegates, for apportionment of delegates within the state on the basis of a formula that gives equal weight to population and to Democratic strength, and for the selection of at least 75 percent of the delegates at the congressional district level or lower (in states using the convention system). The number of delegates to be selected by a party state committee was limited to 10 percent of the total delegation.

One of the most remarkable aspects of this unprecedented action by the national party was the response of the state parties. They accepted the guidelines, altered or abandoned a variety of age-old practices and state laws, and selected their delegations through procedures more open than anyone thought possible. And with "maximum participation" in mind, they produced a convention whose composition—with its emphasis on demographic representation—was vastly different from any previous one.[5] Whether for good or ill, the Democratic party had by 1972 accepted the main tenets of intraparty democracy.[6]

No evidence exists, however, that party democratization has contributed to the development of a more responsible party system. Indeed, the reverse is probably true: the greater the degree of intraparty democracy, the harder it is to develop a coherent program of party policy.[7]

Strengthening the Congressional Parties

Reform, like conflict, is contagious. Essentially the same forces that produced major changes in the electoral structure of the Democratic party have produced major changes in the Democratic congressional party, particularly in the House. The thrust of these changes is clearly in line with the theory of responsible parties. Advocates of this theory have sought not so much to promote the formation of a new party structure in Congress as to breathe new life into existing party structures and procedures. The changes have been impressive. Long dormant, the Democratic caucus is now a more influential force in the affairs of the House, particularly in controlling committee assignments and in shaping rules and procedures. At the opening of the Ninety-fourth Congress (1975), the caucus removed three committee chairmen from their positions, increased party control over the committee assignment process, brought the Rules Committee more firmly under the leadership of the Speaker, and established a requirement that the chairmen of the appropriations subcommittees be ratified by the caucus. These were not stylized or marginal alterations. They should be seen for what they were: as systematically conceived efforts to reshape the power structure of Congress by diminishing the influence of the seniority leaders (who have often been out of step with a majority of the party) and augmenting the power of the party caucus and the leadership. And there have been other demonstrations of caucus power in the 1980s. At the outset of the Ninety-eighth Congress (1983-1984), the Democratic caucus voted to remove a southern party member from the Budget Committee because he had played a key role in fashioning President Reagan's budget strategy in the preceding Congress. Although party disciplinary action is not often taken, it can occur if the provocation is severe.

Organization, Platforms, Nominations, and Elections

A potpourri of other recent reforms was anticipated by the APSA report on responsible parties. Among them are the reassertion of the national convention's authority over the national committee, the selection of convention delegates by direct vote of the rank and file, the allocation of national committee members on the basis of the actual strength of the party within the areas they represent, the use of closed primaries for the selection of convention delegates, the public financing of presidential elections, and the provision for holding a national party conference between national conventions.[8]

In sum, many of the reforms that have been introduced in the party structure and in Congress are consistent with recommendations carried in *Toward a More Responsible Two-Party System*. They touch far more than the outer edges of the party and congressional systems. Nevertheless, there is no good reason to suppose that responsible party government is around the corner—that these reforms will somehow result in the institutionalization of a durable, highly centralized, and disciplined party system. Traditional moorings throughout the political environment make change of this magnitude all but impossible. And the current trends in American politics have in fact done more to disable the parties than to strengthen them.

Trends in American Politics

Office holding in the United States is dominated by the two major parties. The vast majority of aspirants for public office carry on their campaigns under the banner of one or the other of the two major parties. The most important fact to be known about the candidates in a great many electoral jurisdictions throughout the country is the party to which they belong, so decisive is party affiliation for election outcomes. Virtually everywhere, save in nonpartisan environments, the trappings of party—symbols, sponsorship, slogans, buttons, and literature—are in evidence. The parties and their candidates collect money, spend money, and incur campaign deficits on a scale that dwarfs their budgets of a generation ago. Party bureaucracies are larger than in the past. More than two out of three citizens continue to see themselves as Democrats or Republicans, however imperfectly they may comprehend their party's program or the performance of their party's representatives. Party-based voting decisions are common in numerous jurisdictions and especially in congressional elections. These are the signs of party vitality. But in reality they are largely misleading. Major problems confront the party system. Moreover, the key trends in contemporary politics are essentially "antiparty" in thrust:

1. The loss of power by electoral party organizations.

At virtually every point associated with the recruitment and election of public officials, the party organizations have suffered an erosion of power. The reasons are many and varied. At the top of the list, perhaps, is the direct primary. "He who can make the nominations is the owner of the party," E. E. Schattschneider wrote some years ago, and there is no reason to doubt his observation.[9] Given that nonendorsed candidates may defeat party nominees in primaries, one may wonder whether, in some elections and in some jurisdictions, anyone except the candidates really owns the parties. The party label has lost significance as candidates of all political colorations, with all variety of relationships to the organization, earn the right to wear it by capturing primary elections. Most important, a party that cannot control its nominations finds it difficult to achieve unity once it has won office and is faced with the implementation of its platform. Candidates who defeat the organization may see little reason to subscribe to party tenets, defend party interests, or follow party leaders. Not only does the primary contribute to the fragmentation of party unity in office but it also divides the party at large.

> Primaries often pit party leaders against party leaders, party voters against party voters, often opening deep and unhealing party wounds. They also dissipate party financial and personal resources. Party leadership usually finds that it has no choice but to take sides in a primary battle, the alternative being the possible triumph of the weaker candidate.[10]

The weakening of the parties is nowhere more apparent than in the domain of presidential campaign politics. The spread of presidential primaries and the opening up of caucuses introduced a participatory system that undermined the role of party leaders and organizations in the presidential nominating process. Candidates for the nomination touch bases with party leaders as much out of courtesy as out of need, and while presumably leaders' endorsements help, they are surely not critical. The introduction of public funding for presidential campaigns has reduced the party's fund raising role for this office. And it scarcely stretches the facts to argue that the typical national convention is a party conclave in name only. As Byron Shafer has observed, the Democratic reforms "restricted, and often removed, the regular party from the mechanics of presidential selection." [11] Additionally, in the election of the president, the linkage between party and outcome is of no more than modest importance, if that.

Still other reasons may be adduced for the atrophy of the party's role in the electoral process. The great urban machines of a generation ago have practically disappeared. Employing an intricate system of rewards and incentives, the machines dominated the political process—controlling access to power, political careers, and, most important, votes. Their decline, due to a number of reasons, contributed to a growth of independence both within the electorate and among politicians.

More and more candidates bid for elective office outside the major party structures. Defeated in the Republican primary in 1969, John V. Lindsay ran on the ticket of the Liberal party, formed an Independent party to secure another line on the ballot, and won the New York mayor's office in a convincing victory over his Democratic and Republican rivals. In 1974 Maine voters rejected the candidates of both major parties and elected an independent governor. In 1978 Wisconsin elected a governor who did not belong to any party before he sought the Republican nomination—"My mother," he observed, "always told me it was polite to join a party before you take it over." Also in 1978 Alabama elected to the governor's office a "born-again Democrat," a wealthy industrialist who had left the party in 1972 and then served four years as a member of the Republican state executive committee.[12] And in 1980, after faring poorly in the Republican presidential preference primaries, John Anderson entered the presidential race as an independent. Party careers and party endorsements, it is evident, are less important in the new American politics.

Finally, the easing of the party grip on the processes by which a person is recruited and elected to office is explained by a miscellany of reasons: the decline in the volume of patronage due to extension of the merit system, the decline in the attractiveness of patronage jobs, the steady growth of a better-educated electorate, the mobility of voters, the awesome costs of campaigns, the requirement for technical skills in the use of the mass media and in other innovative forms of campaigning, the emergence of the celebrity candidate, and the inability of the parties to capture the imagination and esteem of the voters.

The classic functions of party involve recruitment, nomination, and campaigning.[13] Today's parties are unable to dominate any of these activities, and often their impact is negligible. American politics in the media age is thoroughly candidate-centered. For most offices, major and minor, most of the time, candidates are on their own in making the decisions that count. No party organization or leadership tells them when to run, how to run, what to believe, what to say, or (in office) how to vote. Candidates may tolerate party nudging on some matters while they welcome party money, technical assistance, and services. And they receive them, especially on the Republican side, where a well-developed national system is in place for raising funds and providing services to candidates and state party organizations. But it is unmistakably the candidates who decide what to make of their party membership and party connections—both in and out of government. And there is not much that anyone, including party leaders and party committees, can do about it. In jurisdictions where American parties have more than ordinary importance, they are essentially facilitators, helping candidates who wear their label to do better what generally they would do in any case.

2. The decline of partisanship.

One of the far-reaching changes in American politics during the modern era has been the decline of partisanship in the electorate. For many voters, party no longer carries much weight. A particularly good indication of this is the growing number of independents. Nationwide, nearly one-third of all voters in 1986 described themselves as independents (see Table 6-1). Southerners are becoming more Republican and more independent. To be sure, not all voters who perceive themselves as independents actually behave as independents; doubtlessly some are "undercover" partisans who stay with the same party in most or all elections. Nonetheless, as the proportion of self-styled independents rises, problems mount for the maintenance of a vigorous party system. The party stimulus is weakened all along the line, from the recruitment of candidates, through elections, to office holding. Party electoral prospects become harder to forecast. Voter independence is to party vitality what coalition legislative voting is to party responsibility—a relationship of conspicuous incompatibility.

Every election attests to the "departisanization" of the electorate. In the 1986 House elections, a mere 8.4 percent of all voters said that the candidate's party was the most important factor in influencing their voting choice. The most important consideration was the candidate's character and experience, according to 41 percent of the sample. For 23 percent, state and local issues loomed most important. And of unusual

TABLE 6-1   Political Affiliation in the Nation and in the South, 1960 and 1986

	Democrat	Republican	Independent
Nation			
1960	47%	30%	23%
1986	39	32	29
South			
1960	59	22	19
1986	43	31	26

SOURCE: The 1960 data were taken from *Gallup Opinion Index,* August 1970, 3; the 1986 data appear in *Gallup Report,* July 1986, 21.

interest, in this *national* election, only 20 percent reported basing their decision on *national issues.*[14] The stark fact is that personality factors and parochialism often dominate American elections.

The prevalence of ticket splitting is further evidence of party decomposition. Nearly six out of ten people now cast split ballots in presidential elections, and in elections for local offices the proportion is even larger.[15] This behavior is not surprising since an overwhelming majority of the public believes that "the best rule in voting is to pick the best candidate, regardless of party label." [16] Ticket splitting has major ramifications for the control of government, as can be seen in an examination of the vote for presidential and congressional candidates within congressional districts. Table 6-2 includes data on the number and percentage of congressional districts with split election results— districts won by the presidential candidate of one party and by the congressional candidate of the other party—from 1920 to 1984. The data depict a more or less steady increase in split elections for these offices. A high point was reached in 1972, when 44 percent of all House districts split their results, due largely to the voters' rejection of George McGovern, the Democratic presidential nominee. The proportion of split results was almost as high in 1984 as voters everywhere voted for Ronald Reagan and Democratic House candidates. More split election outcomes occurred in the six elections between 1964 and 1984 than in the eleven elections between 1920 and 1960. Party now provides less structure to voting, in the sense of shaping the choices of voters, than in the past.[17]

Evidence that the party linkage between voters and government has atrophied can also be found in the contrast between presidential votes in the nineteenth and twentieth centuries. In the sixteen presidential elections from 1836 to 1896, only the election of 1872 was of landslide dimensions—that is, an election in which the winning candidate received

TABLE 6-2   Congressional Districts with Split Election Results: Districts Carried by a Presidential Nominee of One Major Party and by a House Nominee of Other Major Party, 1920-1984

Year and party of the winning presidential candidate	Number of districts	Number of districts with split results	Percent
1920 R	344	11	3.2
1924 R	356	42	11.8
1928 R	359	68	18.9
1932 D	355	50	14.1
1936 D	361	51	14.1
1940 D	362	53	14.6
1944 D	367	41	11.2
1948 D	422	90	21.3
1952 R	435	84	19.3
1956 R	435	130	29.9
1960 D	437	114	26.1
1964 D	435	145	33.3
1968 R	435	141	32.4
1972 R	435	193	44.4
1976 D	435	124	28.5
1980 R	435	141	32.4
1984 R	435	191	43.9
Total	6843	1669	24.4

SOURCE: Milton C. Cummings, Jr., *Congressmen and the Electorate* (New York: Free Press, 1966), 32 (as updated).

NOTE: Presidential returns for some congressional districts were not available between 1920 and 1948.

55 percent or more of the two-party vote. By contrast, eleven of twenty-two presidential elections from 1900 through 1984 were decided by landslide margins. Party switching from one election to the next has become increasingly common, and the party-oriented voter of the last century has been displaced by the volatile, candidate-oriented voter of this one. Consider the recent past. Democrats by the millions deserted their party's presidential nominee in 1952, Adlai E. Stevenson, to vote for the Republican candidate, Dwight D. Eisenhower. Similarly, Republicans in droves cast their ballots for Lyndon B. Johnson in 1964 rather than for Barry Goldwater, thus contributing substantially to the landslide Democratic vote. Even more massive switches occurred in 1968 and 1972. In the latter election, one-third of all Democrats voted for the Republican presidential nominee, Richard Nixon. Even in 1976, an election in which party affiliation again surfaced, nearly one out of five

Democratic identifiers voted for the GOP presidential candidate. A major reason for Ronald Reagan's victory in 1980 was that fully one-fourth of all Democrats voted for him, and his support among Democrats was almost as great in 1984.

Departisanization of the electorate contributes significantly to the insularity of politics and elections. John Petrocik and Dwaine Marvick describe this nexus:

> State and local candidates find their fate almost unrelated to the success of the national ticket. With the decline in party loyalty among voters and the development of skills and resources that increase the individuality of any given candidate, only a notoriously weak national ticket seems able to influence congressional, state legislative, or city council elections.[18]

3. The steady weakening of group attachments to the Democratic party in presidential elections.

Since Harry S Truman's election in 1948, the Democratic party has won only three of nine presidential elections—in 1960 (Kennedy), 1964 (Johnson), and 1976 (Carter). Among the explanations for the party's weakness, two stand out. One is that Democratic presidential candidates have been rejected by independents. Between 1952 and 1984, the Democratic presidential candidate gained a majority of the vote of independents only in 1964, a landslide Democratic year. In recent elections, at least two-thirds of this large group of voters (representing perhaps 25 percent of the turnout) have supported the Republican candidate.

But a more important reason is that the Democratic coalition, which emerged during the presidency of Franklin D. Roosevelt, has lost much of its potency. In election after election from the 1930s to the 1960s, Democratic presidential candidates received strong, sometimes overwhelming, support from Catholics, blacks, southerners, blue-collar (especially union) workers, ethnic minorities, big-city dwellers, and young voters. A dramatic shift in support among these groups has occurred (see Table 6-3). The changes among Catholics and white southerners are particularly striking. In 1964 more than three out of four Catholics voted for the Democratic candidate, Lyndon Johnson (about the same percentage as had voted for John Kennedy); in 1984 less than four out of ten Catholics voted for Walter Mondale. A mainstay of the traditional Democratic coalition, southern whites have abandoned the party in droves: a mere 28 percent voted for Mondale. In addition, blue-collar workers and young voters have strayed from the party.

TABLE 6-3   Shifting Groups and Changing Party Fortunes: Major Democratic
             Losses among Demographic Groups since 1964

	Percent Democratic				Percent Democratic loss	
	1964 (Johnson)	1976 (Carter)	1980 (Carter)	1984 (Mondale)	From 1964 to 1984	From 1976 to 1984
Catholics	76	57	46	39	-37	-18
Manual workers	71	58	48	46	-25	-12
Whites	59	46	36	34	-25	-12
Age 18-29	64	53	47	40	-24	-13
Men	60	53	38	38	-22	-15
Union families	73	63	50	52	-21	-11
High school graduates	62	54	43	43	-19	-11
Age 50 and older	59	52	41	41	-18	-11
Southerners	52	54	44	37	-15	-17
Southern whites	a	47	35	28	a	-19

SOURCE: Developed from data in *Gallup Report*, November 1984, 8-9, and in *Public Opinion*, December/January 1985, 4.

[a] Not available.

Group defections have become the norm.

The groups that have remained firmly Democratic are few. Heading the list is the black community, which votes overwhelmingly Democratic in election after election. The black vote for Walter Mondale in 1984 exceeded 90 percent. Also, about two out of three Jews, Hispanics, and unemployed voted for the Democratic candidate; each of these groups, of course, is relatively small. And persons with no religion also favored Mondale.[19]

Republican gains, by contrast, have surged. Support for President Reagan in 1984 increased virtually across the board. Particularly impressive was his showing among white Protestants (73 percent Republican in 1984), white born-again Christians (80 percent Republican), and the wealthy (68 percent Republican among persons with annual incomes surpassing $50,000). White Protestants and white born-again Christians made up nearly two-thirds of the voters in 1984.[20]

The erosion of the Democratic coalition does not necessarily presage an endless stream of Republican presidential victories. Voters who have shifted away from the Democratic party can shift back. Union families and Catholics, for example, gave strong support to Democratic congressional candidates in 1986. Future candidates will of course make a difference. Moreover, the stability of the Republican coalition will be tested—without Ronald Reagan at the head of the ticket. Presidential popularity and party popularity clearly are not the same thing. Nevertheless, it seems improbable that the Democratic coalition fashioned during the Roosevelt era can be generally restored. Too many changes have taken place. The dilemma is that the New Deal (and its successors) turned many "have nots" into "haves" and reduced the saliency and appeal of the party's traditional economic issues. The New Deal, in effect, sowed the seeds of its own destruction. Key elements in the party's traditional following, with their status changed, their confidence in the economy heightened,[21] have found fewer reasons to vote as they did in the past. Switching to the Republican side has not been all that difficult for them. The intriguing question asks what these groups will do in the future.

4. The growth of racial polarization in voting.

Historically, the great divide in racial voting occurred in the 1960s, beginning with a massive shift by blacks in 1964 and continuing with a sizable shift by whites in 1968. In broad outline, this is what happened: Under the leadership of President Lyndon B. Johnson, a bipartisan majority in Congress passed the Civil Rights Act of 1964, the most significant civil rights legislation since Reconstruction. The Republican National Convention shortly chose as its presidential nominee Barry Goldwater, a militant conservative, an exponent of states' rights, and one of the main opponents of the 1964 act. With the lines clearly drawn, blacks voted overwhelmingly (94 percent) for Johnson in November (see Table 6-4). Of the six states carried by Goldwater, five were in the Deep South, where his states' rights/civil rights stance undoubtedly was attractive to white voters. Following Johnson's landslide victory, a top-heavy Democratic Congress passed an even more important civil rights bill: the Voting Rights Act of 1965. (See Chapter 4.) This landmark legislation paved the way for blacks to enter fully into the nation's political life.

By 1968, as a result of movement by white voters, black-white voting divisions intensified; 85 percent of blacks but only 38 percent of whites voted Democratic. With a southerner, Jimmy Carter, at the head of the ticket in 1976, more whites (but less than a majority) voted Democratic than in either of the previous two elections. But this election was merely a "blip"—a modest exception to a profound trend. Today there are no signs that racial cleavages are ebbing, and the current split

TABLE 6-4 Growing Racial Polarization in Voting in Presidential Elections

	1952	1956	1960	1964	1968	1972	1976	1980	1984
Percentage of electorate voting Democratic	45	42	50	61	43	38	50	41	41
Percentage of whites voting Democratic	43	41	49	59	38	32	46	36	34
Percentage of blacks voting Democratic[a]	79	61	68	94	85	87	85	86	87
Racial differential: percentage difference between black and white Democratic vote	36	20	19	35	47	55	39	50	53

SOURCE: Developed from data in *Gallup Report,* November 1984, 8-9.

[a] Technically, this is the nonwhite vote. If the black vote were completely separated from other nonwhite votes, the black Democratic proportion would be several percentage points higher. In 1984, according to a Gallup poll breakdown, the actual black vote was 92 percent Democratic. See *Gallup Report,* November 1984, 7.

is particularly sharp. In 1984 about nine out of ten blacks voted for Walter Mondale, but only one out of three whites. Two out of every three whites thus voted for Ronald Reagan. The division of the races along party lines, grounded in economic policies as well as civil rights, is one of the outstanding facts of contemporary American politics.[22]

5. The emergence of distinctive spheres in party office holding, reflected in the election of Republican presidents and Democratic congressional majorities.

Since 1968 national elections have usually turned on a form of "branch" politics. Republicans regularly have won the presidency (Nixon in 1968 and 1972, Reagan in 1980 and 1984) while Democrats regularly have won Congress (though Republicans held the Senate for six of eight years during the Reagan administration). The data presented in Table 6-5 illustrate this pattern. Of the 370 congressional districts Reagan won in 1984, 257 were carried by decisive margins of at least 59 percent (Reagan's proportion of the national vote). Yet in 97 of these districts, or 38 percent, Democratic congressional candidates also won election— typically by sizable margins. Not even landslide Republican presidential victories apparently threaten Democratic dominance in numerous House districts. As indicated in Table 6-5, the bilevel pattern appears throughout the country but is pronounced in the South.

The Democratic party is the nation's "legislative party," invariably winning the House and ordinarily winning the Senate. From the Eighty-seventh through the One-hundredth Congresses (1961-1988), the Democrats won an average of 60.5 percent of the House seats and 57.4 of the Senate seats. Democratic legislative successes, especially in the House (controlled continuously by the party since 1955), stem largely from four factors, the first three closely related: substantial ticket splitting, growing candidate-centered voting accompanied by defections among Republican partisans, heightened significance of incumbency in elections, and gerrymandering. In recent national elections, about 60 percent of all voters have cast split ballots. The typical pattern shows voters supporting a Republican candidate for president and a Democratic candidate for the House (see Table 6-5). Voters may prefer a Republican in the White House, but to minister to local needs they lean toward Democratic House candidates. It strains the imagination to learn that more than fifteen million persons who voted for Reagan in 1984 did not vote for a Republican House candidate.[23]

Massive split-ticket voting is perhaps the best evidence that party-centered elections have been displaced by candidate-centered ones. And as partisanship has ebbed, the number of party identifiers who vote for the candidate of the other party has grown. Currently, about 20 percent of all party identifiers defect in House elections to vote for the candidate of the other party.[24] And at least three-fourths of these defections take place in the challenger's party, thus strengthening the reelection bids of incumbents.[25] For this and other reasons (see Chapter 5), incumbents are extremely difficult to defeat; in election after election 90 percent or more of all House incumbents on the ballot (98 percent in 1986) are reelected. Long dominant in the House, the Democratic party is the main beneficiary of the voters' decisive preference for incumbents. Put another way, the current successes of Democratic incumbents are derived from their past successes. When incumbency reigns, victories beget victories.[26]

Gerrymandering of congressional districts is the final piece of the puzzle. These district lines are drawn by state legislatures, where the Democratic party typically controls between two and three times as many chambers as the Republicans. Following the 1986 election, for example, Democrats held majorities in sixty-six state chambers as contrasted with twenty-nine for the Republicans. Democrats controlled both chambers in twenty-eight states while Republicans controlled both in only ten.

TABLE 6-5   Congressional Districts Won by Ronald Reagan by 59 Percent or More of the Vote and by Democratic House Candidates, 1984

	Number of districts won by Reagan with 59 percent or more of the vote[a]	Districts won by Reagan with 59 percent or more of the vote and by Democratic House candidates	
		Number	Percent
Northern House districts	162	49	30
Southern House districts[b]	95	48	51
Total	257	97	38

SOURCE: Developed from congressional district data appearing in Michael Barone and Grant Ujifusa, *The Almanac of American Politics* (Washington, D.C.: National Journal, 1986).

[a] Altogether, Reagan won 370 out of 435 House districts. His proportion of the national vote was 59 percent.
[b] States that make up the southern wing of the Democratic party are Alabama, Arkansas, Florida, Georgia, Kentucky, Louisiana, Mississippi, North Carolina, Oklahoma, South Carolina, Tennessee, Texas, and Virginia. The other thirty-seven states are classified as northern in this analysis.

Party control of the legislature is an invitation to draw district lines to serve the interests of party candidates. Leaders of both parties know their way around in gerrymandering, but the weakness of the Republicans at the state legislative level has limited their ability to manipulate district lines for partisan purposes. The Democratic party has been notably successful in getting the most from its electoral support. The evidence lies in the ratio between the national House vote and seats won (see Table 6-6). In 1984 the Democratic party won 52 percent of the nationwide House vote but 58 percent of the House seats—a "profit" margin to which the party has grown accustomed. This persistent imbalance prompts national Republican leaders to argue that gerrymandering has given the Democrats at least twenty House seats that "belong" to the Republicans. It has also prompted them to devote unusual attention and resources in the 1980s to winning state legislatures and governorships, since redistricting legislation will be a major item on state agendas following the 1990 census.

Voting patterns are not static. Although the Republicans have held a House majority for only four years since 1931 (1947-1948, 1953-1954), the party's prospects are now somewhat brighter. In the first place, Republican strength in southern congressional races has grown significantly in the last twenty-five years. Second, when a southern

TABLE 6-6   The Relationship between Nationwide Party Vote Totals and Seats
Won by Parties, U.S. House of Representatives, for Presidential
Election Years 1972-1984, in Percentages

	1972	1976	1980	1984
Nationwide vote for Democratic House candidates	51.7	55.9	50.4	52.1
House seats won by Democrats	55.9	67.1	55.9	58.2
Nationwide vote for Republican House candidates	46.4	42.0	48.0	47.0
House seats won by Republicans	44.1	32.9	44.1	41.8
"Unearned" increment of seats gained by Democrats	4.2	11.2	5.5	6.1

SOURCE: Developed from data in *Congressional Quarterly Weekly Report,* April 13, 1985,
687, and March 31, 1979, 575.

Democratic House incumbent dies or retires, the odds are reasonably
good (about four out of ten from 1952 to 1974) that his successor will be
a Republican.[27] Two out of three southern representatives today are
Democrats; three out of four were Democrats in the 1970s. Third,
congressional redistricting in the 1990s may enhance Republican prospects. And finally, the Supreme Court's new position on gerrymanders,
making flagrant ones subject to invalidation, generally will serve Republican interests more fully than Democratic ones.[28]

    As for the other party sphere, the presidency, there is no reason to
believe that the Republican party has a lock on it. This is a highly
competitive office. Hence the durability of the two-tiered (executive-
legislative) electoral system remains to be seen. In the short run, it is
more likely to be disrupted by a Democratic presidential victory than by
a Republican sweep of both houses of Congress.

6. The escalation of interest-group activity.

The growth in the number and influence of interest groups is one of the
key developments in American politics in recent years. Members of
Congress have become acutely sensitive to the power of lobbies. To quote
former senator Abraham Ribicoff (D-Conn.): "Lobbying has reached a
new dimension and is more effective than ever in history. It has become a
big computerized operation in which the Congress and the public are
being bombarded by single-issue groups." [29]

    The increasing influence of interest groups undoubtedly has con-
tributed to the weakening of the parties. Parties and interest groups
compete for the same political space. When legislators are more con-

cerned with satisfying interest-group claims than with supporting party positions and leaders, the vitality of legislative party organizations is sapped. When party lines collapse, collective responsibility for decisions is diminished. Increasingly, individual members are on their own, crowded and pressured by groups intent on getting their way. Rep. David R. Obey (D-Wis.) has put it this way: "It's a lot more difficult to say no to anybody because so many people have well-oiled mimeograph machines." [30] Or, in the grimly blunt words of Sen. Edward M. Kennedy: "We have the best Congress money can buy. Congress is awash in contributions from special interests that expect something in return." [31]

The current controversy over interest groups focuses on their campaign contributions to candidates for office. Political action committees have become a dominant force in financing congressional campaigns, especially for House seats. Overall, PAC contributions to House and Senate candidates in the 1984 election reached $105 million; in 1986 they grew to $132 million. Roughly 42 percent of all campaign funds received by House incumbents in 1984 came from political action committees. The average House incumbent accepted a total of $142,000 from assorted PACs, about four-and-one-half times as much as PACs gave to the average House challenger.[32] One House incumbent reported PAC receipts of more than $650,000.[33] Currently, about one-fourth of all campaign funds collected by Senate candidates is derived from PACs. For winning Senate candidates in 1986, PAC contributions averaged $833,000; only two of the thirty-four winners accepted less than $500,000 from these committees.[34] The data on funding point in the same direction: congressional candidates have become increasingly dependent on interest-group money. And it is not unreasonable for writers, politicians, public interest groups such as Common Cause, and the public to wonder whether those public officials whose campaigns are heavily financed by PACs find their independence compromised in the policy-making process. Legislation to reduce PAC contributions in congressional campaigns has become a persistent item on the congressional agenda, and prospects for adoption have increased.

Another dimension of the interest-group problem is that of single-issue groups.[35] Their issue is *the* issue; their position is the one on which legislators are to be judged. The compromises that occur naturally to practical politicians seldom carry much weight with the leaders of single-issue groups; members are either for or against the Panama Canal treaties, gun control, abortion, tax reductions, equal rights, nuclear power, environmental safeguards, prayer in the public schools, or any of a number of other issues including certain foreign policies for which there are active domestic constituencies. There are insistent groups on each side of each of these troublesome questions. And legislators do not find it easy to hide from these groups, especially since decision-making processes have become increasingly open as a result of the reform wave of the 1970s.

The broad point is that weakened parties provide slim protection for the harassed legislator in a free-for-all system. Middle-of-the-road politicians find themselves in trouble. Public service itself becomes increasingly frustrating in a politics of tiptoe and tightrope. Shortly before he was defeated for reelection in 1978, a northern Democratic senator observed:

> The single-interest constituencies have just about destroyed politics as I knew it. They've made it miserable to be in office—or to run for office—and left me feeling it's hardly worth the struggle to survive.[36]

The "special cause" quality of much of contemporary politics is also reflected in these comments by a leading official in Minnesota's Democratic-Farmer-Labor party:

> Frankly, there are very few of us in the party leadership now whose primary goal is the election of candidates committed to a broad liberal agenda. Most of the people in control are there to advance their own special causes. From the time we spend on it, you would think the most important problem in the world is whether there should be speedboats on six lakes in northern Minnesota.[37]

The arrival of narrow issue politics has changed the American political landscape. Pragmatic politics has been diminished and compromise has declined as a way of doing business. In forming their positions on certain inflammatory, high-principle issues, members believe that there is a reduced margin for error. A wrong vote can cost them electoral support and produce new challenges to their reelection. And not in a few cases members believe they are faced with a no-win vote—where a vote on either side of a controversial, high-visibility issue appears likely to damage their electoral security.

7. The public's declining confidence in political institutions.

The confidence of the American public in its social and political institutions is substantially lower today than it was two or three decades ago. Nevertheless, it is not as low as it was in the mid-1970s.

Popular disillusionment concerning politics and political institutions did not simply emerge as a result of the revelations of Watergate.

TABLE 6-7   Popular Trust in Government, 1964-1984

	1964	1970	1972	1974	1978	1980	1984
Always	14%	7%	5%	3%	3%	2%	4%
Most of the time	62	47	48	34	27	23	40
Some or none of the time	22	44	45	62	68	73	54
Don't know	2	2	2	1	2	2	2
N [a]	1445	1497	2279	2499	2288	1606	1921

SOURCE: National Election Studies, Center for Political Studies, University of Michigan.

NOTE: Question: How much of the time do you think you can trust the government in Washington to do what is right—just about always, most of the time, or only some of the time?

[a] NAs excluded.

This trend began earlier (see Table 6-7). The disclosures of criminal activities by leading officials of the White House, and President Nixon's role in the coverup, merely accentuated it.

There is no simple explanation for the decline of trust in government. Many factors have been at work, probably the most important of which center in public dissatisfaction with policy outcomes—involving urban unrest and riots in the 1960s, the Vietnam War, and the government's inability to solve certain social and economic problems. It seems likely that the public's negative evaluations of the performance of several presidents also contributed to the erosion of public confidence in government.

Whatever the explanation, many voters have a cynical view of government. About six out of ten people now believe, for example, that "government is pretty much run by a few big interests looking out for themselves." And nearly half of those surveyed agree with the proposition that "public officials don't care much what people like me think" (see Figure 6-1).

Declining trust in government undoubtedly has affected the party system. Though the evidence is elusive, it appears likely that the loosening of ties to party (as manifested in the large number of independent voters and the increase in ticket splitting), the influx and successes of celebrity candidates, the preponderance of candidate-centered campaigns, the popular fascination with anti-establishment candidates, the apparent success of negative campaigns, and the preoccupation with party reform all bear a relationship to the depletion of popular good will

FIGURE 6-1   Evidence of Public Alienation from Government

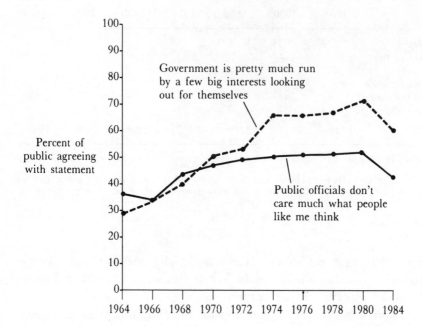

SOURCE: Data drawn from National Election Studies, Center for Political Studies, University of Michigan.

toward government and to the generalized skepticism concerning political institutions.

Nothing about this condition of declining trust is immutable. Changes in political leadership, reorientations in governmental policies leading to amelioration or resolution of nagging problems, successful new policy ventures, and the more complete fulfillment of popular expectations could strengthen trust in government. Positive changes in public attitudes toward government, for example, occurred early in the Reagan administration. Whether this minitrend played itself out, as a result of the Iran-contra scandal and other Reagan administration adventures in misinformation, remains to be seen.[38]

8. The growing importance of professional campaign management firms and the media in politics.

American party organizations no longer dominate the process of winning political support for the candidates who run under their labels. This is one of the principal facts to be known about the party system today. The role of party organizations in campaigns has declined as professional management firms, pollsters, and media specialists—stirred by the prospects of new accounts and greater profits—have arrived on the political scene. Indeed, so important have they become in political campaigns, especially for major offices, that it often appears as if the party has been reduced to the role of spectator. To be sure, the parties continue to raise and spend money, to staff their headquarters with salaried personnel and volunteers, and to seek to turn out the vote on election day. What they do matters, but much less so than in the past.

The center of major political campaigns now lies in the decisions and activities of individual candidates and in their use of consultants, campaign management firms, and the mass media—not in the party organizations or in the decisions of party leaders. Modern political campaigning calls for resources and skills that the parties can furnish only in part (more so on the Republican than Democratic side). Public opinion surveys are needed to pinpoint important issues, to locate sources of support and opposition, and to learn how voters appraise the qualities of the candidate. Electronic data processing is useful in the analysis of voting behavior and for the simulation of campaign decisions. For a fee, candidates with sufficient financial resources can avail themselves of specialists of all kinds: public relations, advertising, fund raising, communications, and financial counseling. They can hire experts in film making, speech writing, speech coaching, voter registration, direct mail letter campaigns, computer information services, time buying (for radio and television), voter analysis, get-out-the-vote drives, and campaign strategy. Fewer and fewer things are left to chance or to the vicissitudes of party administration. What a candidate hears, says, does, wears, and possibly even thinks bears the heavy imprint of the specialist in campaign management.

Campaign consulting is a growth industry. Consultants whose candidates win upset or overwhelming victories are celebrated by politicians and the media alike. They are hot commodities, and candidates vie to purchase their services. Folklore develops that the right consultant is the key to victory. Reportedly, both candidates for the Democratic nomination to the U.S. Senate in New Jersey in 1978 sought to hire the same consultant, one who had gained fame for his victories in the mayoralty race in New York City and the governor's race in New Jersey.[39]

There is, it seems, no end to the variety of services made available to candidates by management firms. The Campaign Communications Institute of America (CCI) has an arrangement under which a candidate low on cash can charge services on his American Express card. A glimpse of other services CCI provides may be gained from this account:

> Under a middleman arrangement with some 35 manufacturing and service firms, [CCI] has produced a swollen bag of personalized vote-getting tricks. There are the routine items—bumper stickers, buttons, litter bags, matchbooks, posters, and flags. But there is also a $19.95 tape-playing machine that enables the candidate to carry his inspirational messages into the homes of voters over the telephone. There are Hertz rental cars equipped with bullhorn sound systems. And there is a $39.95 portable projector that flashes slogans, pictures, and platforms on anything from a living-room wall to the side of an office building. "Our job," the board chairman of CCI has said, "is to enable the low-budget candidate to get the most votes for his bucks."
>
> For well-heeled candidates, CCI will also arrange mass telephone campaigns at a cent and a half a call, state-wide voter polls (sample prices: $4,000 for Vermont, $9,000 for New York) and direct campaigns through Western Union Services or New York's big Reuben H. Donnelly Corporation. . . . "Whenever and wherever people elect people, we'll be there," says the CCI board chairman. "That's our market." [40]

The coming of age of the mass media, technocracy, and the techniques of mass persuasion has had a marked impact on the political system.[41] A new politics has emerged that is dominated by image makers and technical experts of all kinds—organizations and persons who know what the public wants in its candidates and how to give it to them. Consider these views and prognoses for an issueless, pseudopolitics:

> It is not surprising . . . that politicians and advertising men should have discovered one another. And, once they recognized that the citizen did not so much vote for a candidate as make a psychological purchase of him, not surprising that they began to work together. . . . Advertising agencies have tried openly to sell Presidents since 1952. When Dwight Eisenhower ran for reelection in 1956, the agency of Batton, Barton, Durstine and Osborn, which had been on a retainer throughout his first four years, accepted his campaign as a regular account. Leonard Hall, national Republican chairman, said: "You sell your candidates and your programs the way a business sells its products." [42]
>
> Day-by-day campaign reports spin on through regular newscasts and special reports. The candidates make their progress through engineered crowds, taking part in manufactured pseudo events, thrusting and parrying charges, projecting as much as they can, with the help of

makeup and technology, the qualities of youth, experience, sincerity, popularity, alertness, wisdom, and vigor. And television follows them, hungry for material that is new and sensational. The new campaign strategists also generate films that are like syrupy documentaries: special profiles of candidates, homey, bathed in soft light, resonant with stirring music, creating personality images such as few mortals could emulate.[43]

In all countries the party system has folded like the organization chart. Policies and issues are useless for election purposes, since they are too specialized and hot. The shaping of a candidate's integral image has taken the place of discussing conflicting points of view.[44]

[Party] organizations find themselves increasingly dependent on management and consultant personnel, pollsters, and image-makers. The professional campaigners, instead of being the handmaidens of our major political parties, are independent factors in American elections. Parties turn to professional technicians for advice on how to restructure their organizations, for information about their clienteles, for fund-raising, and for recruiting new members. Candidates, winning nominations in primaries with the aid of professional campaigners rather than that of political parties, are increasingly independent of partisan controls. The old politics does not rest well beside the new technology.[45]

No matter what happens, the national political parties of the future will no longer be the same as in the past. Television has made the voter's home the campaign amphitheater, and opinion surveys have made it his polling booth. From this perspective, he has little regard for or need of a political party, at least as we have known it, to show him how to release the lever on Election Day.[46]

9. The increasing nationalization of politics.

So unobtrusively has the change come about that a great many American citizens are doubtless unaware of the extent to which sectional political alignments have been replaced by a national political alignment. The Republican vote in the South in the 1952 presidential election was, it turns out, more than a straw in the wind. Eisenhower carried four southern states, narrowly lost several others, made the Republican party respectable for many southern voters, and, most important, laid the foundation for the development of a viable Republican party throughout the South.

From the latter part of the nineteenth century until recently, the main obstacle to the nationalization of politics was the strength of the

Democratic party in the South. Presidential, congressional, state, and local offices were won, as a matter of course, by the Democrats. No longer is this the case. Republicans now dominate presidential elections in the South. In 1980 and 1984, for example, among southern states only Georgia (in 1980) voted for the Democratic presidential candidate. To recapture the South, popular wisdom suggests, the Democrats may have to nominate a southern candidate.

Republican gains in southern congressional elections have also been impressive (see Table 6-8). The Republican statewide percentage of the vote for representative has grown more or less steadily since the 1950s. About one-third of all House members elected in the South in 1984 and 1986 were Republicans. Vigorous two-party competition occurs even in the states of the Deep South (Alabama, Georgia, Louisiana, Mississippi, and South Carolina). In the 1950s, by contrast, the Republican party rarely even nominated candidates for the House of Representatives in these states. And throughout the South Republican candidates for the Senate now compete much more effectively than in the past. There is a strong breeze of Republicanism coursing through southern electorates.

The movement from parochial to national politics has not been

TABLE 6-8 Republican Percentage of the Statewide Major-Party Vote for the U.S. House of Representatives, Selected Years, Southern States

State	\multicolumn{7}{c}{Republican statewide percentage}						
	1950	1952	1968	1978	1982	1984	1986
Alabama	0.7	5.4	30.8	42.9	32.9	27.3	33.0
Arkansas	0.0	14.3	53.0	66.1	47.6	21.0	41.5
Florida	9.6	25.9	42.8	41.7	40.8	48.9	44.4
Georgia	0.0	0.0	20.5	32.6	33.8	28.3	37.9
Louisiana	0.0	8.7	18.8	50.0	a	a	a
Mississippi	0.0	2.5	7.5	36.9	42.0	38.5	47.3
North Carolina	30.0	32.2	45.4	35.9	44.3	47.6	43.3
South Carolina	0.0	2.0	32.8	37.6	45.5	48.4	42.4
Tennessee	30.3	29.8	51.1	47.3	37.8	44.8	49.2
Texas	9.5	1.3	28.1	40.6	32.4	42.3	50.9
Virginia	24.9	31.0	46.4	50.2	53.1	55.8	54.0

SOURCE: Developed from data in *The 1968 Elections* (Washington, D.C.: Republican National Committee, 1969), 115-116; and *Congressional Quarterly Weekly Report,* November 9, 1974, 3084-3091; November 11, 1978, 3283-3291; November 6, 1982, 2817-2825; April 13, 1985, 689-695; and November 8, 1986, 2864-2870.

[a] In Louisiana, House candidates run on a nonpartisan ballot in the September primary. If no candidate receives a majority in the district, the top two (irrespective of party) face each other in November. Candidates who receive a majority in the primary are considered to be elected.

Growing Republicanism in the South

	Republican party performance in southern states				
	1948	1952	1964	1968	1984
Presidential					
Percentage of two-party popular vote	36	49	47	53	63
Percentage of white popular vote	a	a	a	a	72
States won	0	5	5	7	13
Electoral votes won	0	65	47	74	155
Percentage of electoral votes	0	45	32	51	100
Congressional					
Percentage of House seats held following election	3	8	15	26	36
Percentage of Senate seats held following election	0	4	15	27	46
Gubernatorial					
Percentage of governorships held following election	0	0	8	38	15
State legislative					
Percentage of chambers controlled following election	0	0	0	0	0
Percentage of lower house seats held following election	5	6	9	16	24
Percentage of upper house seats held following election	4	5	8	15	19
Party identification					
Percentage Republican overall	a	a	15	17	36
Percentage of white southerners					
Strong Republicans	a	4	8	5	11
Weak Republicans	a	7	7	8	13
Independent Republicans	a	3	6	12	15

SOURCE: The data are drawn from a variety of sources, including *Congressional Quarterly Weekly Report, Statistical Abstract of the United States, Book of the States,* and *Gallup Opinion Index*. The data on the party identification of white southerners are from the Center for Political Studies, University of Michigan, as reported in Ray Wolfinger and Michael G. Hagen, "Republican Prospects: Southern Comfort," *Public Opinion* 8 (October/November 1985): 9.

NOTE: The data relate only to the South. The states considered southern are Alabama, Arkansas, Florida, Georgia, Kentucky, Louisiana, Mississippi, North Carolina, Oklahoma, South Carolina, Tennessee, Texas, and Virginia.

[a] Not available.

limited to the South. No matter what its history of party allegiance and voting, no state is wholly secure from incursions by the minority party. The vote in presidential elections now tends to be distributed more or less evenly throughout the country; fewer and fewer states register overwhelming victories for one or the other of the major parties. One-party political systems dwindle. "It is probably safe to say that in national and state-wide politics we are in the time of the most intense, evenly-spaced, two-party competitiveness of the last 100 years." [47]

The sources for the growing nationalization of American politics are both numerous and varied. Social changes, rather than conscious party efforts to extend their spheres of influence, have provided the principal thrust for the new shape given to American party politics. Among the most important of these has been the emergence and extraordinary development of the mass media in political communications. Through the electronic media, national political figures can be created virtually overnight, national issues can be carried to the most remote and inaccessible community, and new styles and trends can become a matter of common knowledge in a matter of days or weeks. Insulation, old loyalties, and established patterns are difficult to maintain intact in the face of contemporary political communications. Consider these observations by Harvey Wheeler:

> Eisenhower was himself a newcomer to party politics. . . . He was heavily financed. He employed expensive and sophisticated mass media experts. "Madison Avenue" techniques were devised to project a predesigned "image." A new kind of electoral coalition was formed, composed largely of urban, white-collar people dissociated from the grass roots traditions of the agrarian past. His campaign cut across traditional party lines to orient itself about the personality of the candidate rather than the machine or the party. The new coalition of voter groups was socially and geographically mobile. The new politics required image manipulators rather than ballot box stuffers. The new organizations were ad hoc affairs created overnight by national cadres of advance men. The presidential primary overshadowed the party convention. This was to be the wave of the future. Television truly nationalized campaign communications and undermined the federal structure of the old machines. Party politics gave way to personality politics.[48]

For all their importance to the changes under way, the electronic media have not by themselves transformed the face of American politics. Changes in technology, the diversification of the economic bases of the states, the growth of an affluent society, the higher educational attainments of voters, the mobility of the population, the migration of black citizens to the North, the illumination of massive nationwide problems, the growth of vast urban conglomerations, and the assimilation of immigrant groups have all contributed to the erosion of internal barriers and parochialism and, consequently, to the strengthening of national political patterns. Whatever the complete explanation for this phenomenon, one thing is clear: the forces for the nationalization of politics are far more powerful today than the forces for localism and sectionalism. A changing party system is the inevitable result.

10. A continuation of party competition based on meaningful policy differences between the parties.

The American parties are often criticized for being Tweedledum and Tweedledee—for being so similar that even attentive voters can miss the alternatives they present. This criticism has limited merit. Consider, first of all, the ideology and policy attitudes of Democratic and Republican elites during the Reagan era. The differences contrast sharply in how Democratic and Republican delegates to the 1984 national conventions classified themselves in terms of ideology (see Figure 6-2). Sixty percent of all Republican delegates emerged as conservatives, while 50 percent of all Democratic delegates described themselves as liberals. Only 1 percent of the Republican delegates were liberals and only 5 percent of the Democratic delegates were conservatives. It is thus unsurprising that the party platforms diverged. The Republican platform endorsed such conservative proposals as a constitutional amendment to require a balanced federal budget, right-to-work laws, a ban on abortions, voluntary prayer in the schools, increased military spending, an easing of gun controls, restrictions on the jurisdiction of federal courts, and work requirements for welfare recipients. On nearly all of these issues, the Democratic platform provided clear-cut contrasts.

Party conflict in Congress also occurs along liberal-conservative lines. Over the years most Democratic members have supported labor-endorsed legislation, measures to provide for government regulation of business, social welfare bills of great variety, civil rights legislation, federal aid to education, and limitations on defense expenditures. By contrast, Republican members have generally favored business over labor, social welfare programs of more modest proportions, private action rather than government involvement, state rather than federal responsibility for domestic programs, the interests of higher-income groups over those of lower-income groups, and a greater emphasis on

FIGURE 6-2   The Ideology of National Convention Delegates, 1984

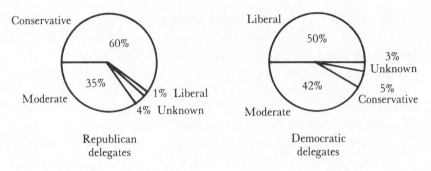

Republican
delegates

Democratic
delegates

SOURCE: Developed from survey data gathered by CBS and the *New York Times*. See the *New York Times*, July 15, 1984, and August 2, 1984.

NOTE: Ideological positions are based on self-classification.

national defense. When viewing the economy, party members typically focus on different problems: Republicans are more concerned about inflation, Democrats more concerned about unemployment.[49] During the Reagan presidency, party conflict in Congress was particularly intense over the defense budget, arms control, and the administration's support for guerrilla movements opposing leftist regimes.

The important point to recognize is that the parties' weaknesses— particularly apparent in the electoral process—have not clouded the ideological differences between their leaders. Meaningful differences separate the parties in Congress (or at least majorities of the two parties). Even larger differences divide the parties' national convention delegates. Quite plainly, Democratic and Republican party elites do not evaluate public problems in the same light. Nor are they attracted to the same solutions.

Differences between the parties can also be examined from the perspective of the public. In a survey of how individuals see themselves in ideological terms and how they perceive the ideology of each party, people who view themselves as middle-of-the-roaders are most numerous (see Figure 6-3). Interestingly, more people now see themselves as conservatives than formerly; the proportion of conservatives increased from 31 percent in 1976 to 36 percent in 1984, a gain roughly parallel- ing the increase in the number of Republican party identifiers. The number of self-described liberals has slipped sharply—from 24 percent during the Carter administration to 18 percent during the Reagan administration.

The public's assessment of each party's ideological position is close

FIGURE 6-3   Ideology and Party in the 1980s

How people see themselves:
The political ideology of the public, 1976 and 1984

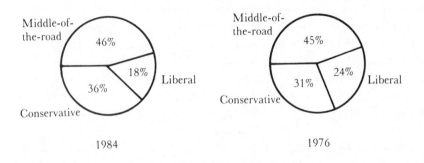

1984   1976

The public's perceptions of each party's ideology, 1984

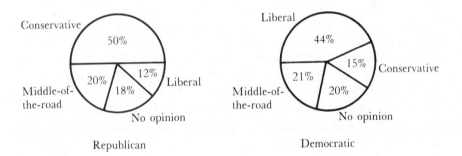

Republican   Democratic

SOURCE: Developed from data in *Gallup Report*, November 1984, 23.

to the mark. Fifty percent of the public finds the Republican party to be conservative, while 44 percent views the Democratic party as liberal. Each party is categorized as middle-of-the-road by about one-fifth of the electorate—a label that may well fit the facts in certain areas. The people who are analytically out of focus are not numerous: the 12 percent who see the Republican party as liberal and the 15 percent who see the Democratic party as conservative (though southern respondents who find the Democratic party to be conservative can find abundant local evidence to support their view). The broad point is simple but important: The public's ideological development and its understanding of the ideological leanings of the parties are generally consistent with the idea of programmatic parties.

Other evidence on the public's general awareness of party positions is available. Gallup poll survey data presented in Figure 6-4 show the distribution of voters on the recurrent question of which party best represents certain interests, for example, labor or business. Prior to the Reagan administration, the typical survey findings showed that at least one-third of the voters saw no difference between the parties or had no opinion. Since then, the lines between the parties have been drawn more clearly. The Democratic party has consistently emerged as the party of the working class, while the Republican party has been viewed as the party most responsive to the interests of business and professional people as well as white collar workers in general. These perceptions of interest group orientations form a classic distinction in American politics. They are salient for many voters, helping them to organize political information and to evaluate candidates. Hence in the policy orientations of their elites and in the public mind, the parties do stand for something—almost surely for more than they are given credit.

11. An era of party and governmental reform.

Ordinarily, changes in American politics do not come easily. No democratic political system anywhere rivals the American system for the number of opportunities present to prevent or delay the resolution of public problems or the adoption of new forms and practices. American politics is slow politics. Nonetheless, during the current era many large-scale reforms have found their way into the party structure, into Congress, and into public policies that shape and regulate the political process. In the main, these changes took shape and were adopted during a time in which the political system was in substantial disarray. In the midst of an unpopular war, challenged on all sides, President Johnson withdrew from the presidential election campaign of 1968. Robert F. Kennedy was assassinated. The 1968 Democratic convention, meeting in Chicago, was an ordeal of rancor, tumult, and rioting. And then came the Watergate affair—an assault on the political process itself. It is not surprising that public alienation from the political system, which had been building for years, reached a high point. The stage was set for reform. The success of those who brought it about was due to their ability to seize upon these unusual and transitory circumstances to develop new ways of carrying on political business.

From almost any perspective, the changes were remarkable. More reforms were adopted between 1968 and 1974 than at any time since the early nineteenth century.[50] The power of national party agencies to

FIGURE 6-4   The Public's Perception of the Party Best for Unskilled Workers,
Business Owners and Professional People, and White Collar
Workers, 1947-1984

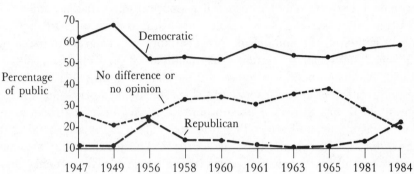

Party best for unskilled workers

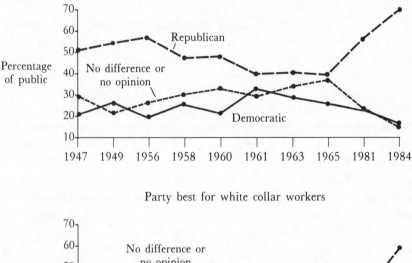

Party best for business owners and professional people

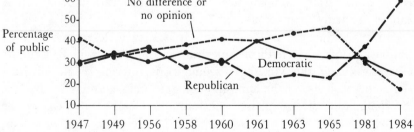

Party best for white collar workers

SOURCE: Developed from data in *Gallup Report*, November 1981, 29-45, and January/
February 1985, 21-34.

establish standards for state party participation in national nominating conventions was established—and the Supreme Court added its imprimatur to this development. The first national party charter was adopted by the Democrats. At the state level, a number of presidential primary laws were adopted to broaden political participation, and caucus-convention systems were opened up—thus contributing to the democratization of the nominating process. Nor was Congress immune to change. The seniority system was modified by providing for secret caucus ballots on nominees for committee chairmen, thus increasing the responsiveness of these leaders to fellow party members. Committee power itself was dispersed as subcommittees and their chairmen won new measures of authority. The filibuster rule was revised, making it easier for a Senate majority to assert itself. The party caucus took on new roles and new vigor. To reduce the influence of private money and big contributors in political campaigns, the Federal Election Campaign Act was adopted, with its provision for public financing of presidential campaigns. In sum, numerous new choices and opportunities were presented to politicians and public alike.

For the most part, the party reforms of the modern period were designed to democratize political institutions and processes. Concretely, reformers set out to reduce the power of elites (that is, party leaders or "bosses") and to augment the power of ordinary citizens. And they were clearly successful, at least on the surface. But as Nelson W. Polsby has shown, the reforms led to numerous other, unanticipated consequences, particularly on the Democratic side: state party organizations were weakened; party elites lost influence to media elites; candidate organizations came to dominate the presidential selection process; presidential candidates were encouraged to develop factionalist strategies (in seeking to differentiate their candidacies) rather than to build broad coalitions; and the national convention fell under the sway of candidate enthusiasts and interest group delegates as its role in the presidential nominating process shifted from candidate selection to candidate ratification.[51] These changes are truly momentous.

In evaluating the party reforms, it is easy to lose sight of their relationship to the strength of American parties. As David B. Truman observed recently, the McGovern Commission reforms "could not have been accomplished over the opposition of alert and vigorous state parties. The commission staff exploited the limitations and weaknesses of the state parties; they did not cause them." [52] The reforms, in other words, weakened an institution already in more than a little trouble.

Party reform is thus not the same as party strengthening. A more open political process, for example, does not necessarily contribute to the increased participation of the general public, to a heightening of political trust, or to popular acceptance of the parties. A demographically representative national convention, a central objective of the Democratic reforms, has not led to the selection of candidates who can best represent the party, unify it, or be elected. The public financing of presidential election campaigns has not by any means solved the problem of money in politics, as the spiraling costs of elections and the growing power of PACs clearly show. Changes in party-committee relations in Congress have not changed congressional behavior in significant ways—Congress remains an institution whose members have an unusually low tolerance for hierarchy in any form. The adoption of a national party charter has not diminished the prevailing federalism of American politics or reduced the autonomy of state and local parties on most matters that count.[53]

The reform of the party system must therefore be taken with a grain of salt—for a reason that is obvious to anyone who began reading this book somewhat in advance of this page. American parties are to an important extent the dependent variable in the scheme of politics, more the products of their environment than the architects of it. The only governmental system the parties have known is Madisonian, marked by division of power and made to order for weak parties. Federalism, the separation of powers, and all manner of structural arrangements and election laws (for example, direct primary, candidate-oriented campaign regulations, nonconcurrent terms for executive and legislature, nonpartisan elections, and staggered elections) militate against the development of strong parties. And by diminishing party control over the presidential nominating process, the reforms weakened the only national institution fully empowered to represent the party's constituent elements.[54] The massive use of television for political campaigns, the increasing power of special-interest groups, and the arrival of public relations, media, survey, computer, and fund-raising experts have also contributed heavily to the current candidate-centered system that stresses personality over party and, frequently, style over substance. And for an American public that has never had much enthusiasm for parties, their current desuetude is not likely to be cause for popular concern.

12. A growing effort to professionalize and strengthen party organization.

In this era of overall party decline, there is one bright spot: the increasing strength of parties in organizational terms. Evidence of professionalization and organizational strength is varied. It appears, for example, in the significant growth of permanent and professional party staffs at both national and state committee levels. The national committee's functions have been broadened and diversified, as the committee has shifted from an exclusive preoccupation with presidential matters. The Republican National Committee has become heavily involved in a range of party-building activities that include serious efforts to promote party fortunes in state and local election campaigns. Operating budgets for the national committees have grown markedly. The capacity of the national parties to raise funds, particularly in direct mail campaigns, has improved dramatically—in this respect, the Republican party again led the way, but the Democrats have been gaining ground. On the Democratic side, national party authority has been substantially enlarged through the development of rules for state party participation in national nominating conventions. While the Democratic party has increased the legal authority of its national organization, the new importance of the national Republican apparatus has stemmed from successful fund raising that permits it to offer extensive services to state party organizations and candidates.[55]

The strength of state party organizations, a recent study finds, is partly a function of the party-building activities of the national party organization, leading to greater national-state party integration. State party organizational strength is reflected in matters of *program, recruitment,* and *bureaucratization;* specifically, it appears in services to candidates, headquarters' staff size and complexity, newsletters, voter mobilization programs, public opinion polling, headquarters accessibility, candidate recruitment, issue leadership, leadership professionalism, and money contributions to candidates. Many Republican state party organizations score high on these indicators. Virtually without exception, Democratic state organizations are substantially weaker than their Republican counterparts. Nonetheless, the weaker Democratic National Committee seems to have had more success than the stronger RNC in adding to the capabilities of its state party organizations, perhaps because any addition in resources for a weak organization renders it more effective. For the most part, national-state party integration (or influence) is a one-way street, since most state parties rank low in the degree to which they are involved in (and thus influence) national committee affairs.[56]

Professionalism of the parties is clearly on the rise. At the national level, the parties' financial strength never has been greater. Staff development has been impressive. The parties, through their staffs, have become sophisticated in the use of modern campaign technologies that involve computers, electronic mail, television, marketing, advertising, survey research, data processing, and direct mail solicitations. And of considerable interest, influence generally flows from the national level downward, a distinctly different pattern from the state-dominated party structure of the past.[57]

Intriguing to consider is whether the structural changes and other developments have arrested the parties' downward slide and strengthened their capacity to function as parties. Are they better able to discharge the traditional functions of party involving recruitment, nominations, campaigns, and control of government? Specifically, how strong is party performance today in grooming and recruiting candidates, controlling nominations, controlling campaign resources (money, manpower, expertise), electing their candidates and controlling a range of offices simultaneously, mobilizing voters, stimulating competition, maintaining effective coalitions and inhibiting factional conflict, illuminating issues and fashioning policy alternatives, representing and integrating group interests, making public policy, enforcing discipline, providing public instruction, winning public acceptance and loyalty, and providing voters with a means for keeping government accountable? Exactly what a resurgence of the parties would consist of is hard to say, but it would seem to require them to conduct these activities, or at least most of them, reasonably well. National fund raising and provision of services aside, the reality is that the parties are unable to do most of these things much if any better than in the past. And in certain key respects, the parties seem to be doing substantially worse.

In the old-fashioned sense of party organization as a network of individuals that does grass-roots party work, as Byron Shafer observes, the parties are in "precipitous decline."[58] Unquestionably, the party-in-the-electorate has never been weaker.[59] Partisanship is at low ebb. Candidates and incumbents dominate the electoral system. Party coalitions, the quintessence of American parties, have atrophied. Control over nominations, the sine qua non of strong parties as E. E. Schattschneider and others have argued, is thin and insubstantial at all levels.[60] (And in an ecumenical spirit, but only 5-4, the Supreme Court recently opened the door for independents to vote in party primaries, if the parties approve.)[61] Split-election outcomes and divided government are the norm in nation and state. Party control over government continues to be uneven and unpredictable, and programmatic responsibility, which is occasionally impressive, is typically elusive and erratic. The influence of the media and interest groups in key phases of politics has probably never been greater. Indeed, in the presidential selection process, the media have simply supplanted the parties. The overall condition of American parties thus leaves a great deal to be desired. All things considered, and despite their heightened professionalism and enhanced bureaucratization, the parties are in about the same shape as observers have long known them, which is to say that, at best, they are no more than moderately successful in some of the things they do.

The Prospects

The American party system has been shaped more by custom and environment than by intent. Indeed, in broad contour, the parties of today resemble closely those of previous generations. For as long as can be remembered, the major parties have been loose and disorderly coalitions, heavily decentralized, lacking in unity and discipline, preoccupied with winning office, and no more than erratically responsible for the conduct of government and the formation of public policy. There is, of course, another side to them. They have performed at least as well as the parties of other democratic nations—and perhaps far better. Democratic politics requires the maintenance of a predictable legal system; institutionalized arrangements for popular control of government and the mobilization of majorities; methods and arenas for the illumination, crystallization, and reconciliation of conflict; and means for endowing both leaders and policies with legitimacy. To each of these requirements the parties have contributed steadily and often in major ways.[62]

A truism of American politics is that it is invariably difficult to cut free from familiar institutions. Old practices die hard. Conventional arrangements hang on and on. Change arrives incrementally and unnoticed. Not only are most Americans habituated to weak parties but the parties themselves are accustomed to the environment in which they function. It would seem that prospects for the development of a system of responsible parties are thin at best. But the matter deserves a closer look.

It seems clear that on most counts the parties have lost ground in recent years. The electoral party organizations undoubtedly have been weakened. Their control over the nominating process, once a virtual monopoly, has gradually slipped away. Primary battles for major offices appear to occur more and more freqently. So-called independent candidates seem to be more numerous and more successful than in the past. Indeed, many candidates use the party label "in the same spirit that ships sail under Liberian registry—a flag of convenience, and no more." [63] More voters have come to regard themselves as independents in recent years than ever before—occasionally, in fact, independents outnumber Republicans (though not since early in the Reagan administration). The power of local party leaders probably never has been less than it is today. The media, public relations consultants, campaign management firms, and political action committees are now as much a part of campaigns as the party organizations—at least when important offices are at stake. In sum, American parties compete within the political process but do not dominate it. In some jurisdictions they are all but invisible. A great deal of contemporary politics lies outside the parties and beyond their control.

The weakness of the parties makes the prospects for the development of a full-blown responsible party system anything but bright. Too many obstacles—constitutional, political, and otherwise—stand in the way. But this is not to say that responsible party performance in government is unattainable. The way in which parties govern is far from dependent upon the strength and vitality of the electoral party organizations or upon the way in which men and women are elected to office. The party-in-the-government, it is worth remembering, is both different from the party-in-the-electorate and largely independent of it.

The essence of a responsible party system is not to be found in party councils, closed primaries, demographically representative national conventions, off-year party conventions, government financing of elections, or intraparty democracy. Instead, the key idea is represented in party responsibility for a program of public policy. Such responsibility requires, in the first place, a strong measure of internal cohesion within the party-in-the-government in order to adopt its program, and, in the second place, an electorate sufficiently sensitive to party accomplishments and failures that it can hold the parties accountable for their records, particularly in the case of the party in power. At times, neither requirement can be met to any degree. Nevertheless, there are occasions when American political institutions function in a manner largely consonant with the party responsibility model.

A responsible party system at the national level demands a particular kind of Congress—one in which power is centralized rather than dispersed. Over long stretches of time, Congress has not been organized to permit the parties, *qua* parties, to govern. The seniority system, the independence of committees and their chairmen, the filibuster, the weaknesses present in elected party positions and agencies, and the unrepresentativeness of Congress itself have made it difficult for party majorities to assert themselves and to act in the name of the party. Nevertheless,

---

What Would "Strong" Parties Look Like?

In the electorate:

1. Public perception of parties as legitimate and fair.
2. Party electioneering, broad electoral appeal, and well-established "mainstream" constituencies.
3. Sufficient power to limit fragmentation by keeping the nomination stage from becoming a free-for-all among numerous candidates.
4. Sufficient resources (for example, money, manpower, expertise) to perform their functions adequately.

In the government:

5. Power associated with responsibility: the capacity to govern through distinctive cooperation and cohesion among fellow partisans in the policy process.

In electorate and government:

6. The presence of sufficient rewards and incentives to induce support and secure compliance among activists and officeholders.
7. Capacity to limit disaffection and conflict among groups that compose the party coalition.
8. Capacity to adapt in response to changes in the political environment.

SOURCE: This is a modest adaptation of a list of attributes developed in David E. Price, *Bringing Back the Parties* (Washington, D.C.: CQ Press, 1984), 123.

NOTE: Do the parties meet these broad requirements? In my view, the answer is "hardly at all" in the case of 1, 2, 3, and 6 and "moderately at best" in the case of 4, 5, 7, and 8.

---

these barriers to party majority building have been notably diminished in recent years.

Every so often the congressional party comes fully alive. Consider the first session of the Eighty-ninth Congress (1965)—"the most dramatic illustration in a generation of the capacity of the president and the Congress to work together on important issues of public policy":

> In part a mopping up operation on an agenda fashioned at least in spirit by the New Deal, the work of the 89th Congress cut new paths through the frontier of qualitative issues: a beautification bill, a bill to create federal support for the arts and humanities, vast increases in federal aid to education. . . . [The] policy leadership and the legislative

skill of President Johnson found a ready and supportive response from a strengthened partisan leadership and a substantial, presidentially oriented Democratic majority in both houses. A decade of incremental structural changes in the locus of power in both houses eased the President's task of consent-building and of legislative implementation. Yet Congress was far from being just a rubber stamp. On some issues the President met resounding defeat. On many issues, presidential recommendations were modified by excisions or additions—reflecting the power of particular committee chairmen, group interests, and bureaucratic pressures at odds with presidential perspectives.

[The lessons of the Eighty-ninth Congress] proved that vigorous presidential leadership and sizable partisan majorities in both houses of the same partisan persuasion as the President could act in reasonable consonance, and with dispatch, in fashioning creative answers to major problems. The nation's voters could pin responsibility upon a national party for the legislative output. If that partisan majority erred in judgment, it could at least be held accountable in ensuing congressional and presidential elections.[64]

Party responsibility came to the fore again in the Ninety-seventh Congress (1981-1982). President Reagan was the beneficiary of the highest party support scores received by any president over the last three decades. His legislative proposals received unusually strong support in Congress. During the first session of the Ninety-seventh Congress, Senate Republicans voted in agreement with the president 80 percent of the time and House Republicans 68 percent of the time.[65] At session end, Republicans could reasonably claim that their party had moved the nation in a new direction. The major elements of their program consisted of major budget cuts, sizable reductions in individual and business taxes, the largest peacetime defense appropriation in the nation's history, a significant cutback in federal regulations, and a moderate reordering of federal-state relations that gave the states greater discretion in the use of funds provided through federal aid. Consonant with the party responsibility model, the performance of the Reagan administration was the overriding issue in the off-year election of 1982, in which Republicans lost twenty-six seats in the House while holding Democrats to a standoff in Senate races. In sum, presidential leadership, in concert with Republican congressional leaders and bolstered by party imagination and discipline, characterized the Ninety-seventh Congress (especially the first session) almost as much as it had the Eighty-ninth. From the perspective of the president, these were halcyon days, but they passed by quickly. Conflict between the branches intensified, the president's legislative successes declined, and legislative assertiveness during the latter stages of the Reagan administration, and particularly during the One-hundredth Congress (1987-1988), became manifest.

No one should expect party-oriented Congresses to be strung together, one following another. The conditions must be right: a partisan majority in general ideological agreement (or an effective majority, such as the Republican-led conservative coalition in the House during the Ninety-seventh Congress) and a vigorous president are essential. A long or innovative policy agenda may also be required. In any case, the point not to be missed is that, under the right circumstances, the deadlocks in American politics can be broken and the political system can function vigorously and with a high degree of cooperation between the branches of government. Party responsibility can thrive even if unrecognized and unlabeled. The evidence of these Congresses suggests that the first requirement for government by responsible parties—a fairly high degree of internal party agreement on policy—can, at least occasionally, be met.

The second requirement—an electorate attuned to party performance in government—is a different matter. This is the point at which the total system of responsible parties tends to break down.

> What the public knows about the legislative records of the parties and of individual congressional candidates is a principal reason for the departure of American practice from an idealized conception of party government. . . . The electorate sees very little altogether of what goes on in the national legislature. Few judgments of legislative performance are associated with the parties, and much of the public is unaware even of which party has control of Congress. . . . Many of those who have commented on the lack of party discipline in Congress have assumed that the Congressman votes against his party because he is forced to by the demands of one of several hundred constituencies of a superlatively heterogeneous nation. In some cases, the Representative may subvert the proposals of his party because his constituency demands it. But a more reasonable interpretation over a broader range of issues is that the Congressman fails to see these proposals as part of a program on which the party—and he himself—will be judged at the polls, because he knows the constituency isn't looking.[66]

Experiments with forms of party responsibility, like fashion, will perhaps always possess a probationary quality—tried, neglected, forgotten, and rediscovered. The tone and mood of such a system will doubtless appear on occasion, but without the public's either anticipating it or recognizing it when it arrives. More generally, however, the party system is likely to resemble, at least in broad lines, the model to which Americans are adjusted and inured: the parties situated precariously atop the political process, threatened and thwarted by a variety of competitors, unable to control their own nominations or to elect "their" nominees, active in fits and starts and often in hiding, beset by factional rifts, shunned or dismissed by countless voters (including many new ones), frustrated by the growing independence of voters, and moderately irresponsible. From the vantage point of both outsiders and insiders, the party system ordinarily will appear, to the extent that it registers at all, in disarray. And indeed it is in disarray—more so than at any time in the last century—but not to a point that either promises or ensures its enfeeblement and disintegration.

Notes

1. All of the proposals for reforming the party system cited in this section, along with quoted material, are drawn from the Committee on Political Parties of the American Political Science Association's report, *Toward a More Responsible Two-Party System* (New York: Holt, Rinehart and Winston, 1950). The longer quotations appear on these pages of the report: 1, 2, 22 (definition of party responsibility); 61-62 (seniority); 66 (intraparty democracy); and 69-70 (party membership).

2. For a comprehensive development of the themes of this and the preceding paragraph, see Austin Ranney, *The Doctrine of Responsible Party Government* (Urbana: University of Illinois Press, 1954), 10-16.

3. There are a number of excellent analyses of party responsibility. See Austin Ranney, "Toward a More Responsible Two-Party System: A Commentary," *American Political Science Review* 45 (June 1951): 488-499; T. William Goodman, "How Much Political Party Centralization Do We Want?" *Journal of Politics* 13 (November 1951): 536-561; Evron M. Kirkpatrick, "Toward a More Responsible Two-Party System: Political Science, Policy Science, or Pseudo-Science?" *American Political Science Review* 65 (December 1971): 965-990; Gerald M. Pomper, "From Confusion to Clarity: Issues and American Voters, 1956-1968," *American Political Science Review* 66 (June 1972): 415-428; Michael Margolis, "From Confusion to Confusion: Issues and the American Voter (1956-1972)," *American Political Science Review* 71 (March 1977): 31-43; and David S. Broder, "The Case for Responsible Party Government," in *Parties and Elections in an Anti-Party Age,* ed. Jeff Fishel (Bloomington: Indiana University Press, 1978), 22-32.

4. The recommendations of the commission are found in *Mandate for Reform* (Washington, D.C.: Commission on Party Structure and Delegate Selection, Democratic National Committee, 1970).

5. The price of these reforms was high. Delegates of the new-enthusiast variety were far more numerous than party professionals. Moreover, the ideological cast of the delegates was markedly different—that is, much more "liberal"—from that of the general run of Democrats. And fewer delegates belonging to labor unions were present than is ordinarily the case. In some respects the new rules produced a most unrepresentative convention. The candidate it nominated,

George McGovern, was overwhelmingly defeated in the election—undoubtedly due in part to the defection of party moderates and conservatives. Ironically, though it was expected that the quota system for blacks, women, and youth would increase support among these groups in the election, nothing of the sort occurred. Blacks and youths supported the 1972 Democratic presidential candidate in about the same proportion as they did the 1968 candidate. Support among women voters declined notably. See Austin Ranney, *Curing the Mischiefs of Faction: Party Reform in America* (Berkeley: University of California Press, 1975), 153-156, 206-208.

6. To achieve a system of responsible parties, according to *Toward a More Responsible Two-Party System,* "The internal processes of the parties must be democratic, the party members must have an opportunity to participate in intraparty business, and the leaders must be accountable to the party." Committee on Political Parties of the American Political Science Association, *Toward a More Responsible Two-Party System,* 23.

7. See the analysis by Kenneth Janda, "Primrose Paths to Political Reform: 'Reforming' versus Strengthening American Parties," in *Paths to Political Reform,* ed. William J. Crotty (Lexington, Mass.: D.C. Heath, 1980), especially 319-327.

8. In addition, though tangential to this account, certain major recommendations of the report have been met through action by the federal government. A number of barriers to voting were eliminated as a result of the passage of the Voting Rights Act of 1965 and the adoption of the Twenty-sixth Amendment to the Constitution in 1971.

9. E. E. Schattschneider, *Party Government* (New York: Holt, Rinehart and Winston, 1942), 64.

10. Frank J. Sorauf, *Political Parties in the American System,* 102. Copyright © 1964 Little, Brown and Company Inc. Reprinted by permission.

11. Byron E. Shafer, *Quiet Revolution: The Struggle for the Democratic Party and the Shaping of Post-Reform Politics* (New York: Russell Sage Foundation, 1983), 529.

12. See an account of "party crashers" in *Congressional Quarterly Weekly Report,* October 28, 1978, 3107-3109.

13. David B. Truman, "Party Reform, Party Atrophy, and Constitutional Change: Some Reflections," *Political Science Quarterly* 99 (Winter 1984-1985): 167.

14. These data are derived from a *New York Times*/CBS News poll, as reported in the *New York Times,* October 7, 1986.

15. Martin P. Wattenberg, *The Decline of American Political Parties, 1952-1984* (Cambridge, Mass.: Harvard University Press, 1986), 21.

16. See Jack Dennis, "Public Support for the Party System, 1964-1984" (Paper delivered at the annual meeting of the American Political Science Association, Washington, D.C., August 28-31, 1986), 19, and Wattenberg, *The Decline of American Political Parties,* 22.

17. See an analysis that finds ideology supplanting party as the primary structuring agent in presidential elections: George Rabinowitz, Paul-Henri Gurian, and Stuart Elaine Macdonald, "The Structure of Presidential Elections and the Process of Realignment, 1944 to 1980," *American Journal of Political Science* 28 (November 1984): 611-635.

18. John R. Petrocik and Dwaine Marvick, "Explaining Party Elite Transformation: Institutional Changes and Insurgent Politics," *Western Political Quarterly* 36 (September 1983): 350.

19. See the exit interview data assembled by the *New York Times*/CBS News poll, as reported in the *New York Times,* November 8, 1984, and the ABC exit poll,

as reported in the *Washington Post,* November 8, 1984.

20. *New York Times,* November 8, 1984.
21. Confidence in the president's economic policies was the main reason cited by Reagan voters for their vote in 1984. By contrast, four years earlier numerous Reagan voters offered anti-Carter reasons for their vote. See *Gallup Report,* November 1984, 10-11.
22. For analysis of the voting patterns of blacks and whites, see Harold W. Stanley, William T. Bianco, and Richard G. Niemi, "Partisanship and Group Support over Time: A Multivariate Analysis," *American Political Science Review* 80 (September 1986): 970-976, and Edward G. Carmines and James A. Stimson, "Racial Issues and the Structure of Mass Belief Systems," *Journal of Politics* 44 (February 1982): 2-20.
23. *Congressional Quarterly Weekly Report,* April 13, 1985, 687. Concerning the two-tier voting system, see Everett Carll Ladd, "On Mandates, Realignments, and the 1984 Presidential Election," *Political Science Quarterly* 100 (Spring 1985): 1-25.
24. Norman J. Ornstein, Thomas E. Mann, Michael J. Malbin, Allen Schick, and John F. Bibby, *Vital Statistics on Congress, 1984-1985 Edition* (Washington, D.C.: American Enterprise Institute for Public Policy Research, 1984), 58-59.
25. Thomas E. Mann and Raymond E. Wolfinger, "Candidates and Parties in Congressional Elections," *American Political Science Review* 74 (September 1980): 620.
26. The success of incumbents is high, to be sure, but they are no safer today than they were in the 1950s. The key to incumbent survival is to maintain "an image of invulnerability" to discourage activists of the other party from mounting a major challenge. Steady attention to the district is essential in this strategy. See Gary C. Jacobson, "The Marginals Never Vanished: Incumbency and Competition in Elections to the U.S. House of Representatives, 1952-82," *American Journal of Political Science* 31 (February 1987): 126-141. And on the general subject of legislative-constituency relations, see David R. Mayhew, *Congress: The Electoral Connection* (New Haven, Conn.: Yale University Press, 1974), and Richard F. Fenno, Jr., *Home Style: House Members in Their Districts* (Boston: Little, Brown, 1978). As a general rule, college students majoring in political science should not be permitted to graduate, or at least not with distinction, until they have read these books.
27. Richard G. Hutcheson III, "The Inertial Effect of Incumbency and Two-Party Politics: Elections to the House of Representatives from the South, 1952-1974," *American Political Science Review* 69 (December 1975): 1399-1401.
28. *Davis v. Bandemer,* 106 S. Ct. 2797 (1986).
29. *Time,* August 7, 1978, 15.
30. *Time,* January 29, 1979, 12.
31. *U.S. News & World Report,* January 29, 1979, 24.
32. *Congressional Quarterly Weekly Report,* April 13, 1985, 701. 1986 data from press release, Federal Election Commission, May 10, 1987.
33. Press release, Federal Election Commission, May 16, 1985.
34. *New York Times,* February 8, 1987.
35. See a discussion of single-issue and ideological PACs in William J. Crotty and Gary C. Jacobson, *American Parties in Decline* (Boston: Little, Brown, 1980), 117-155.
36. *Washington Post,* September 13, 1978. The comment was made by Sen. Wendell R. Anderson (D-Minn.) to columnist David S. Broder.
37. *Washington Post,* September 13, 1978.
38. Late in the Reagan administration, a *U.S. News & World Report*-CNN poll

286 *Parties, Politics, and Public Policy in America*

reported that only 30 percent of Americans believe that congressional leaders always or almost always tell the truth and only 38 percent believe that the president does; these figures represented the poorest showing since the Watergate scandal. *U.S. News & World Report,* February 23, 1987, 57.

39. See an account in *Congressional Quarterly Weekly Report,* July 22, 1978, 1857-1860. The consultant was David Garth. He chose to work for Richard Leone, former New Jersey state treasurer. Bill Bradley, known for moving without the ball better than anyone on the Knicks and probably better than anyone else in the National Basketball Association except John Havlicek, then hired Michael Kaye. Bradley overwhelmed Leone, and a new star was born: Michael Kaye.

40. *Newsweek,* April 29, 1968, 76. For a comprehensive study of the public relations person in politics, see Stanley Kelley, Jr., *Professional Public Relations and Political Power* (Baltimore: Johns Hopkins Press, 1956).

41. See an analysis by Benjamin Ginsberg, "Money and Power: The New Political Economy of American Elections," in *The Political Economy,* ed. Thomas Ferguson and Joel Rogers (Armonk, N.Y.: M. E. Sharpe, 1984), 163-179.

42. Joe McGinniss, *The Selling of the President,* 1968, 27. © 1969 by Joemac Inc. Reprinted by permission of Trident Press/Division of Simon and Schuster Inc.

43. Robert MacNeil, *The People Machine: The Influence of Television on American Politics* (New York: Harper and Row, 1968), xvii.

44. Marshall McLuhan, as quoted by McGinniss, *The Selling of the President,* 1968, 28. © 1969 by Joemac Inc. Reprinted by permission of Trident Press/Division of Simon and Schuster Inc.

45. Dan Nimmo, *The Political Persuaders: The Techniques of Modern Election Campaigns* (Englewood Cliffs, N.J.: Prentice-Hall, 1970), 197.

46. Harold Mendelsohn and Irving Crespi, *Polls, Television, and the New Politics* (Scranton, Pa.: Chandler, 1970), 310-311.

47. From Frank J. Sorauf, *Party Politics in America,* 48. Copyright © 1968 Little, Brown and Company Inc. Reprinted by permission.

48. Harvey Wheeler, "The End of the Two Party System," *Saturday Review,* November 2, 1968, 20. Copyright 1968, Saturday Review Inc.

49. Concerning this point, see Edward R. Tufte, *Political Control of the Economy* (Princeton, N.J.: Princeton University Press, 1978), especially Chapter 4.

50. Ranney, *Curing the Mischiefs of Faction,* 3.

51. For an elaboration of these themes, see Nelson W. Polsby, *Consequences of Party Reform* (Oxford, England: Oxford University Press, 1983), especially Chapter 2.

52. Truman, "Party Reform, Party Atrophy, and Constitutional Change: Some Reflections," 639.

53. Apart from its provisions concerning intraparty democracy, very little is new in the Democratic party charter. The midterm party convention that adopted the charter in 1974 rejected numerous provisions designed to centralize the party and to alter its federal character, including a dues-paying membership, a mandatory national party conference every other year, an independent national chairman elected for a four-year term (to reduce the presidential nominee's influence over the chairman), an elaborate regional party organization, and a strong national party executive committee. Few changes were made in the major organs of the party: the national convention, national committee, and the office of the national chairman. The vast majority of the compromises reached both prior to and during the convention were struck on the side of those who wanted to preserve a party system notable for its decentralization. See an interesting account of the convention's issues involving centralization versus decentraliza-

tion by David S. Broder, *Washington Post,* December 1, 1974.

54. See a provocative essay by Jeane Jordan Kirkpatrick, which argues that the most important cause for the decline of the parties has been the reforms of the 1970s. She recognizes, of course, that social, cultural, and technological factors have also contributed to their weakening. *Dismantling the Parties: Reflections on Party Reform and Party Decomposition* (Washington, D.C.: American Enterprise Institute for Public Policy Research, 1978).

55. Cornelius P. Cotter and John F. Bibby, "Institutional Development of Parties and the Thesis of Party Decline," *Political Science Quarterly* 95 (Spring 1980): 1-27. For a close analysis of the services made available to congressional candidates by national party committees, especially those of the Republican party, see Paul S. Herrnson, "Do Parties Make a Difference? The Role of Party Organizations in Congressional Elections," *Journal of Politics* 48 (August 1986): 589-615.

56. Robert J. Huckshorn, James L. Gibson, Cornelius P. Cotter, and John F. Bibby, "Party Integration and Party Organizational Strength," *Journal of Politics* 48 (November 1986): 976-991.

57. For the development of these and cognate themes that point to a "political rebirth" of the American party system, see Xandra Kayden and Eddie Mahe, Jr., *The Party Goes On: The Persistence of the Two-Party System in the United States* (New York: Basic Books, 1985). And also of interest, see Xandra Kayden, "The New Professionalism of the Oldest Party," *Public Opinion* 8 (June/July 1985): 42-44, 49.

58. Byron E. Shafer, "The Democratic Party Salvation Industry," *Public Opinion* 8 (June/July 1985): 47. And see the analysis of Michael Margolis and Raymond E. Owen, "From Organization to Personalism: A Note on the Transmogrification of the Local Political Party," *Polity* 18 (Winter 1985): 313-328. For a finding that local parties have not become less active and less organized in the current era, see James L. Gibson, Cornelius P. Cotter, John F. Bibby, and Robert J. Huckshorn, "Whither the Local Parties?: A Cross-Sectional and Longitudinal Analysis of the Strength of Party Organizations," *American Journal of Political Science* 29 (February 1985): 139-160. In addition, see Barbara C. Burrell, "Local Political Party Committees, Task Performance and Organizational Vitality," *Western Political Quarterly* 39 (March 1986): 48-66.

59. No study documents and explains this better than Wattenberg, *The Decline of American Political Parties, 1952-1984.*

60. E. E. Schattschneider, *Party Government* (Holt, Rinehart and Winston, 1942), 64ff.

61. *Tashjian v. Republican Party of Connecticut,* 107 S. Ct. 544 (1986).

62. To explore the literature that defends the American party system, see in particular Herbert Agar, *The Price of Union* (Boston: Houghton Mifflin, 1950); Pendleton Herring, *The Politics of Democracy* (New York: Norton, 1940); Arthur N. Holcombe, *Our More Perfect Union* (Cambridge, Mass.: Harvard University Press, 1950); and Edward C. Banfield, "In Defense of the American Party System," in *Political Parties, U.S.A.,* ed. Robert A. Goldwin (Chicago: Rand McNally, 1964), 21-39.

63. *Time,* November 20, 1978, 42.

64. Stephen K. Bailey, *Congress in the Seventies* (New York: St. Martin's Press, 1970), 102-103. Among the other major accomplishments of the first session of the Eighty-ninth Congress were the passage of bills to provide for medical care for the aged under Social Security, aid to depressed areas, the protection of voting rights, federal scholarships, the Teacher Corps, immigration reform, and

a variety of programs to launch the War on Poverty.

65. *Congressional Quarterly Weekly Report,* January 2, 1982, 20-21.
66. Donald E. Stokes and Warren E. Miller, "Party Government and the Saliency of Congress," in *Elections and the Political Order,* ed. Angus Campbell (New York: Wiley, 1966), 209-211.

Index